Syntactic Islands

The phenomenon of the syntactic 'island' – a clause or structure from which a word cannot be moved – is central to research and study in syntactic theory. This book provides a comprehensive overview of syntactic islands. What are they? How do they arise? Why do they exist? Cedric Boeckx discusses the pros and cons of all the major generative accounts of island effects, and focuses the discussion on whether islands are narrowly syntactic effects, are due to interface factors, or are 'merely' performance effects. Thanks to the diversity of island effects, readers are given a unique opportunity to familiarize themselves with all the major research styles and types of analysis in theoretical linguistics and have the chance to reflect on the theoretical implications of concrete natural language examples, allowing them to develop their own synthesis.

CEDRIC BOECKX is Research Professor at ICREA (The Catalan Institute for Advanced Studies) and is also a member of the Department of Linguistics at the University of Barcelona.

KEY TOPICS IN SYNTAX

"Key Topics in Syntax" focuses on the main topics of study in syntax today. It consists of accessible yet challenging accounts of the most important issues, concepts, and phenomena to consider when examining the syntactic structure of language. Some topics have been the subject of syntactic study for many years, and are re-examined in this series in light of new developments in the field; others are issues of growing importance that have not so far been given a sustained treatment. Written by leading experts and designed to bridge the gap between textbooks and primary literature, the books in this series can either be used on courses and seminars, or as one-stop, succinct guides to a particular topic for individual students and researchers. Each book includes useful suggestions for further reading, discussion questions, and a helpful glossary.

Forthcoming titles:

Argument Structure by Alexander Williams

The Clitic by Francisco Ordóñez

Ellipsis by Kyle Johnson

Syntactic Agreement by Roberta D'Allesandro

Clause Structure by Elly Van Gelderen

The Evolution of Syntax by Brady Clark

Syntactic Islands

CEDRIC BOECKX

ICREA/University of Barcelona

CAMBRIDGE UNIVERSITY PRESS
Cambridge, New York, Melbourne, Madrid, Cape Town,
Singapore, São Paulo, Delhi, Mexico City

Cambridge University Press
The Edinburgh Building, Cambridge CB2 8RU, UK

Published in the United States of America by
Cambridge University Press, New York

www.cambridge.org
Information on this title: www.cambridge.org/9780521138789

First published 2012

Printed and Bound in the United Kingdom by the MPG Books Group

A catalog record for this publication is available from the British Library

Library of Congress Cataloging in Publication data

Boeckx, Cedric.
  Syntactic islands / Cedric Boeckx.
    p.   cm. – (Key topics in syntax)
  ISBN 978-0-521-19146-3 (Hardback) – ISBN 978-0-521-13878-9 (Paperback)
  1. Grammar, Comparative and general–Syntax.   2. Minimalist theory (Linguistics)   I. Title.
  P291.B647 2012
  415–dc23

                                                                    2012000481

ISBN 978-0-521-19146-3 Hardback
ISBN 978-0-521-13878-9 Paperback

For Youngmi

In gratitude for the love and support through thick and thin

Contents

Preface

This book is an insider's reflection on 'syntactic islands.' I am a syntactician by training, and much of my work, including my Ph.D. dissertation, has revolved around *island effects*: What are they? How do they arise? and Why do they exist?

Most modern grammarians would agree with me if I said that island effects are perhaps the most important empirical finding in modern theoretical linguistics, which I understand to refer to the generative/biolinguistic enterprise, broadly construed.[1]

About fifty years ago, syntacticians observed that the sort of seemingly unbounded dependencies ('movement dependencies') that natural languages exhibit appears to be subject to certain restrictions, as the following paradigm illustrates:

(1)   guess *who* John saw ___
          who Mary said that John saw ___
          who Bill believes that Mary said that John saw ___
          who Sue thought that Bill believed that Mary said that John saw ___

(2)   guess *who John saw Harry and ___
          *who Mary contested the claim that Bill saw ___
          *who Bill arrived after Mary said that John saw ___
          *who Sue met the man who believed that Mary said that John saw ___

Some of the sentences in (1) may sound a bit baroque, but there is no denying that native speakers of English can produce and understand them effortlessly. By contrast, the sentences in (2) strike the same speakers as distinctly odd, un-English, unacceptable. It's not the case that they sound strange or foreign (all the words in them are part of a native speaker of English's vocabulary). Nor is it difficult to see what they are meant to express. They are all requests for information of the sort one finds (in a different discourse context) in (3):

(3)   Tell me again: John saw Harry and *who*?!
          Mary contested the claim that Bill saw *who*?!
          Bill arrived after Mary said that John saw *who*?!
          Sue met the man who believed that Mary said that John saw *who*?!

Informally speaking, 'island effect' refers to whatever happens in (2) that makes these sentences unacceptable. For John R. ('Haj') Ross, the linguist who, with characteristic word flair, came up with the very term *island*, islands were structural domains that impose constraints on certain grammatical operations, the image being that of syntactic elements marooned on certain portions of the sentence.

This book is meant to provide an overview of the major views that linguists have entertained in this domain of research, and also to point to the sort of answers that appear to be more promising based on the evidence currently available and the stage of conceptual development that theoretical linguistics is in.

This is, to say the least, no easy task. Islands have figured prominently in virtually all the major stages of development of linguistic theory since the 1970s. The sophisticated analyses that have been put forth in order to capture island effects offer perhaps the strongest case for a rich, abstract, domain-specific mental module for language ('Universal Grammar'). In addition, because the structures that appear to give rise to island effects are quite rare in everyday speech, certainly quite rare in child directed speech, island constraints offer a classic case of poverty of stimulus (no wonder the most widely discussed illustration of poverty of stimulus, Chomsky's *Is the man who __ tall is happy?*, involves an island violation), and thus raise serious learnability issues.

It is something of an understatement to say that the sort of constraints Ross uncovered has proven to be one of the most productive areas of research in linguistics. The size of the literature on islands is truly overwhelming, not only in terms of theoretical proposals that have been put forth to account for them, but also in terms of data, for the level of generality at which Ross and Chomsky formulated constraints on transformations made it possible to start a new era in comparative syntax: once extracted from their specific constructions, Rossian constraints became the basis for cross-linguistic comparisons. As a result we now have available extremely detailed descriptions of how general locality conditions interact with the subtle, and not so subtle, differences across languages.

For this reason alone, I could not possibly intend to capture everything we know about islands in this book, so I decided to be more pragmatic and offer something that I had the capacity to write and that, in my opinion, would be useful in the current context of linguistic theory. Accordingly, what the reader of this book will find in the chapters that follow is not a 'summa,' it's far less than an encyclopedia on islands, it's much more modest, something that reflects the limitations (and, I want to be honest, the theoretical inclination) of the author. I have decided to offer a guide to how linguists (not only syntacticians) have come to think about islands, and what they currently think islands will turn out to be. Accordingly, the reader will find little in terms of new data, indeed, there will be relatively few data points explicitly discussed here. Instead, the reader will be introduced to core empirical generalizations and a comprehensive discussion of the theoretical significance that researchers have ascribed to these generalizations. Put differently, the overarching concern in this book will be on the architecture of the language faculty as seen from the unique perspective offered by island effects: what do these effects tell us about the nature of syntax and the systems that the syntactic component interacts with? Put yet another way: why should there be islands?; and why precisely these islands (and not equally conceivable others)?

I thought this focus would be useful and rewarding because, due to the centrality of island phenomena, I believe that the story I tell in this book traces the history of the field, it reflects the various styles of analysis that have come and gone (and come back!), the types of answers favored at one point, but ignored, or dismissed at other times, the avenues that once looked more promising but now seem doomed (only to be revived later), and also because it allows me to highlight what remains to be understood.

It is true that the architectural concerns I took as the organizing principles in writing this book can be said to be 'minimalist' in the sense that the discussion centers around why-questions of the sort that defines minimalism (see Boeckx 2006), but readers who are skeptical about the specific lines of approach developed under the rubric of linguistic minimalism these days should not dismiss this book offhand. As Noam Chomsky has stressed on numerous occasions, minimalism *as a program* is fairly theory-neutral, and the questions that define this program arise, and are of interest, no matter which particular technical idiom one writes in. Indeed, I have tried to be as theory-neutral as possible in the pages that follow. As a matter of fact, readers will find many critical remarks concerning mainstream minimalist approaches to islands in Chapter 3.

I also would like to point out that the material on islands is so huge that I had to be highly selective at times, especially when it came to sketching what looked to me like promising avenues for future research. Inevitably, in such places, I have favored views that are close to my own reflections on islands, though I have tried to point to the limitations of my own analyses as much as I could. I ask for the reader's forgiveness if he/she thinks that I have indulged in too much self-citation in some parts of this work.

Having said this, the reader should rest assured: I think that I have managed to represent virtually all the major theoretical positions on islands, though perhaps not in an orthodox or chronological fashion. I have favored a more thematic approach. And I have tried to be eclectic. As I hope the text makes abundantly clear, I think that the correct approach to islands is inherently pluralist. The empirical landscape is so complex and varied that I'm almost sure that every theoretical proposal about islands will turn out to be right about something. The problem with most proposals is that they all too often claim to be right about everything.

By the end of this book I am confident that the reader will be familiar with the shape of each major theoretical proposal concerning islands, with all the main arguments in favor of each, and also all the counterarguments that can be found in the literature (and all those I could think of while writing!).

However, let me emphasize that this is not a textbook: though the reader will gain acquaintance with all the theoretical landmarks in the domain of islands, the discussion presupposes a fair amount of background knowledge. I have not sought to scrutinize or delve into all the technical terms that I used if they did not immediately pertain to islands. All of them, I'm sure, can be found in standard textbooks on syntax. I have tried to keep the technical discussion to a minimum, only using what I thought was necessary to reveal the major insights behind the approaches I was discussing. If the reader wants more technical detail, I urge him/her to turn to the primary literature. What this book aims for is to give the reader enough information for him/her to be able to see through the technical details and interpret/understand the theoretical content and import of the claims that have been made regarding islands.

This book is structured in a way that would have pleased Hegel: it begins with a thesis, moves to an anti-thesis, and concludes with an attempt at a (more personal) synthesis. I see theories of islands as constantly fluctuating between two extremes: on the one hand, the Einstein-like dream of a final theory (a unified theory of islands), and on the other, the acknowledgement that this Quixotic quest has been populated by mirages (the denial of the existence of syntactic conditions on transformations). Chapter 1 describes the thesis, giving pride of place to the early works on islands by Ross and Chomsky, and emphasizes the early desire to unify all island effects. The chapter also discusses how the dream of a unified theory of islands quickly began to break down in light of ever increasing amounts of data. Chapter 2 presents the anti-thesis, revolving around so-called reductionist attempts intent to show that there are no syntactic constraints on transformations, and that alleged island effects reduce to processing difficulties. At the end of the chapter, I offer a critique of such accounts, while acknowledging their merits. Chapters 3 and 4 seek to offer a synthesis amidst the more recent ('minimalist') literature on islands, highlighting the differences between derivational theories, which take islands to be constraints on certain rule applications, and representational theories, which take islands to filter out the outputs of certain rule applications. Chapter 3 highlights the limitations of purely syntactic accounts of islandhood, while Chapter 4 stresses the empirical and conceptual virtues of more interface-oriented proposals. Finally, Chapter 5 wraps up the entire volume, highlighting the enduring character of Ross's insights.

Before thanking the people that helped me write this book, let me say a few words about its title. The book is entitled *Syntactic Islands*, not just *Islands*, if only to prevent the book from ending up on the shelves of travel agencies. The adjective *syntactic* was added primarily because I see this book as a modest tribute to the work of John R. Ross, who included the word 'syntax' in the title of his (1967) thesis, and also in the (1986) book version of the latter. As I discuss in Chapter 2, many linguists have come to deny the existence of syntactic constraints underlying island effects, and I certainly don't want the title of the book to be seen as a rejection of this line of research; indeed I hope that this book will be of interest to non-syntacticians as well. If some take offense at the adjective 'syntactic,' I ask them to bear in mind that the islands I am talking about are after all not real islands, so I think it's ok to adopt a title like 'syntactic islands' even if islands turn out not to be really syntactic after all.

DISCUSSION QUESTIONS

1. This is a good time to make sure you are familiar with the basics of 'A-bar'/ 'Wh-' movement. Do you know what its major motivations are? Can you easily identify its prototypical landing site?

2. (If you are not yet familiar with the literature on islands at all): Just by looking at the examples in (1), (2), and (3), can you try to guess what may be the source of the unacceptability in (2)?

Acknowledgements

In writing this book I have benefitted from the help of various people and institutions, and I would like to take this opportunity to thank them. First and foremost I would like to acknowledge the enormous debt I owe to my teacher, Howard Lasnik, who introduced me to the topic of islands, and made me appreciate the beauty and enduring relevance of classic works like Ross's. I also want to thank Norbert Hornstein for the numerous discussions we have had over the years regarding the nature of island effects, and for his comments on a penultimate draft of the manuscript. Thanks also to Juan Uriagereka, Noam Chomsky, Željko Bošković, Kleanthes K. Grohmann, Colin Phillips, Jon Sprouse, Bridget Samuels, Dennis Ott, Hiroki Narita, and the late Jean-Roger Vergnaud for helping me understand various aspects of locality through discussions over the years.

The present volume has its roots in an overview article I was invited to write for the *Language and Linguistics Compass* in 2008. I am very grateful to the editors of this journal for commissioning this work, as I am to Helen Barton for offering me the opportunity to contribute to the new Cambridge University Press series "Key Topics in Syntax," and for her patience and advice during the writing process. Thanks also to Evelina Leivada for indispensable help with the manuscript, and to Jon Billam for expert copy-editing.

In organizing the material I have benefitted from the comments I received at conferences dedicated to islands which I was fortunate enough to take part in: The 2008 Mayfest at the University of Maryland, the 2009 conference on minimalist perspectives on locality in Budapest, the workshop on chains at Yokohama National University in 2011 and the 2011 conference on islands at the University of the Basque Country. I am deeply grateful to the organizers for inviting me to these thought-provoking meetings, where I never failed to be reminded of the numerous kinds of approaches one can develop in the context of islands.

And, of course, thanks to Haj Ross.

The preparation of the present work was supported by a Marie Curie International Reintegration Grant from the European Union (PIRG-GA-2009−256413), research funds from the Universitat de Barcelona, as well as grants from the Spanish Ministry of Science and Innovation (FFI-2010−20634; PI: Boeckx), and from the Generalitat de Catalunya. The financial support of all these organizations is gratefully acknowledged.

The last, but by no means the least, lines of these acknowledgements I would like to devote to my wife, Youngmi, whose love and encouragement not only gave me the confidence to finish this project, but make life so pleasant and meaningful. No words of gratitude are enough to express what I feel towards her, and what she does for me.

1 Never such innocence again

1.1 A SHOT THAT THANKS TO ROSS WAS HEARD AROUND THE WORLD

It all began so innocently. While discussing issues regarding levels of adequacy in the formulation of grammatical theories, Chomsky 1964 touched on the formulation of transformations such as relative clause formation and question formation, and in so doing proposed what is, to the best of my knowledge, the very first general constraint on long-distance dependencies in natural languages – the very constraint that Ross took as his point of departure in his 1967 thesis, where the notion of island was introduced in linguistic theory.

Chomsky (1964:930–931) writes the following (the original numbering of the examples has been retained):

Consider the sentences:

(6) (i) Who(m) did Mary see walking toward the railroad station?
(ii) Do you know the boy who(m) Mary saw walking to the railroad station?
(7) Mary saw the boy walking toward the railroad station

(7) is multiply ambiguous; in particular it can have either the syntactic analysis (8i) or (8ii)

(8) (i) NP – Verb – NP – Complement
(ii) NP – Verb – NP

where the second NP in (8ii) consists of an NP ("the boy") with a restrictive relative clause. The interpretation (8ii) is forced if we add "who was" after "boy" in (7); the interpretation (8i) is forced if we delete "ing" in (7). But (6i, 6ii) are not subject to this ambiguity; the interpretation (8ii) is ruled out, in these cases. Once again, these are facts that a grammar would have to state to achieve descriptive adequacy...

The problem of explanatory adequacy is again that of finding a principled basis for the factually correct description. Consider how (6i) and (6ii) must be generated in a transformational grammar of English. Each must be formed by a transformation from a terminal string

S underlying (7). In each case, a transformation applies to S which selects the second NP, moves it to the front of the string S, and replaces it by a wh-form ... But in the case of (7) with the structural description (8ii), this specification is ambiguous, since we must determine whether the second NP – the one to be prefixed – is "the boy" or "the boy walking to the railroad station", each of which is an NP. Since transformations must be unambiguous, this matter must be resolved in the general theory. The natural way to resolve it is by a general requirement that the dominating, rather than the dominated, element must always be selected in such a case. This general condition, when appropriately formalized, might then be proposed as a hypothetical linguistic universal. What it asserts is that if the phrase X of category A is embedded with a larger phrase ZXW which is also of category A, then no rule applying to the category A applies to X but only to ZXW.

Let me unpack this important passage a little. Basically, in the paragraphs I have just reproduced, Chomsky points out that the relevant[1] ambiguity that exists in *Mary saw the boy walking to the railroad station* (either Mary saw the boy who was walking to the station or Mary saw the event of walking by the boy) is lost if we relativize or question the sentence as Chomsky does in sentences (8i, 8ii). Chomsky's concern is: Why should this be? The great novelty of Chomsky's (1964) proposal concerns the general nature of the constraint he proposes (cf. "this matter must be resolved in the *general* theory"; "resolve it ... by a *general* requirement"; "this *general* condition"; "a hypothetical linguistic *universal*"; "*no* rule ..."): if there is a case where a rule can apply to either a dominating or a dominated element of a given type A, pick the dominating, not the dominated, element. This constraint, which is unnamed in Chomsky (1964) (notice that the constraint is not even presented in indented form, or anything of the sort), but which came to be known as the "A-over-A condition" after Ross referred to it that way in his 1967 thesis, is quite different from something that Chomsky could have suggested: instead of proposing a constraint that covers all movement transformation (cf. "*no* rule ..."), Chomsky could have tried to incorporate the relevant constraint into the relevant individual transformations he was discussing (question-formation, relative clause-formation, etc.). By formulating the A-over-A condition as a general requirement, Chomsky essentially freed up the individual transformations from the burden of having to incorporate the restriction. As a result, the transformations themselves can be stated in simpler ways.

Ross stresses this very point at the beginning of his thesis (pp. 6–7):

> It is probably unnecessary to point out that it is commonplace to limit the power of the apparatus which is available for the description of particular languages by 'factoring out' of individual grammars

principles, conditions, conventions and concepts which are necessary
in all grammars: to factor out in this manner is to construct a theory of
language. So, for example, when the principle of operation of the
syntactic transformation cycle has been specified in linguistic theory,
it is unnecessary to include another description of this principle in a
grammar of French. ... The present work should be looked upon as an
attempt to add to this list a precise specification of the notion *syntactic
variable*. The notion is crucial for the theory of syntax, for without it
the most striking fact about syntactic processes – the fact that they
may operate over indefinitely large domains – cannot be captured. And
since almost all transformations either are most generally stated, or
can only be stated, with the help of variables, no transformation which
contains variables in its structural index will work properly until
syntactic theory has provided variables which are neither too powerful
nor too weak. It is easy to construct counterexamples ... for almost every
transformation containing variables that has ever been proposed in the
literature on generative grammar. It is for this reason that attempts to
constrain variables ... are so important: without the correct set of
constraints, it is impossible to formulate almost all syntactic rules
precisely, unless one is willing to so greatly increase the power of the
descriptive apparatus that every variable in every rule can be constrained
individually. But one pursuing this latter course will soon come to
realize that many of the constraints he imposes on individual variables
must be stated again and again; that he is missing clear generalizations
about language. Thus, the latter course must be abandoned: the only
possible course is to search for universal constraints.

I think that Ross's words are very clear to the modern reader, except
perhaps the notion of 'variable.' Recall that in those early days transformations were formulated *Syntactic Structures*-style: in terms of a
structural analysis ("If you find a string such and such ...") and a
structural change ("Turn string such and such into ...").[2] So, for
example, "If you find the following string, 'C_x WYZ X', turn it into
'X-C_x WYZ.'" WYZ were called variables, which provided the context
around which the relevant transformation (in our example, joining C_x
and X) operated. What Chomsky discovered in 1964 was the need to
impose a general constraint on variables in syntax: if you try to move
an element of category A, and the context of that transformation is
such that this element of category A is dominated by an element of the
same category, you must move that bigger, dominating element.

As Ross's remarks make clear, it wasn't the first time that linguists
realized that not every property involved in the formulation of a given
transformation must be stated in the transformation: there are notions
that belong to the general (meta)theory. You don't want to define the
notion of phrase as part of the transformation that moves, say, *wh*-phrases.

Likewise, you don't want to have to define the notion of 'verb' every time you want to express that a certain suffix attaches to verbs. Already in the work that provided the context for his own Ph.D. thesis, "The logical structure of linguistic theory" (1955/1975), Chomsky formulated general properties of the theory of grammar. For example, he noted that passive questions (e.g. *Was Bill killed by Sue?*) don't require a special transformation, as they emerge naturally from the interaction of two independently needed transformations (passivization and question-formation). Nevertheless, in that same work, Chomsky missed the opportunity to formulate the very first general locality constraint on long-distance dependencies.[3] On p. 437, Chomsky observes a certain restriction on question-formation by giving the following unacceptable example:

(1)   *Whom did [your interest in __] seem to me rather strange?

But unlike what he did in 1964, Chomsky suggested incorporating whatever constraint is operative in (1) into the transformation itself. This suggests that different transformations could be subject to different locality constraints.

The perspective in Chomsky (1964) and in Ross (1967), and for much of subsequent linguistic theorizing,[4] was dramatically different. The focus there was on extracting general conditions and formulating hypothetical linguistic universals – in Ross's terms, quoted above, "to construct a theory of language." Not individual grammars, but universal grammar. I am stressing this because without this theoretical stance, without this universalist aspiration, islands would not be a topic of inquiry (nor would linguistic theory be what it is today). Without this universalist craving, islands would not have been discovered. Islands indeed offer a powerful and enduring illustration of the idea that theories act like microscopes and telescopes; theories are perhaps the most powerful tools for empirical discovery.

There is a final remark I want to make in the context of the passage from Chomsky (1964) quoted above before I turn to later developments in the theory of islands. As I mentioned above, this passage by Chomsky is rightly regarded as the seed that gave birth to Ross's dissertation and all subsequent works on locality, but I think that it is in fact even richer than it looks. It certainly contains the A-over-A constraint, but examining it more closely, it becomes clear that this passage contains a second condition (constraint) on transformations. It is stated even more innocently than the A-over-A condition, as part of "background knowledge," buried in a *since*-clause: "since transformations must be unambiguous, . . ." This too is a general constraint, to be stated "in the general theory," a property of Universal Grammar.

As far as I know, Ross also took this condition for granted, but, as we will see later on in this book (Chapter 4), several linguists subsequently elevated the concern for unambiguity to the level of important principles responsible for island effects (though they did not, as far as I know, point out that the first hint of such principles went back to Chomsky's famous A-over-A passage).

1.2 ISLAND HO!

Be that as it may, Ross did not ignore Chomsky's A-over-A condition. In fact, his entire thesis revolves around it. More precisely, Ross's entire thesis tries to 'fix' the A-over-A condition, for, as Ross pointed out, Chomsky's proposal is both too weak and too strong. It's too weak because there are many examples of illicit question formation about which the A-over-A hypothesis is silent. For instance, nothing seems to ban extraction of the adjective from the Noun Phrase in (2c), even though the moving element is not of the same type/category as the domain it moves from (NP):

(2) a. You have a very nice car
     b. How nice a car do you have?
     c. *How nice do you have [__ a car]?

The A-over-A is too strong in ruling out acceptable examples of extraction of a Noun contained inside a bigger Noun Phrase, as the following examples show:

(3) a. Who would you approve of [my seeing __]?
     b. Which author did you read [a book about __]?

After pointing out that none of the solutions that Chomsky proposed in other versions of his (1964) work were successful, Ross went on to propose more adequate constraints on variables in syntax. Most of these came to take the form "transformational rules of type such and such cannot take place in environment so and so," and 'environment so and so' came to be called an island. Thus, Ross was the first to observe that extraction was not possible out of (among other structural domains) "complex Noun Phrases" (say, an NP modified by a relative clause), "coordinate structures," "sentential subjects," and "left branches" (NPs on the left branches of bigger NPs):

(4) a. *Which book did John meet [a child who read __]?   *Complex NP*
     b. *What did you eat [ham and __]?   *Coordinate Structure*
     c. *Who did [that Mary kissed] bother you?   *Sentential Subject*
     d. *Whose did you buy [__ book]?   *Left Branch*

Ross's main concern in his thesis was to characterize as accurately as possible the contexts in which transformations could apply. In so doing, Ross made crucial observations concerning the nature of islands. Let me list those that I think continue to play a significant role in current linguistic theorizing.

First, Ross observed that at least some of these island constraints were language-specific. For example, the Left Branch condition ("No NP which is the leftmost constituent of a larger NP can be extracted out of that NP"), illustrated in (4d), does not appear to hold in many Slavic languages. Likewise, Ross observes that many languages impose a ban on NP-extraction out of a PP ("Preposition-stranding"), but English is not one of them:

(5)   Who did you talk [to __]?

Second, Ross noted that languages resort to a variety of strategies to circumvent islands. Thus, many languages, including English, allow for extraction out of a coordinate structure if said extraction takes place "across the board" (in parallel from both conjuncts), as shown in (6).

(6)   a. *Which movie did [John hate __ and Bill criticize the book]?
       b. Which movie did [John hate __ and Bill criticize __]?

In the same vein, Ross pointed out that many islands can be circum-vented if the island is carried along with the element to be moved (a process that Ross made famous by the name of Pied-Piping). This is how English gets around Left Branch Condition violations, and how many languages avoid stranding prepositions.

(7)   a. *Whose did you read [__ book]?
       b. [Whose book] did you read?

Finally, Ross also pointed out that islands should not be defined in absolute terms. That is to say, Ross showed that it is simply not the case that no rule of any sort is blocked in the presence of an island. Ross's main concern was with a certain class of so-called "reordering trans-formations"; in a more traditional idiom: with movement processes that leave a gap (so-called "chopping rules"). Other transformations, for example reordering ('movement') rules that leave a pro(nominal) form (a so-called 'resumptive' element) instead of a gap – "copying rules" – appear to be immune to island effects. Witness the difference in behavior in a Complex NP environment in (8):

(8)   a. *Who did Sue read [the claim that __ was drunk] in the *Times*?
       b. That man, Sue read [the claim that *he* was drunk] in the *Times*

In fact, these are Ross's last words on this matter in his Ph.D. thesis (right before the concluding chapter):

> Variables in chopping rules, feature-changing rules, and unidirectional rules of deletion cannot cross island boundaries; variables in other rules can (p. 289)

In those days, it was standard to distinguish among various kinds of rules, and Ross certainly did so. In addition to deletion rules ('ellipsis'), he appealed to feature-changing rules (e.g., today's Negative Polarity Item licensing operation, which in those days was a rule turning *some* into *any*), and re-ordering rules, and in the context of the latter, he distinguished among those reordering rules which left a pro(nominal) form (copying rules), and those that left a gap (chopping rules). He furthermore distinguished between chopping rules that were leftward-oriented and those that were rightward-oriented because only leftward chopping rules allowed for Preposition stranding in English, and were not upward bounded as rightward chopping rules were (rightward chopping rules were restricted to apply to their own clause; i.e., they were "clause-bounded," which Ross dubbed the Right-Roof Constraint).

I am stressing this fact because as we are about to see, subsequent theorizing on islands, probably under the influence of Chomsky (1973, 1977), has tended to view islands as domains out of which any form of movement was prohibited, and has treated those dependencies crossing islands in non-movement terms (so-called "rules of construal"). For this reason, it is common to come across definitions of islands, in textbooks and elsewhere, as the following:[5]

> We say that a phrase is an "island" if it is immune to the application of rules that relate its parts to a position outside of the island. Thus to say that a *wh*-clause is an island is to say, in particular, that the rule of *wh*-movement that forms questions and relatives by moving such expressions as *who*, *what, what sonatas*, etc., to the left of a clause cannot be applied in general to a *wh*-expression with a *wh-clause*. (Chomsky 1980:194)

> "Islands" are syntactic configurations ... into which the relation of *wh* binding may not reach. (McCloskey 1988:23)

> islands ... Syntactic configurations which do not permit movement rules ... to move categories from positions inside them to positions outside them. (Roberts 1997:284)

> "Islands" is the cover term for nodes which obstruct syntactic movement (Szabolcsi and den Dikken 2002:213)

A quote from an anonymous reviewer reported in Postal (1997:2), sums up the standard take on islands rather well: "If something allows extraction, then it is not an island. This is at least the current view of the notion island. The copying rules of Ross (1967) today would not be taken to involve extraction, at least not when they are not island-sensitive."

The following quote, from Freidin (1992:94),

> A construction from which a constituent may not be moved by a transformation is designated as an island (following Ross 1967)

illustrates that this standard position is often attributed to Ross, but this is inaccurate. Ross's position on this point was far more nuanced, far more flexible, and, as we will see as we proceed, quite likely also much closer to the truth. (I suspect that Ross's more qualified stance on islands stems from the starting point of his thesis: the recognition that Chomsky's A-over-A hypothesis turned out to be too strong.)

What is accurate about Ross's position, and – as Postal (1997) insightfully remarked – not obviously true, is that he took syntactic domains to be non-islands by default. That is, as Ross stresses throughout his thesis, he took as a fundamental, basic property of human language (indeed, as Ross says on p. 7, "the most striking fact about syntactic processes") that syntactic dependencies were unbounded; they may operate over indefinitely large domain. Alongside Postal, I want to point out that this is a reasonable, but by no means obvious, assumption, certainly from a modern viewpoint where the family of domains that count as islands has grown a lot since Ross's early proposals. Perhaps the domains that allow for chopping rules that leave a gap are the exception rather than the rule.

Be that as it may, looking back at Ross's study, syntacticians like myself feel very fortunate indeed that Ross did not ignore Chomsky's brief discussion of the A-over-A condition, for it led to a reorientation of linguistic theory. As Postal (1986:xvii) writes in his Foreword to *Infinite Syntax!* (the long-awaited book-version of Ross's thesis),

> Previously, attempts to construct fragments of transformational grammars had overwhelmingly tended to assume that restrictions on particular constructions relevant to a hypothesized rule had to be built into the structure of that rule. In practice, this led to postulated rules of extraordinary complexity, involving myriads of *ad hoc* constraints. It further led to a lack of comparability between rules for different constructions, and still more for different languages. It obscured the possibility that large classes of different constructions were subject to similar constraints.

In sum, Ross's study, by "concretiz[ing] the abstract possibility of general constraints on rules in a set of actual proposals [that], while hardly perfect or the last word on the matter, were sufficiently close to the mark to have continued to be the basis for further work through the present day" (Postal 1986:xviii–xix), planted the seeds of a theory of Universal Grammar, where constructions in specific languages are epiphenomena, and the seeds of the new, revitalized, Comparative Syntax of today, where constructions can be compared across languages, and in doing so, Ross pointed to a very fruitful way of addressing "Plato's problem," the logical problem of language acquisition.

1.3   FIRST DREAMS OF A FINAL THEORY

The first author to fulfill the potential of Ross's proposals was Chomsky who, in his (1973) article "Conditions on transformations," took the goal of extracting general conditions from specific constructions to new heights, as he set out to uncover what the various island configurations discovered by Ross had in common. In fact, Chomsky did more than this. His (1973) article is an attempt to uncover and unify all the locality principles constraining transformations. Thus, Chomsky does not begin "Conditions on transformations" with island effects, but with more stringent locality conditions, such as the impossibility of relating an anaphor to its antecedent across a tensed clause or across an overt, lexical (there called "specified") subject:

(9) a. *John said [that himself was smart]
     b. *John said [that Sue liked himself]

Based on the observation that the same constraint appears to hold of movement (10), Chomsky proposed the following conditions (11)/(12), which he named the "Tensed-S Condition" and the "Specified Subject Condition," respectively.

(10) a. *John seems [that __ is smart]
     b. *John seems [that Mary likes __]

(11) No rule can involve X, Y in the structure
     $\ldots X \ldots [_\alpha \ldots Y \ldots] \ldots$
     where α is a tensed sentence.

(12) No rule can involve X, Y in the structure
     $\ldots X \ldots [_\alpha \ldots Z \ldots -WYV \ldots] \ldots$
     where Z is the specified subject of *WYV* in α.

Notice the universalist character of the rule "no rule ..."; no rule ... of any kind (recall, and contrast with, Ross's careful distinctions among rules that can or cannot cross islands). The rigidity of the conditions, however, turned out to be too strong. As Chomsky realized, some dependencies can be formed across tensed clauses and specified subjects:

(13) a. Who do you believe [___ likes Mary]?
      b. Who do you believe [Mary likes ___]?

Accordingly, Chomsky had to qualify his original conditions to allow for those instances of movement. Chomsky noticed that the dependencies in questions involved elements that typically occupy complementizer positions (today's CP area) and, moreover, that the conditions could only be violated if the movement really targets the complementizer domain and if there is an unoccupied complementizer position at the edge of the domain out of which movement takes place. The first observation accounts for the fact that it is possible to move a *wh*-word as was done in (13) but impossible to have the *wh*-word land in the subject (non-complementizer) position of the higher clause:[6]

(14) *Who is said that [Mary likes ___]?

The second observation captures the fact that the type of movement allowed in (13) is ruled out in the presence of a filled complementizer domain of the relevant Tensed/Specified Subject extraction site:

(15) *Who did you ask [where John saw ___]?

The outcome of these observations led to the following revised locality condition:

(16) No rule can involve X, Y in the structure
    $\ldots X \ldots [_\alpha \ldots Z \ldots -WYV \ldots] \ldots$
    where (a) Z is the specified subject of *WYV*
    or   (b) Y is in COMP and X is not in COMP
    or   (c) Y is not in COMP and α is a tensed S.[7]

From this perspective, Chomsky suggested that the reason that the movement in (13) can violate his original conditions is due to the fact that the moving element can first land in the intermediate COMP position, at the edge of the locality domain characterized by his original conditions, and in so doing circumvent their effects. Thus was born the idea that long-distance movement proceeds in small steps, COMP-to-COMP, or, as it soon came to be known, successive cyclically.

Chomsky then observed that the COMP position that movement exploits to reach the final landing site (the other COMP) should not be "too far away" from the latter. To characterize the right distance, Chomsky made use of the notion of *cycle*, thereby linking the two most innovative ideas of generative grammar.

Along with islands or the concerns with locality constraints more generally, the principle of the cycle, first proposed in the area of phonology by Chomsky, Halle, and Lukoff (1956) and codified in Chomsky and Halle (1968), constitutes a genuinely new idea in grammatical theorizing. As Tobias Scheer has noted on several occasions (see, e.g., Scheer 2011), the idea of a cyclic derivation was absent from linguistic thinking in Antiquity and the Middle Ages, and from the neogrammarian and structuralist paradigms in modern times. It's a genuinely new idea introduced by generative grammarians.

The core idea of the cycle[8] is that complex structural domains (words in phonology, sentences in syntax) have nested internal structure, and that certain rules apply first to the most deeply embedded constituent, then to the next most deeply embedded, and so on.

In those early days, cyclic nodes in syntax were NP and S, and Chomsky noticed that the COMP positions targeted by movement should not be separated by any cyclic node: they should be on adjacent cycles, or, as Chomsky dubbed the relation, "subjacent" (the COMP position used as an escape hatch should be on the cycle that is immediately embedded inside the cycle offering the next COMP position/ target of movement). Thus, the distance between COMPs is ok in (17), but not in (18).

(17) COMP he believes [COMP that John saw who]
     cf. Who does he believe John saw ___?

(18) COMP he believes [the claim [COMP that John saw who]]
     cf. *Who does he believe the claim that John saw ___?

Chomsky seized this opportunity to point out that his subjacency condition on rules that apply cyclically straightforwardly captures many of the examples that fell under Ross's Complex NP Constraint. Chomsky went on to propose further refinements of the subjacency condition to capture other islands (such as the sentential subject condition[9]), but he also suggested that some other islands, such as the Coordinate Structure Constraint, may be of a different nature. Thus, Chomsky points out that in coordinate structures, "it is generally the case that operations must apply uniformly through the coordinated terms; for instance, verbal affixes must be assigned uniformly, so that we have *John has flown planes and driven cars* but not **John has flown planes and drive cars*. Correspondingly, in a structure . . . where *Y* is a term of a conjunct, no rule, *syntactic or semantic*, can involve *X* and *Y*" (emphasis mine).

Like Ross's "Constraints on variables in syntax," Chomsky's "Conditions on transformations" contains a lot more than what I have covered here. For example, Chomsky formulates the Superiority condition that says that within a certain domain and given a choice of two elements to which a certain rule can apply, the higher element should be selected (a condition that is very reminiscent of the A-over-A condition, except that the latter concerns relations of domination, while the Superiority condition concerns relations of what came to be known as c-command[10]). Chomsky also sought to derive Ross's observation that rightward movement is more restricted than leftward movement by appealing to the idea (attributed to Joan Bresnan) that movement to COMP positions, those used as escape hatches, is overwhelmingly to the left.

Finally, Chomsky also briefly addressed a question raised in the concluding chapters of Ross's thesis, and a topic to which we will return in subsequent chapters: why should islands exist? In Section 11 of "Conditions" Chomsky points out that some of his locality conditions have a certain naturalness to them. For example, the A-over-A condition and the Specified Subject Condition have the effect of "reducing ambiguity," or of "increasing the reliability of a reasonable perceptual strategy that seeks the nearest" appropriate element, or of "guaranteeing a correspondence between deep structure position and scope."

Setting aside the fact that "Conditions" was written 40 years ago, and therefore inevitably contains proposals that now look dated or baroque, there are two central features of the paper that continue to dominate modern reflections on islands: First, and foremost, the ambition to provide a unified account of locality conditions; and second, the idea that locality restrictions impose severe conditions on extraction; in fact, they impose conditions that appear far too severe (recall that the original Tensed-S condition and Specified subject conditions would rule out run-of-the-mill extractions like *who did John say that Mary kissed?*) and must therefore be relaxed in a very particular way, by means of successive cyclic movement through escape hatches.

As we will see in Chapter 3, this idea of severe conditions accompanied by windows of relaxation (escape hatches) has remained a constant in Chomsky's theorizing about locality over the years (it is at the heart of his (1986) *Barriers* account, and also a central ingredient of his more recent *phase*-based approach, outlined in Chomsky 2000, 2001, 2008). Indeed, the subjacency account has remained the strategy of choice among syntacticians to account for island effects. To a certain extent, "Conditions" departs from Ross's idea that domains are non-island by default: for Chomsky, the locality conditions are so severe that the main task of the theoretician becomes one that focuses less on which movements are allowed, and more on how to allow for acceptable cases of movement not to violate islands. In saying this, I depart from Postal's (1997) contention that it has been a constant of syntactic theorizing on islands that domains are non-islands by default. It seems to me that the growing list of cyclic nodes, beginning with Williams's (1974) suggestion that all categories are cyclic, quickly leads to the question of how any movement is possible if subjacency holds.

1.4 A FIRST RETRACTION

Shortly after "Conditions," Chomsky returned to the topic of islands in his other epoch-making paper, "On wh-movement" (1977). Although it clearly builds on and extends the subjacency-based reasoning of "Conditions," "On wh-movement" is worth a separate section, for in a certain way it constitutes a significant retraction from the ambition expressed in "Conditions."

Before we get to the retraction, let me highlight a few things that Chomsky stressed in (1977) regarding his (1973) approach. The first issue concerns exceptions to the conditions Chomsky proposed, some of which can already be found in Ross's thesis (I will discuss several examples in the next chapter). Chomsky points out that the conditions hold only of a certain class of transformations, those called cyclic. Post-cyclic transformations need not abide by the same rules. Chomsky goes on to express the following (p. 76)

> In Chomsky (1973), two approaches to interpretation of conditions on rules are contrasted, an absolute and a relative interpretation; and the relative interpretation is proposed for conditions of the sort discussed there . . .. Under this interpretation, a condition does not impose an absolute restriction against rules of a certain type . . .; rather a rule must be interpreted in accordance with the condition unless otherwise specified. Thus, one might construct a rule to "violate" the A-over-A condition, but only at a cost: the rule would have to make explicit the relevant structures so that it can apply without failing under the condition. "The logic of this approach," as noted, "is essentially that of the theory of markedness."

In the next chapter we will come back to issues raised in this passage, for it is the case that in the standard treatment of islands, apparent subjacency-violations have always received a peripheral treatment.

Finally, let me point out that Chomsky, like Ross, stresses the need to make sure that apparent exceptions to his conditions receive an adequate analysis: in many such cases, Chomsky points out, the relevant examples can receive a different structural analysis, one according to which the relevant condition is satisfied. Thus, Ross already pointed out in his discussion of the Complex NP constraint that cases like (19) may receive an analysis where *make the claim* amounts to a single verb (equivalent to *claim*), and therefore do not involve extraction from a complex NP.

(19) ?The money which I am making the claim that the company squandered amounts to $400,000.

The second issue I want to mention in the context of Chomsky's (1977) discussion of his (1973) proposal is that, like Ross, he recognizes that some island constraints ought to be parametrized. Here is the relevant passage, which in many ways foreshadows the subjacency parameter proposed by Rizzi in (1978) (following a suggestion of Chomsky's, in fact) to account for differences in extraction possibilities between English and Italian:

> Plainly, rules can vary from language to language within the constraints imposed by UG, but it is often assumed that conditions on rules must be invariant. This assumption is somewhat arbitrary. . . . There is no a priori reason not to assume the opposite, and in fact, a very high level of explanatory adequacy might well be attained by a theory of UG that permitted either rules or conditions to vary, within fixed limits. (p. 75)

Chomsky goes on to say that what counts as a tensed S (relevant for the Tensed-S Condition) may vary (within limits) from language to language. Likewise, "application of the [Specified Subject Condition] in a language depends on the characterization of the notion 'subject' in this language."

Chomsky concludes this discussion by stating that "[f]or the moment, I would prefer to think of the conditions cited as instances of condition-schemata." (pp. 75–76)

The big difference between "Conditions on transformations" and "On wh-movement" concerns the realization on Chomsky's part that the final formulation of his central condition (cf. (16)) was in fact quite complex, and that the complexity was actually due to the fact that in 1973 Chomsky was assuming that all (extraction) transformations obeyed the same set of conditions. In "On wh-movement," Chomsky states that the rule system he assumes consists of not one but *two* transformational rules, Move NP and Move *wh*-phrase (now known as A- and A-bar movement, respectively), and construal rules that are now called binding conditions, but that were part of the rules subject to extraction conditions in (1973). Once the distinction between A- and A-bar movement is taken into account, the subjacency condition can be simplified. Put differently, island constraints cease to restrict all chopping rules, they restrict only a subtype of chopping rules, those involving wh-movement.

On this basis Chomsky goes on to withdraw the key suggestion he had made to Ross, who discusses it in the following quote:

> At the outset of my research on variables, . . . I concluded that the way to explain the similarity of the constraints on these rules was to assume that one rule was basic, and was a component of the operations of the other . . . rules. But Noam Chomsky pointed out to me an alternative possibility: this similarity of constraints might be derivable from some formal property shared by the four rules, rather than from some assumed common function or component. My further research proved Chomsky correct: there are a large number of transformations which obey the same constraints as the four rules that I had originally noticed, rules whose operations are far too dissimilar for it to be possible that there is one rule which is basic to each of these. (Ross 1967:383–384)

In "On wh-movement" Chomsky adopts Ross's original idea that those transformations to which islands apply are those that have a *wh*-movement component in common. In (1977), Chomsky in fact defines wh-movement as the process that leaves a gap and observes island constraints:

> When we find such a configuration [a dependency involving a gap, and obeying island constraints] in the data, [we can] explain it on the assumption that the configuration results from wh-movement. In other words, the conditions [presence of a gap, and island constraints] serve as a kind of "diagnostic" for wh-movement (p. 86)

This I take to be the origin of the now standard view that islands serve as a diagnostic for movement, a view which we will see at various points in this book has been repeatedly questioned, although it remains the textbook characterization, for reasons that are not entirely clear to me.

1.5 FURTHER BREAKDOWNS OF LOCALITY

Geologists, who study real islands, distinguish between two kinds of islands: continental islands and oceanic islands. Continental islands are those islands once connected to a continent but later separated either by rising sea levels that flooded former land bridges or by moving continental plates. Oceanic islands, by contrast, are those islands that were never connected to a continent; they arose from the sea floor, initially bereft of life, as growing volcanoes or coral reefs.

Linguists, too, have come to divide islands into subtypes. Perhaps the most well-known distinction is that between strong and weak islands, the subject of an extensive overview by Szabolcsi (2006) (for a condensed version, see Szabolcsi and den Dikken 2002). The need for such a distinction came from the realization that not all subjacency violations have the same (unacceptable) 'feel' to them. Consider the following pair of examples:

(20) Which girl did John refute [the claim that Bill kissed __]?

(21) Which girl did John wonder [whether Bill kissed __]?

Both examples are classic cases of island violations: (20) is a standard example of the Complex NP constraint, and (21), a standard example of a *wh*-island. But it's been repeatedly pointed out in the literature that the violation in (20) feels worse than the one in (21). There are sharper contrasts still. Thus, (22) or (23) sound much worse than (21).

(22) *Which girl did John arrive [after Bill kissed __]?

(23) Which (other) girl did John kiss [Mary and __]?

On the basis of such contrasts syntacticians came to the conclusion that islands come in two flavors: strong/absolute islands, and weak/ selective islands. Some islands are called strong or absolute because they appear to block all kinds of extraction. Other islands are called weak or selective because they appear to be islands for certain types of extraction elements only. This is the spirit of the distinction, at least. Many linguists readily acknowledge that the dichotomy is not always straightforward, and that at times the borderline between strong and weak islands is not very firm, but that some such distinction exists is now standard opinion. The basic diagnostic for the distinction often revolves around the adjunct/argument distinction or the NP/PP distinction: if crossing an island with an argument or an NP yields a deviant output that is roughly on a par with crossing that same island with an adjunct or a PP, the island is said to fall into the strong/absolute category. This is the case for the so-called Adjunct Condition (the ban on extraction from adjoined phrases).

(24) a. *Who/Which girl did John arrive [after Bill kissed __]?
       b. *How/In what way did John arrive [after Bill kissed Mary __]?

If the island effect is only strongly felt in the case of adjunct/PP-extraction (and even then, it may be weaker than the corresponding extraction out of strong islands), then we are dealing with a weak island. The *wh*-island is of this type:

(25) a. ??Who/Which girl do you wonder [whether Bill kissed __]?
      b. *How/In what way do you wonder [whether Bill kissed Sue __]?

The sensitivity to NP vs. PP extraction manifests itself in a variety of ways. For example, in the so-called parasitic gap construction[11] – a construction where a gap inside an island is rendered licit thanks to the presence of another gap, outside the island (26b) – the gap inside the island can only be an NP, it cannot be a PP (27).

(26) a. *Which paper did you read the book [before filing __]?
      b. Which paper did you read __ [before filing __]?

(27) a. *How important can one become __ [without feeling __]?
      b. *How many weeks will you spend __ in Berlin [without wanting to spend __ in Madrid]?

On the basis of such examples, Cinque (1990) – a classic work on the strong/weak island distinction – claimed that strong islands, like the Adjunct Island in (26/27), at best allow NP-gaps. He then proposed that such gaps were not real gaps, in the sense of Chomsky (1977) (recall his diagnostics for *wh*-movement), but were instead phonetically null 'resumptive' pronouns. In Ross's terms, such 'gaps' were the result of a copying, rather than a chopping, rule. Cinque based his proposal on the fact that in languages/constructions where resumptive pronouns are overt, they are only available for NPs (arguments), not for PPs (adjuncts). Thus, in dislocation contexts, it's possible to find a resumptive pronoun in (28), but not in (29).

(28) That guy, I told you that Mary likes $him_{res.\ pro.}$

(29) For that reason, I told you that Mary left Bill *??res. pro.??*

Thanks to this contrast, Cinque could maintain the idea that no genuine extraction ('movement') takes place out of strong islands, and in fact proposed that the strong vs. weak island distinction be defined in terms of the possibility of NP-'gaps': If an island domain completely rules out a PP-gap, it is a strong island.

    Incidentally, the idea that the gaps that one would standardly analyze as the results of movement operations are in fact null (resumptive) elements (proforms) is not unique to Cinque's study. Obenauer (1984) already put forth the idea that whenever a gap is found inside an island, it is a proform (thereby perpetuating the idea that 'islands block movement'). Even before Obenauer, in fact, shortly after Ross completed his dissertation, Perlmutter (1972) suggested that *all* instances of extraction (not just extractions out of islands) could be analyzed as leaving (sometimes phonetically null) proforms. Perlmutter's proposal is the first of a series of technical solutions that can serve as an alternative to the standard idea of movement in generative grammar to capture long-distance dependencies, a line pursued in various ways in frameworks like GPSG (Generalized Phrase Structure Grammar), HPSG (Head-Driven Phrase Structure Grammar), LFG (Lexical-Functional Grammar), as well as in more 'representational' formulations of more narrowly Chomskyan models such as Koster (1978a, 1987) and Brody (1995), where 'movement' is reanalyzed in terms of binding at-a-distance.

Postal (1997, 1998) took the possibility of reanalyzing gaps-left-by-movement as (null) proforms to mean that there are many more island domains than previously thought; in fact, Postal suggested, in a departure from standard practice, that categories are islands by default.[12]

Postal's (1997, 1998) reflections on islands, though couched in a less standard framework, strike me as very insightful. By expanding the scope of proform-based dependencies, Postal can reach the conclusion that Ross already reached in (1967): that there are no absolute islands. Put differently, no domain bans all dependencies of all kinds. Instead, what one finds is a variety of domains that are more or less 'selective' in their islandhood. Postal goes on to distinguish between locked and unlocked islands. Those that are locked are those that only allow dependencies of the (left) dislocation sort, with an overt proform (*That man, Sue arrived after Mary kissed him*). Unlocked islands are those that require licensing of null proforms. The distinction is reminiscent of the strong vs. weak island treatment, but some strong islands are assigned an unlocked domain status, on a par with traditionally weak islands.

Postal also points out that his treatment distinguishes between externally determined and internally determined islands. Externally determined islands are those domains that are islands in virtue of the function they fulfill in larger structures, whereas internally determined islands are those domains that block certain dependencies in virtue of their internal structure, irrespective of their global function. I mention this distinction here because it really suggests that not all islands are created equal.

Pursuing my discussion of breakdown of the unified picture that was the ambition of Chomsky's "Conditions on transformations," I would

like to say a few words about what has become the standard, if health-
ily controversial, treatment of weak islands: Rizzi's (1990) *Relativized
Minimality*-based analysis. Though not without antecedents,[13] Rizzi's
analysis established an influential way of thinking about (some)
islands that views them not as domains that elements can 'escape'
from, but rather as intervention effects caused by the presence of
certain elements along movement paths.

Building on original observations by Ross (1984) concerning the
blocking effect of negation[14] and by Obenauer (1984) concerning
the blocking effect of certain quantificational adverbs, Rizzi proposed
that some island effects can be characterized in terms of dependencies
being formed across an element that 'stands' in between the original
extraction site and the desired landing site (more accurately, the
intervener c-commands the launch site of the moving element) and
moreover, that is similar in nature to the moving element. Rizzi's
original characterization of 'similarity' was in terms of the movement
rules discussed in Chomsky (1977) (*Wh*-movement/A-bar movement,
and NP-movement/A-movement).[15]

In this way, Rizzi could account for why, for example, *wh*-elements
cannot undergo A-bar movement across a range of operators (regarded
as 'A-bar elements') c-commanding their launch sites, which includes
wh-elements, of course, but also topics, negation markers, certain
quantificational elements, etc.:

(30)   a. *Please tell me [*what* who bought __]
       b. **When* did John wonder [who kissed Mary __]
       c. *What* did John say [that to Bill Sue gave __ __]
       d. *I asked [*how* John did not behave]
       e. *How* did only John think [that you behaved __]
       f. *How* did you deny [that you behaved __]

Since Rizzi's original proposal much effort in linguistic theory has
been devoted to characterizing precisely the range of interveners for
all the types of dependencies that natural languages exhibit. Today,
the consensus is that intervention should be defined in featural terms,
rather than in terms of movement types: intervention obtains when a
certain element (say, a *wh*-word) tries to cross an element with which it
shares features (e.g., another *wh*-word) to reach a higher position that is
also associated with an element sharing the relevant features (an
interrogative C^0).

Relativizing intervention to features in this way allows for a very
flexible model,[16] ideal to capture weak island effects, which, as we saw
above, depend crucially on the lexical nature of the moving element.
Thanks to Rizzi's Relativized Minimality principle, it became possible

to say that weak island effects arise when the moving element and the intervener along its path have many features in common, but disappear as soon as the sets of features characterizing the moving element and the intervener become sufficiently distinct. Currently, the most promising way of defining distinctness seems to be in terms of subset-superset relation: intervention arises if the set of features of the intervener exhausts the features of the moving element and those of the target landing site; intervention is circumvented if the set of features of the moving element is a superset of the features of the potential intervener. (See Starke 2001 for the origin of this type of reasoning, and Boeckx and Jeong 2004 and Rizzi 2004, 2011 for extensions and refinements.)

The success of Relativized Minimality also stems from the fact that it is easy to think of it in terms of an economy principle ("You are only allowed to pick the closest element of a given type if you want to fill a particular landing site by movement"), as Chomsky and Lasnik (1993) suggested. This is particularly significant in the context of the minimalist program being pursued in theoretical linguistics (see Chomsky 1993, 1995, Boeckx 2006, 2010b, 2011a, among many others). Relativized Minimality became one of the core principles within minimalism, as it embodies the minimalist claim that the design of the core of natural language syntax is determined by principles of efficiency, nonredundancy, least effort, and the like.

In closing, I would like to stress a point made in the very first line of the very first page of Rizzi (1990), and stressed again by Szabolcsi in her (2006) review of the literature on weak vs. strong islands: Relativized Minimality is only intended to be "a partial characterization of the locality conditions" holding in syntax. While proponents of theories of (strong) islands have often tried to extend their approach to weak islands (witness Chomsky 1986 and Lasnik and Saito 1984, to cite but two of the most prominent locality analyses in the *Government-and-Binding* [GB] era, to which I will return later on in this book), proponents of theories of weak islands typically do not try to extend their accounts to strong islands, thereby acknowledging that the locality landscape in syntax is not uniform. (As a matter of fact, some theoreticians even suggest that weak islands may not form a natural class; see Szabolcsi 2008 for relevant discussion.)

On the strong island part of the spectrum, the dominant view remains the one intuited by Cattell in (1976), and consolidated in terms of government during the 1980s ('GB period'), arguably the most extensive period of investigation of island effects. Today this view is usually designated by Huang's (1982) CED acronym, short for "Condition on Extraction Domain," which Huang phrased in terms of (proper) government: strong islands are those domains that are not properly governed. Without going into the details of proper government (a structural relation that received many modifications during the 1980s, due to the large amount of data that it was meant to cover, and that syntacticians have been trying to avoid ever since), one can say that only those domains that are complements, or in a close structural relation with predicates, count as extractable domains. Thus, the two major domains that count as strong islands are non-complements: adjuncts (31) and subjects (32) (especially those subjects that have moved away from the predicate, as is standard under the VP-internal subject hypothesis, often attributed to Ken Hale, which takes sub-jects to raise out of their thematic positions to reach their surface positions).

(31) a. *Who did you get upset [because I talked to __]?
      b. *Who did they arrive [after I talked to __]?

(32) a. *Who did [comments about __] annoy you?
      b. *Who did [pictures of __] cause Mary to cry?

These examples contrast sharply with instances of extraction from complement domains:

(33) a. Who did you talk [to __]?
      b. Who did you make [comments about __]?
      c. Who did you take [pictures of __]?

Over the years,[17] the ban on extraction out of adjuncts (the Adjunct Condition) has been extended from straightforward adjoined domains (*because-*, *after-*, *since*-clauses) to relative clauses, sentential comple-ments of nouns like *the claim that 2 + 2 = 4* (treated as appositives; Stowell 1981), sentential 'subjects' (said to be appositives/'satellites' linked to a possibly null subject pronoun, and not genuine subjects themselves; see Koster 1978b), sentential 'complements' of certain verbs (e.g., manner-of-speaking verbs like *grunt*, which Ross 1967 already noted are islands, and which are analyzable as satellites/ complements of nouns, once such verbs are decomposed into a light verb + a noun: *grunt = give a grunt*) – all of which are islands, as the following examples illustrate.

(34) a. *Who did John arrive [after Bill kissed __]?
      b. *Who did John meet [the woman [that said that Bill kissed __]]?
      c. *Who did John listen to [rumors [that Peter kissed __]]?
      d. *Who did John grunt [that Mary likes __]?

In a similar vein, the Subject condition (ban on extraction out of (displaced) subjects) has also been extended to all displaced arguments, be they subjects, direct or indirect objects:

(35) a. *Who did [pictures of __] annoy Bill?
      b. *Who did you give [friends of __] three books?
      c. *Who did you believe [friends of __] to be fools?
      d. *Who did you pick [friends of __] up?

Since Huang's crisp CED formulation, numerous authors have tried to find a way to treat subjects and adjuncts as a natural class, to the exclusion of complements. I will review the major attempts to achieve this in Chapter 4. Suffice it to say for now that it's been far from an easy task, especially in light of the growing skepticism towards government relations (and relations defined over government, such as 'proper government,' which Huang resorted to); a skepticism that culminated in the complete rejection of such a notion in the current era of linguistic minimalism (Chomsky 1993 *et seq.*). The leading idea to account for the (generalized) subject condition goes back, again, to Ross, who in his thesis put his finger on the role of displacement[18] in situations like (35) and suggested the idea that displaced domains are frozen. This condition was dubbed "the freezing principle" in Wexler and Culicover (1980). The idea behind freezing is that once an XP has been treated as a unit (say, for purposes of displacement), it must remain a unit (hence no subunit can extract). The freezing metaphor illustrates yet again the standard take on islands: domains become (are frozen into) islands. They are not 'born' islands.

When it comes to the (generalized) adjunct condition, most accounts have tried to blame islandhood on the special character of adjunction, but, leaving details aside for now, let me point out that this too has been far from easy given that adjuncts, and adjunction, stick out like sore thumbs in most theoretical (phrase structural) treatments (see Chametzky 2000, 2003 for extensive discussion).

Not surprisingly, it's occasionally been suggested that it is a mistake to try to unify the (generalized) subject condition and the (generalized) adjunct condition. Stepanov (2001, 2007), who calls for such a rejection of the CED, points out that in addition to finding a common denominator for both conditions, empirical considerations suggest that the two island cases behave differently. Stepanov notes[19] that cross-linguistically[20] the adjunct condition is much more robust than the subject condition and takes this to mean that the two conditions should not be treated on a par. Accordingly, even strong islands may not form a natural class.

1.6   GLIMMER OF HOPE FOR UNITY?

We have come a long way since Chomsky's seemingly innocent remark in (1964). True, Ross had shown that the A-over-A condition fell short of descriptive adequacy, but in "Conditions on transformations" Chomsky had hinted at an important underlying unity: subjacency.

Today, the island landscape resembles a fragmented mosaic. Nevertheless, there remain a few signs pointing to the unity of old. In her review of the literature on weak vs. strong islands, Szabolcsi (2006) notes that while the weak/strong distinction is well established, there remain "some intriguing similarities between the phrases that may or may not escape from the two types of islands." In particular, Szabolcsi notes that just like it is easier to extract an NP, instead of a PP, out of weak islands, it is also easier to find acceptable examples of NP- (but not PP-) extraction out of, say, adjuncts, which typically qualify as strong islands:

(36) a. Which politician did John wonder [whether to interview __]?
      b. *?How much gravy did John wonder [whether to cook __]?

(37) a. ?Which politician did you go to England [after meeting __]?
      b. *How much water did you make the pasta [after boiling __]?

In addition, as many syntacticians have pointed out, the standard, modern treatment of weak islands within syntax, Relativized Minimality, and the updated subjacency accounts in terms of phases in current minimalism (Chomsky 2000 *et seq*.), which remain the method of choice to tackle strong islands, offer partially redundant accounts of locality effects. For instance, both principles rule out unacceptable examples like:

(38)   *John seems [that it was told __ [that Bill left]]

Under Relativized Minimality, (38) is out because movement of *John* crosses a c-commanding element of the same type (*it*); for the subjacency-type account, movement is out because of the ban on Improper Movement already posited in Chomsky (1973) to account for the badness of *Who is said [that Mary likes __]?* To escape from the embedded finite clause, *John* in (38) would have to first move to SpecCP, and doing so, would be banned from returning to a non-SpecCP position.

I do not claim, of course, that Relativized Minimality and subjacency accounts always overlap, but the sort of redundancy just illustrated suggests that perhaps we are missing some higher-level generalization.

Thirdly, although I have discussed views that stress the diversity of locality conditions in syntax, not all such views are equally compelling. For example, Stepanov's argument against a unified, CED-style treatment of strong islands rests on the different cross-linguistic profiles of the (generalized) adjunct condition and (generalized) subject condition. It is true that the adjunct condition appears to be more robust cross-linguistically, but, as I already pointed out in Boeckx (2008b), this may be for reasons unrelated to islandhood. As Chomsky (1977) already observed, what counts as a subject varies cross-linguistically, much more so than what counts as an adjunct, in part because adjunction may be a primitive of the theory, whereas as Chomsky (1965) already stressed, there is no primitive notion of subject in (generative) syntax. For this reason, the cross-linguistic fluctuation of the subject condition may simply reflect the fact that what we call extractions out of subjects may not be cases of extraction out of the same domains. For example, some of these subjects may have been displaced, while others not. I should also note, stressing a point made by Uriagereka (2011), that the adjunct condition is robust only insofar as we try to extract elements from adjuncts that are very high in the syntactic hierarchy. As soon as extraction takes place out of non-tensed low adjuncts, the operation improves (a fact already noted in Uriagereka 1988, Browning 1987, and explored more systematically in Truswell 2007). Consider the following cases:

(39) *Who did John leave the room [because Mary kissed __]?

(40) a. What did John drive Mary crazy [whistling __]?
      b. What did John leave the room [whistling __]?
      c. Which book did John design his garden [after reading __]?
      d. What are you working so hard [in order to achieve __]?
      e. Who did John travel to England [to make a sculpture of __]?

Taking both the difficulty of defining the notion of 'subject' cross-linguistically, and the violability of the adjunct condition in cases like (40) into account, it seems to me that the case against a unified treatment of strong islands is not very strong.

In fact, the violability of both the subject condition and the adjunct condition reinforces Postal's claim (see also Boeckx 2003a) that no syntactic domain constitutes an absolute island, in the sense of prohibiting all syntactic dependency of all kinds. Readers of this chapter will recall that this was already the conclusion reached by Ross in (1967).

But notice now that we have managed to find something that unites all islands: no island is absolute. In other words, all islands are selective. Put differently, Ross's (1967) conclusion may provide a useful starting point to unify all islands. Not surprisingly, it has been argued in recent years that since all islands are selective, a unified theory of islandhood should take the form of a Relativized Minimality account, given the success of the latter in the context of the prototypically selective domains called weak islands (see Starke 2001, Abels 2003, and Rizzi 2009 for suggestions along these lines). Unfortunately, discussion in this area remains more suggestive than conclusive, in large part because the attempted unification remains rather artificial. This is in no small part due to the fact that in order to account for strong islands (which, in general, block a broader range of dependencies than weak islands do), it has turned out to be necessary to endow the relevant intervening nodes with many features whose existence is ad hoc (only justified on the basis of island effects). This is perfectly understandable: the bigger the number of dependency-types an element block ('the stronger the island'), the bigger the number of feature-types that element will have to bear. And alongside the rich number of features, such an account has to posit a fair amount of lexical structure among those features to ensure the relevant subset-superset relation that governs minimality violations (see Starke 2001, and the discussion above). All of this renders current minimality-based attempts at unification more technical than natural.

An alternative take stemming from the selectivity of all island domains has been that perhaps islands are just not there. Perhaps we were wrong in taking the unacceptable cases to be the baseline; perhaps we should have argued from the opposite direction: take the acceptable cases to be basic (showing that there are no constraints on variables in syntax, no syntactic conditions on transformations), and try to explain the bad cases, the 'island' effects, in some other way. This antithetical position is the topic of the next chapter.

DISCUSSION QUESTIONS

1. Going through Ross's thesis, list all the constraints on variables he identified, and provide an example illustrating each.
2. Compare the positions of Chomsky (1973) and Chomsky (1977) regarding "conditions on transformations." Resort to one or two concrete examples to illustrate the differences.

2 What is really all just a mirage?

The position – or I should say, positions, for there is more than one way of articulating the perspective at the heart of this chapter – that I will focus on here exists in both a radical and a more conservative version. Usually, the more radical version – 'there are no islands in syntax!' – is presented in the abstract and introductory sections of the relevant article, presumably to catch the reader's attention. But this is such a radical version that it often proves too difficult to maintain, so much so that towards the end of the more careful papers, it is claimed that at least some island effects, though by no means all such effects, could be explained in a non-syntactic fashion.

As I already mentioned in the concluding part of the previous chapter, the plausibility of such a view, which is often called 'reductionist,' stems from the fact that as data regarding island phenomena accumulated, and problematic cases for the proposed constraints came to light, some theoreticians came to the conclusion that the data set used to motivate island constraints was, in the words of Hofmeister and Sag (2010), "slippery at best."[1] Gradually, counterexamples to nearly every structure-based island constraint ever proposed in the literature came to light, and linguists began to wonder whether there was anything left of Ross's and Chomsky's original conditions, or modern refinements of them. Already back in the 1970s, a few linguists suggested that island effects were not effects of syntax (or grammar) proper, but rather, the unacceptability of certain extractions was due to processing factors, or discourse factors, or semantic factors, or pragmatic factors, or a combination of all of these, but crucially not due to syntactic factors.

Here is what Postal (1986:xix) has to say in his foreword to Ross's *Infinite Syntax!*:

26

Although CVS ["Constraints on variables in syntax"; Ross 1967] argued
for the relevance of island constraints to a wide range of
phenomena, these were all roughly of the sort generally known as
"syntactic." One of the more interesting and at the time quite
unsuspected developments of CVS was the discovery that island
constraints play a role in a much broader range of phenomena,
governing to some extent: (a) the scope of semantic operators and
quantifiers; (b) the possibilities of well-formed lexical items; and
(c) even certain phenomena often taken to involve discourses rather
than sentences proper. Thus, although islands were shown in CVS to
have a quite broad scope, the actual domain for which they are
relevant has turned out to be far broader.

The view that islands may not be purely syntactic after all did not
emerge on the basis of empirical considerations only. As soon as
syntacticians began to ask why island constraints should exist, and
why they should take the form(s) that they do, they began to think of
non-syntactic factors. Thus, at the very end of his thesis (p. 291), Ross
asked "Why should complex NP's, coordinate nodes, sentential subject
clauses, and NP's on the left branches of larger NP's all function the
same in defining islands? Can islands be shown to behave like psycholinguistic entities?"

Reflecting on his "Conditions," Chomsky (1973) pointed out that
some of them at least have the effect of "increasing the reliability of
a reasonable perceptual strategy that seeks the nearest" appropriate
element. Chomsky and Lasnik (1977) noted that "[i]t is possible, though
hardly necessary, that general properties of grammar might be
explained, at least in part, in terms of the exigencies of performance."
This naturally led to 'grammaticization' accounts of island effects, best
represented by Berwick and Weinberg (1984). The idea of such accounts
is that certain kinds of syntactic dependencies (those crossing island
nodes) would lead to real-time processing difficulties. Accordingly,
the grammar prohibits those movements, and in that way could be
said to be 'adaptive' to the real-time parser. Put differently, the existence of grammatical constraints is rationalized on the basis of parsing
considerations: without a grammar with island constraints, the nature
of the parser would be less deterministic, more complex, etc. Put yet
another way, the grammar is complicated by restrictions on possible
rules, and the complication is directed specifically towards avoiding
the generation of structures that would strain the parser.

Such grounded accounts of island effects should, however, be kept
separate from the more reductionist accounts that are the focus of the
present chapter.[2] Grounded accounts do not deny the existence of
grammatical constraints. What they do is offer a rationale for them

in terms of extra-grammatical considerations. But they make roughly the same kind of (synchronic) empirical predictions as standard grammatical accounts.[3] By contrast, reductionist accounts claim that the grammar does not ban movement across islands; rather, it is the task of extra-grammatical accounts to capture why certain, in and of themselves completely licit, instances of movement across certain domains traditionally referred to as islands lead to unacceptability.

Such accounts cannot simply be ignored because if successful, they remove one of the most pervasive arguments for abstract, complex theories of grammar. They also potentially remove one of the classic motivations for domain-specific constraints on language acquisition, as data illustrating island constraints are vanishingly rare in everyday speech, which begs the question of how come they end up being part of our knowledge of language – a classic 'poverty of stimulus' argument.

Reductionist accounts, then, have far-reaching implications for the architecture of the language faculty, much more so than grounded accounts. It is therefore no surprise that reductionist attempts have re-emerged with greater enthusiasm in recent years in the context of linguistic minimalism, where even syntacticians try to keep the content of Universal Grammar to the bare minimum. As Hofmeister and Sag (2010) point out, a grammar without island conditions is (potentially) "even more minimal than current minimalist characterizations of grammatical knowledge."

2.2   A BRIEF NOTE ON 'DISCOURSE-BASED' ACCOUNTS

As always in such situations, when the stakes are so high, the final word must come from the data and from the strength of the alternative theories. In the remainder of this chapter I will focus on two major reductionist views: (i) the processing view, which takes (some) island effects to be due to parsing difficulties, and (ii) the semantico-pragmatic view, which takes (some) islands to arise at the level of sentence interpretation. My choice does not exhaust the realm of possible reductionist accounts. For example, it has sometimes been suggested (see Erteschik-Shir 1973, Goldberg 2006) that island effects are to be understood in terms of discourse cohesiveness. Reviewing work by Erteschik-Shir (1973), Morgan (1975), and others, Goldberg claims that (certain) island domains correspond to domains of back-grounded information at the level of discourse structure – neither the primary topic of the sentence, nor the focus domain, and suggests that islands are therefore not the result of grammatical constraints, but rather are due to principles of discourse structure. She also points out that such a discourse-based account would be flexible enough to accommodate the weakening of island effects (in her view, to be captured in terms of context effects).

While it is tempting to attribute the 'slippery' nature of island effects to contextual factors, the fact remains that certain violations (e.g., *What did John eat ham and __?*) do not appear to go away no matter what context they are presented in (it is for this reason that the otherwise very reductionist Hofmeister and Sag treat the coordinate structure constraint as a case of irreducibly grammatical island). But more importantly, suggestions like Goldberg's are only compelling insofar as the discourse principles that are meant to induce island effects are well articulated. It is fair to say that investigation of discourse structure is far less developed than grammatical theory, and, as a result, the equation 'island = backgrounded information,' to the extent that it holds, remains at this point mere curiosity. I should also point out that it is not at all clear to me that discourse structure is so independent from grammatical structure. There exist many (to my mind, quite compelling) attempts to reduce topic-focus articulation to grammatical structure,[4] in which case Goldberg's suggestion, once fully developed, would in fact boil down to a grammatical theory.[5]

To repeat, then, alternative, extra-grammatical accounts of islands are only compelling insofar as they offer theoretical, explanatory models that are as detailed as those used in grammatical approaches. Merely pointing to correlations, contextual effects, intriguing examples, and the like won't do.

The views discussed below have been chosen for purposes of exposition because they have been relatively well articulated, well enough to make novel, testable predictions.

2.3 HARD TO PROCESS

On the first page of the (1986) *Barriers* monograph, arguably his most ambitious attempt to unify locality conditions since 1973, Chomsky writes:

> I want to explore some rather murky questions concerning the theories of government and bounding, including, in particular, the possibility of a unified approach to these topics. The intuitive idea is that certain categories in certain configurations are barriers to government and to movement (application of the general rule Move-α). A natural speculation would be that the same categories are barriers in

the two cases. As is well known, however, government is a stricter and "more local" relation. We might therefore expect that one barrier suffices to block government, whereas more than one barrier inhibits movement, perhaps in a graded manner. One of the questions I want to explore is whether there is a reasonable notion of barrier that has these properties.

The concept of government enters into a broad range of considerations; as a result, any proposal concerning its formulation has many and intricate consequences. Furthermore, many of the empirical phenomena that appear to be relevant are still poorly understood. With regard to the theory of movement, it appears that a number of different factors enter into informant judgments, including lexical choices to which they are sensitive; it is therefore necessary to proceed on the basis of some speculations concerning the proper idealization of complex phenomena: how they should be sorted out into a variety of interacting systems (some of which remain quite obscure), which ones may tentatively be put aside to be explained by independent (sometimes unknown) factors, and which others are relevant to the subsystems under investigation. I will consider several paths through the maze of possibilities that come to mind.

Some of the "different factors" to which Chomsky is here referring are illustrated in the following examples.[6] (As always, judgment indications such as *, ?, are meant to be contrastive, differentiating the pair of examples under discussion, not absolute.)

(1)   a. *A person who Robin got real drunk [after she thought about __]
      b. A person who Robin got real drunk [after thinking about __]
      c. *A person who Robin went to Washington [so that her daughter could work with __]
      d. ?A person who Robin went to Washington [in order for her daughter to work with __]

(2)   a. *Who does [baking ginger cookies for __] give her great pleasure?
      b. ?Who does [baking ginger cookies for __] seem useless?
      c. *A person who [that Robin attacked __ so viciously] didn't surprise me
      d. ?A person who [for Robin to attack __ so viciously] wouldn't surprise me
      e. ?A person who [Robin's vicious attack on __] didn't surprise me

(3)   a. *The campaign that [someone who could actually spearhead __] was finally thought of
      b. That's the campaign that I finally thought of [someone to spearhead __]

(4)   a. *She is a person who [whether or not the President should talk to __] is unclear
      b. ?She is a person who [whether or not to talk to __] is unclear

(5)   a. *Who did you make dinner and Robin talk to __ all evening?
      b. ?Who did you make dinner and talk to __ all evening?
      c. Who did you sit around and talk to __ all evening?

Facts like these are of the kind that Ross used to cast doubt on the inadequacy of Chomsky's A-over-A condition, which the reader will recall from our discussion in Chapter 1 Ross found both too weak and too strong. Gradations of the sort just illustrated are also found in Chomsky (1973), who observed that the following (a) example is worse than the (b) example, which is in turn worse than the (c) example.

(6)   a. *Who did you discover [Mary's poem about __]?
      b. ??Who did you discover [the poem about __]?
      c. Who did you discover [a poem about __]?

But both Ross and Chomsky, and many syntacticians following them, sought to find structural, grammatical differences to account for the various degrees of acceptability. (For example, many of the examples just illustrated involve the effect of tense and/or definiteness, which figure prominently in Manzini's 1992 grammar-based theory of islands.)

Other theoreticians take the relevant pairs of examples to be structurally on a par, and conclude that the differences in acceptability must be due to something else. Specifically, they take the acceptable cases to directly reflect the products of the grammar, concluding that the latter is island-free, and view the unacceptable cases as the result of extra-grammatical complications. This is not an innocent point. Logically speaking, it is equally possible that it is the bad cases that are closer to what the grammar dictates, and that it is the more acceptable cases that should be explained in terms of extra-grammatical factors (e.g., some violations are easier to recover from, figure out the meaning of, . . . hence feel more acceptable). As Phillips (2011) correctly points out, "it is important to remember that evidence that a speaker is able to represent a given structure does not entail that the speaker treats that structure as well-formed."

I will come back to Phillips's assessment of reductionist theories of the processing sort. But for now, let me provide a detailed sketch of how reductionist arguments are structured. Most of the time, I will be relying on Hofmeister and Sag (2010), whose very clear exposition I found very useful.

2.3.1   The logic of the argument

Already back in (1979), Givon pointed out that unacceptable cases like those in (7) were probably due to processing, as opposed to grammatical, factors:

(7)   a. *The man who I saw [the dog that bit __] fell down
      b. *Who did you see [the dog that bit __]?

Givon claimed that the examples like (7a) "are difficult to process because the grammatical-functional relations in the deeply embedded clause are hard to reconstruct, given the deletion, the lack of morphological indicators, and the fact that there is a large gap between the head noun (*the man*) and the verb of which this is the object (*bit*)."

This early argument is not compelling at all, given that the following examples, which also involve deletion, lack morphological indicators, and exhibit a large gap (of roughly the same length as what we find in (7)) between the extracted element and the verb it is the object of, are fully acceptable.

(8)   a. The man who you think that Mary said that [the dog bit __]
      b. Who do you think that Mary said that [the dog bit __]?

But Givon's argument contains the general idea of the standard reductionist argument, well expressed by Deane (1991) in terms of "attention": Extraction consists in the establishment of a long-range grammatical relation. An obvious prerequisite to establishing a relation between two concepts is that one be paying attention to both concepts at the same time. This presents no problem with local grammatical relations (they are directly adjacent). In long-distance extraction, however, the two concepts to be linked are separated far enough from one another that some means must be provided to focus attention on both.

The general intuition behind reductionist arguments is that island constraints reflect cognitive limits, e.g., on attention: island domains are defined by elements that divert the limited resource of attention away from filler and gaps. Put differently, the idea is that there is a processing cost associated with the operations necessary to build the syntactic structures that we have come to call islands, but, according to the reductionists, islands do not reflect structural constraints. Rather, the perception of unacceptability arises as a by-product of the processing requirements of the relevant sentences.

Deane chose to frame his argument in terms of attention, but as Phillips (2011) points out, there are many different possible 'bottlenecks' in comprehension and production (often reductionist arguments are not very explicit about which one(s) they assume, expressing satisfaction as long as one extra-grammatical factor can be found): the parsing difficulty could be due to misanalysis caused by temporary ambiguity, much like in the well-known garden-path sentences (*the horse raced past the barn fell*), or the sentence may have a degree of complexity that exceeds the comprehender's capacity ('overload' effects). Or the sentence may be difficult to interpret because it overburdens the comprehender's ability to relate the

utterance to a suitable mental model. Or a specific portion of the
sentence may be difficult to construct due to the left-to-right presentation of the sentence, which often conflicts with its hierarchical
representation. Or something else. In sum, many things could go
wrong, in processing terms, and perhaps different things go wrong
in different island cases. In my opinion, one of the points to stress in
the context of reductionist accounts is that they do not seek a unified
(processing) theory of islandhood. What unites such accounts is their
attempt to remove islands from the purview of syntactic theory.

The inspiration for reductionists is often said to come from Miller
and Chomsky (1963), who pointed out that the general unacceptability
of center-embedding (*[the cheese [(that) the rat [(that) the cat chased] ate] was
from France]*) had to be due to processing considerations, which crucially they tried to be precise about, because ruling out such structures
in syntax would lead to unnecessary complications of grammatical/
syntactic rules. The fact that it is possible to find reasonably acceptable
cases of center embedding (*[The reporter [(that) everyone [(that) I met] trusts]
reported the coup]*)[7] was taken to reinforce this claim.

The Miller and Chomsky (1963) strategy was replicated in a few
cases (Bever 1970 is a personal favorite of mine): find a constraint, try
to explain the constraint in grammatical terms. If the explanation becomes too complex, ad hoc, unnatural, consider an extra-
grammatical explanation, be as explicit as you can about the latter,
and find acceptable examples that are as close as possible to the
original and suggest that the grammar can indeed generate the
structures, thereby strengthening your case for an extra-grammatical
account of the original data.

This is the roadmap that Hofmeister and Sag (2010) follow, and
which I will sketch here for the sake of illustration.

Hofmeister and Sag (2010) begin by expressing their dissatisfaction
with the way counterexamples to island constraints have typically
been dealt with in the syntactic literature. Faced with the breakdown
of locality conditions already reviewed in Chapter 1, as well as the
sort of data that I began this chapter with, generative grammarians
have not hesitated in (i) introducing ad hoc exception principles,
(ii) assigning marginal, peripheral status to the counterexemplifying
data, and (iii) claiming that certain dependencies that crossed islands
without leading to unacceptable results were in fact not instances of
movement, but involved base-generation of the head of the dependency binding a (possibly null) proform instead of a gap. In addition,
syntacticians have typically failed to appreciate the fact that extra-
grammatical factors may be highly relevant.

Everyone would agree that it would be a step forward if ad hoc conditions could be avoided, of course. And although base-generation + binding of a proform have emerged as a real theoretical possibility, Hofmeister and Sag are correct in pointing out that far too often in the grammatical literature a given construction is said to involve base-generation solely because if it were analyzed in terms of movement, some island condition would be violated. Such circularity is, of course, not a theoretical virtue. Finally, it is also fair to say that extra-grammatical considerations have been underutilized by syntacticians.

Hofmeister and Sag contend, relying in part on original arguments by Kluender (1991, 1992, 1998, 2004), that "many island constructions have features that are known to produce processing difficulties," and moreover, "controlling for these [independent] factors that make processing more difficult improve the acceptability of island-violating sentences."

For example, Hofmeister and Sag point out that it has become standard since at least Pesetsky (1987) for syntacticians to appeal to 'D(iscourse)-linking' to capture the fact that extraction involving *which*-phrases is less island-sensitive than their plain *wh*-counterparts:

(9)   a. Which of the three articles do you wonder [whether Bill read __]?
      b. ??What (on earth) do you wonder [whether Bill read __]?

The notion of D-linking is intended to capture the idea that the set of possible answers is pre-established or otherwise (discourse) salient. But, as Hofmeister and Sag point out, it is unclear why conditions like subjacency should be sensitive to discourse properties like salience. In the current syntactic literature, it's often said that D-linked *wh*-phrases are base-generated in their surface position, or can move to their final landing site in one fell swoop (as opposed to successive cyclically, as subjacency would dictate), but as Chung (1994:39) writes:

> Why should long movement be legitimized in just those cases where the trace [left by movement] ranges over a sufficiently restricted set? To put the question differently, what is it about the ability to narrow down the domain of *wh*-quantification 'enough' that makes it possible for strict locality to be violated?

According to Hofmeister and Sag, a processing-based account is better equipped to capture the nature of the improvement caused by D-linking: D-linked *wh*-phrases "narrow down the range of alternatives that have to be considered, thereby reducing computational effort." (They state that "computing an answer to a question is easier when the scope of the question is narrowed by the discourse.")

In general, Hofmeister and Sag adopt the perspective of Deane (1991), Hawkins (1999), and others, according to which expending cognitive resources in one part of a sentence reduces the availability of resources to process other parts of that sentence. Accordingly, completing a linguistic dependency successfully "is contingent on processing demands imposed by material between the endpoints of a dependency [(the filler and the gap)]."

As many have pointed out, merely identifying the gap is no small task: it's an empty element, which can often be ambiguously posited at various points in the sentence due to sentence processing taking place one word at a time. In addition, at the same time in fact, the filler must be kept in working memory. To top it all off, all the intervening material separating the filler and the gap must be processed as well.

Hofmeister and Sag claim that from this perspective one can understand why "informationally-heavy," "referentially rich" expressions (tensed domains; specific (complex) NPs, etc.) cause 'island effects': the effort such expressions require to access their mental referents disrupts the processing of the filler gap dependency. For example, Hofmeister and Sag point out that Complex NP Constraint examples (e.g., *Which politician did you read [reports that we had impeached __]?*) typically require processing at least three nominal references (*you*, *reports*, and *we*) inside the dependency (*which politician ... __*), in addition to crossing a (relative) clause boundary, and claim that it is no surprise, under a processing account, that Complex NP Constraint examples can be made quite acceptable by using semantically rich fillers, intervening NPs of 'high accessibility,' choosing intermediate verbs that reduce the risk of garden-path/ wrong attachment, etc.

To account for why adjuncts (PP-gaps) are more island-sensitive than arguments (NP-gaps), Hofmeister and Sag follow previous accounts such as Pritchett (1991) in pointing out that adjuncts have multiple association sites, and are therefore more prone to garden-path effects. They also follow Kluender and Kutas (1993) in taking "information-rich clausal boundaries" (elements like *if*, *whether*, etc.) to impose processing demands that create disruption. And they stress the role of frequency of certain collocations, degree of contextualization difficulty, and so on, to account for contrasts like those that follow:

(10) a. Which book did you see [pictures of __]?
  b. ??Which book did you destroy [pictures of __]?

(11) a. Who did you say [that John believes you saw __]?
  b. ??Who did you lisp [that John believes you saw __]?

(12) a. Who did you obtain votes for the impeachment of __?
      b. ?Who did you find votes for the impeachment of __?
      c. ?*Who did you buy votes for the impeachment of __?
      d. *Who did you criticize votes for the impeachment of __?

Everyone would agree with Hofmeister and Sag's claim that "processing differences are influencing perceptions of acceptability." Indeed, this is close to being a truism. And everyone would also agree that all else equal it is better to resort to independently motivated factors, perhaps not even specific to language, to account for islands or whatever else one wishes to explain, rather than positing some highly specialized linguistic machinery that has a fair amount of arbitrariness to it. As minimalists now keep stressing, cost-free explanations should be strongly desired.

It is also true that far too often in syntactic theory island constraints have been embellished with additional featural specifications that are fundamentally ad hoc. As we saw in the case of D-linking above, there is usually no accompanying theory of why these extra features should impact syntactic dependency formation.[8]

In the end, these extra features amount to the special rules alluded to in the following passage from Chomsky (1973:244):

> Some speakers seem to accept such forms as *What did he wonder whether John saw? What crimes did he wonder how they solved?* For me, these are unacceptable. It would be possible to add special rules to allow for these examples by a complication of the particular grammar, given the suggested interpretation of the conditions.

It may be useful at this point to repeat a passage from Chomsky (1977), already quoted in the previous chapter:

> In Chomsky (1973), two approaches to interpretation of conditions on rules are contrasted, an absolute and a relative interpretation; and the relative interpretation is proposed for conditions of the sort discussed there. . ... Under this interpretation, a condition does not impose an absolute restriction against rules of a certain type . . .; rather a rule must be interpreted in accordance with the condition unless otherwise specified. Thus, one might construct a rule to "violate" the A-over-A condition, but only at a cost: the rule would have to make explicit the relevant structures so that it can apply without failing under the condition. "The logic of this approach," as noted, "is essentially that of the theory of markedness."

The logic of markedness or, for that matter, the logic of *Barriers* briefly mentioned above (the more barriers an element crosses, the worse the dependency) is not the problem for the advocates of reductionist accounts. It's the arbitrariness of the solutions used to capture the counterexamples that makes one grow skeptical about the whole approach.

2.3.2   Puzzles for the reductionists

But the crux of the matter for Hofmeister and Sag, or indeed any such reductionist attempt, lies in the "all else equal." And it seems to me that, for the moment, there is quite a bit of basic explaining that remains to be done on the part of the reductionists. For even if it is true that combining long-distance dependencies and various other factors independently known to render processing more difficult (some clausal boundaries, information-rich NPs, and the like) causes problems, why should it be that the difficulty (severe unacceptability) arises only in certain configurations, those where the gap is inside "islands"?[9] More concretely, why is (13) much better than (14), despite the fact that, in linear terms, the filler is separated from the gap by an information-heavy NP?

(13) Who did John give [the report that Mary died] to __?
(14) Who did John read [the report that Mary kissed __]?

And why does (15) sound much better than (16), even if in (15) the filler is separated from the gap by an embedded interrogative clause?

(15) Who did John ask, setting aside [whether Mary was there or not], __ to write the report?
(16) Who did John ask [whether Mary kissed __]?

In all these cases, a long-distance dependency must be constructed, a filler must be kept in working memory for a long time, while various elements (complex NPs, embedded interrogative clauses) have to be processed, which, by hypothesis, renders the completion of the filler-gap dependency more difficult.

   And, come to think of it, why should information-rich *wh*-phrases make it easier to cross islands (cf. "D-linking"), while information-rich NPs create islands? If it's easier to maintain D-linked elements in working memory, why is accessing their mental referents so disruptive?

   Elsewhere in their paper, Hofmeister and Sag (2010) point out that "an assortment of processing difficulties that are absent in argument dependencies" render adjunct-dependencies more island-sensitive, but they forget to point out that this assortment of processing factors (lack of a close association with a verb, optionality, multiple modification sites, and so on) finds a direct reflex in grammar (lack of a theta-role, optional character of adjunction, etc.). While it is true that some factors may have been 'brute-forced' into the grammar by syntacticians, not all the ingredients of grammatical theories of islands have an arbitrary character. And while it is true, as Hofmeister and Sag (2010) write, that some conditions on transformations appear "complex, arbitrary, and ultimately either too strong or too weak," it is not the case that none of them are "arbitrary in the sense that they bear no relationship to other constraints, emanate from no general principles of language." In fact, principles like cyclicity, or Relativized Minimality appear to have the right 'generic' character to qualify as genuine explanations. If they can account for some island effects, why should processing accounts be preferred? Explanations that follow from these principles are potentially as cost-free as processing-based explanations.

It is significant that Hofmeister and Sag (2010) conclude that some island effects are irreducibly syntactic (part of grammar proper). What they fail to consider is what shape the grammatical conditions would take to account for this grammatical island residue. What if the conditions needed turn out to extend naturally to many cases for which Hofmeister and Sag favor a processing account? In such a situation, wouldn't it be better to try to explain counterexamples to the grammatical condition in processing terms?

Ironically, one of the examples of a purely grammatical island that Hofmeister and Sag highlight is the Coordinate Structure Constraint. I say 'ironically,' for there is a growing consensus among syntacticians that this constraint is to be understood as a more general cognitive condition on parallelism (as already hinted in Chomsky 1973), defined over semantic representations (see Fox 2000, Goodall 1987, Kato 2006, Kehler 1996, Lin 2001, Moltmann 1992, Muadz 1991, Munn 1993, Ruys 1993). The reason for such growing consensus is that no other grammatical condition ever proposed appears to be able to subsume the Coordinate Structure Constraint. The reasoning here is quite different from Hofmeister and Sag, for whom the Coordinate Structure Constraint must be the result of a grammatical condition since "there is sparingly little counterevidence to" it. Hofmeister and Sag seem to exclude the possibility that cognitive (non-strictly grammatical) constraints are inviolable. But why should this be? As I pointed out above in the context of discourse-structure-based accounts of islands, in the absence of a *theory* of cognitive constraints, why should we trust intriguing facts or potential factors more than grammatical theory?[10]

Here is what Phillips (2011) has to say about the general form of reductionist arguments, specifically those such as Hofmeister and Sag (2010) that are based on "amelioration effects."

An argument from amelioration involves two assumptions. First, the argument assumes that acceptability entails grammatical well-formedness. ... Second, the argument relies on the assumption that superficially similar sentences have the same syntactic structure. ... These are reasonable initial assumptions, but unfortunately there are a number of reasons to doubt both assumptions.

Phillips observes that it is fairly easy to find counterexamples to the assumption that acceptability entails grammaticality. As he writes, "we have all been witnesses to assertions that taken literally fail to convey what the speaker intends." There also exist numerous cases of so-called grammatical illusions: sentences that are judged acceptable despite being ill-formed. The most famous illusion of this kind is due to the linguist Mario Montalbetti: *More people have been to Russia than I have.* But there are many more, such as the example in (17), which sound relatively good to many people when they are asked to judge it, despite the fact that it is missing a verb:

(17) The patient that the nurse that the clinic had hired met Jack.

Such cases show that although grammatically ill-formed sentences tend to lead to unacceptable results, there are also numerous circumstances where ill-formed sentences are judged acceptable, with the parser improving the status of syntactic outputs.

Phillips also offers counterarguments to the second assumption of the case for processing accounts based on amelioration: that superficially similar sentences share the same syntactic structure. Far too often, non-syntacticians suffer from a certain 'wysiwyg' (what-you-see-is-what-you-get) attitude, which is unfortunate, given the wealth of evidence that sometimes small surface variations entail massive structural differences. As we already saw in Chapter 1, Ross was the first to point out that apparent violations of his Complex NP Constraint need not entail the rejection of the constraint, given that the counterexamples can receive an alternative structural characterization that complies with the constraint. For example, Ross proposed that in (18), we are not dealing with extraction from a complex NP, because *make the claim* can be represented as a (complex) Verb equivalent to *claim*:

(18) How much money are you making the claim that the company squandered __?

Phillips (2011) cites work by Kush (2010) (see also Kush and Lindahl 2011), where standard examples of what appear to be 'acceptable island violations' in certain languages like Swedish (cited by Hofmeister and Sag 2010) are shown to be cases of alternative structures that merely resemble islands, but do not violate any constraints. For example, Kush argues that cases like (19) do not involve extraction from a Complex NP, but instead involve extraction from a small clause.

(19) Den teorin känner jap ingen   som tror   på
     That theory know I   nobody that believes in
     'That theory, I know nobody who believes in (it)'

To support his argument, Kush shows that when examples like (19) are modified in such a way as to block construal as a small clause (e.g., using a different main verb), the island effect surfaces, as the grammatical theory predicts.

(20) * Den här teorin, finns det ingen   som tror   på
     That here theory exists it nobody that believes in
     'That theory there is nobody who believes in (it)'

Phillips is right to use such cases as useful reminders of structural ambiguity in language.

In sum, amelioration effects do not wear theoretical conclusions on their sleeves. They are certainly quite informative, and should not be discounted offhand. Not all such amelioration effects are illusions or subject to structural ambiguity. I'm quite sure that some of them are real, but, as Phillips (2011) concludes, this is to be done on a case-by-case basis, and everyone should bear in mind that "amelioration effects do not immediately reveal the underlying nature of unacceptability effects. Rather they serve as useful starting points for further investigation."

Incidentally, in his (2011) survey, Phillips also addresses the 'gradation argument' that is often used in advocating processing-based accounts of grammatical constraints, and has this to say:

> The existence of gradedness is sometimes seen as evidence for a reductionist account of a syntactic phenomenon. The argument runs as follows: if the putative grammatical constraint affects ratings in the same way that manipulations of processing difficulty do, then surely it is more parsimonious to assume that the phenomena have the same origin (Hofmeister and Sag 2010).
>
> This argument is straightforwardly dispatched. If speakers are asked to judge a sentence using a 1-dimensional scale, then it is unsurprising that they give judgments that make use of that scale. If the question under investigation is whether variation in acceptability judgments reflects one, two, or more orthogonal cognitive dimensions (e.g., difficulty vs. grammaticality), then we should not expect to resolve that question by asking speakers to give 1-dimensional ratings, and checking whether manipulation of an extra-grammatical factor modulates ratings in the same manner as the putative grammatical constraint.

The issue of judgment variability[11] bears directly on how to interpret the phenomenon of "satiation" (amelioration upon repeated exposure), which was first discussed by Snyder (2000). While it has often been noted anecdotally among linguists that repeated exposure renders judgments less sharp, Snyder was to my knowledge the first to suggest that not every violation is subject to satiation. Specifically, Snyder tested standard island effects and claimed that only some are subject to satiation. He went on to suggest that these may be amenable to extra-grammatical explanations. (This suggestion was later used by Stepanov 2007 to argue against the unity of the CED (cf. Chapter 1).[12])

In an attempt at replication, Sprouse (2009) obtained different results from Snyder's, and concluded that satiation was most likely an artifact of the methodology used by Snyder. In fact, Sprouse found a couple of problems with the original design of Snyder's experiments (which Sprouse suggested may account for the difficulty of replicating his results in the literature). In addition to only allowing for either yes or no judgments, Snyder's samples were unbalanced: they contained significantly more unacceptable examples than acceptable ones, and Sprouse suggested that rather than satiating, informants were trying to equalize their ratings during the task (i.e., give roughly the same number of yes and no). Once these design flaws were addressed, Sprouse found out that island effects showed up robustly.

On the one hand, this is good news for the grammarians: it shows that the standard judgments reported in the literature are reliable. On the other, the absence of true satiation effects means that we have to abandon Snyder's suggestion that violations due to processing factors are subject to satiation, while violations due to grammatical constraints are not.

Before concluding this overview of attempts to offer processing-accounts of island effects with what is currently the strongest empirical counterargument against it, I would like to briefly mention two more phenomena that bear on the issue. The first is due to Lasnik (1999); the second, to Phillips (2006).

Lasnik (1999) points out that while one may be sympathetic to attempts to reduce island constraints to processing factors, it is difficult to imagine[13] how such accounts could extend to island effects where there is no overt filler-gap dependency, as is the case with certain *wh*-in-situ constructions in languages like Chinese or Japanese (see Huang 1982, Lasnik and Saito 1984 for seminal discussion).[14] As Lasnik observes, adjunct wh-phrases in situ such as those illustrated in

(21) are sensitive to islands, even if the filler is pronounced in the position where languages like English exhibit a gap.

(21) a. *Ni xiangxin Lisi weisheme lai de shuofa?   [Chinese]
        You believe Lisa why came that claim
        'You believe the claim that Lisa came why'
     b. *John-wa Mary-ga naze sore-o katta kadooka siritagatte-iru no?   [Japanese]
        John-nom. Mary-nom. why it bought whether want-know Q
        'John wants to know whether Mary bought it why'

Phillips 2006 brings up another problematic set of data for processing accounts. He points out that if island constraints are indeed the effects of limitations on on-line sentence processing, we should not find cases where the constraint is violated during on-line structure building. That is, we should not find evidence of speakers spontaneously positing a gap in island domains (domains that are by hypothesis too complex to posit a gap in), and yet this is exactly the sort of thing that Phillips (2006) found. Phillips used the phenomenon of parasitic gaps, extensively discussed in the 1980s in theoretical syntax, and discovered using a self-paced reading experiment that speakers were positing a gap inside 'islands' during on-line sentence constructions, but crucially only in those cases where grammatical theory allows for parasitic gaps. The relevant paradigm appears in (22).

(22) a. *Which parts did [the attempt to repair __] ultimately damage the car?
     b. *Which parts did the attempt to repair the car ultimately damage __?
     c. Which parts did [the attempt to repair __] ultimately damage __?

Whereas speakers were positing a gap in the bracketed phrases in (22) during on-line processing (subsequently ruling out (22a), but not (22c)), they showed no sign of positing a gap in those domains that cannot license parasitic gaps, as in (23).

(23) a. *What did [the reporter that criticized __] eventually praised the Mayor?
     b. *What did the reporter that criticized the Mayor eventually praised __?
     c. *What did [the reporter that criticized __] eventually praised __?

As Hofmeister and Sag (2010) conceded, facts of this kind suggest that some island domains are best treated in grammatical terms.[15] Here it is important to stress again that once the door to grammatical accounts is reopened, one must be precise about which accounts one is willing to accept (which theory one adopts), for most accounts that exist do not seem to make the cut that reductionists want: they often naturally extend to situations that reductionists would like to fall under the purview of 'pure' processing analyses.

2.3.3   A serious empirical problem for the reductionists

Let me conclude this overview with what I take to be currently the strongest empirical argument against existing processing accounts, found in its clearest expression in Sprouse, Wagers, and Phillips (to appear).

Sprouse *et al.* decided to take seriously and test the basic idea behind Kluender's (1991, 1992, 1998, 2004) processing account of islands, arguably the best worked out reductionist accounts. Kluender's analysis rests on the natural assumption that humans have limited processing resources and that island effects result when these limited processing resources are overtaxed. Specifically, island effects emerge when we have to process long-distance dependencies, which have an inherent processing cost to them, across structures that are known independently to impose processing demands (e.g., relative clauses), which Sprouse *et al.* call "island structures." According to Kluender, it is the conjunction of these two resource intensive processes that leads to unacceptable results when they must be deployed simultaneously.

The key factor to explain though is what Sprouse (2007a) emphasized: the independently attested acceptability-lowering effects of both dependency length and 'island structures' are not additive; they are *super*additive.

Let me explain this further. Sprouse tested the interaction of the two factors at the heart of Kluender's account by manipulating length and structure, using sentences involving (i) a short-distance wh-question, (ii) a long-distance wh-question, (iii) a short-distance wh-question combined with an embedded interrogative, and (iv) a long-distance wh-question combined with an embedded interrogative, as illustrated here:

(i) Who __ thinks that John bought a car?
(ii) What do you think that John bought __?
(iii) Who __ wonders whether John bought a car?
(iv) What do you wonder whether John bought __?

The experimental set up allowed Sprouse to isolate the effect of each of the individual factors on continuous acceptability ratings (so-called magnitude estimation). For example, the effect of processing long-distance wh-dependencies can be seen by comparing the short, non-island condition in (i) to the long, non-island condition (ii), and the effect of processing 'island-inducing' structures can be seen by comparing the short, non-island condition (i) to the short, island condition (iii).

This allowed Sprouse to understand and quantify the interaction of the two factors – the superadditive effect that needs explaining: If

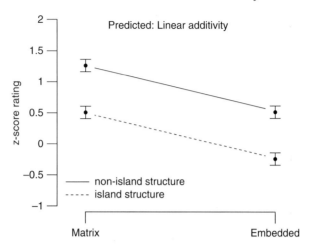

Figure 1 (courtesy of J. Sprouse)

there were no interaction between the two factors (i.e., if the two sets of processes affected acceptability ratings independently), we would expect a graph like that in Figure 1. Figure 1, in the words of Sprouse *et al.*, "is an example of simple linear additivity between each factor in which the cost of each process leads to a decrease in acceptability ratings, and in which each cost sums linearly with respect to the short/non-island condition." This linear additivity leads to two parallel lines. (If length causes a decrease in acceptability of, say, 1 degree on a given scale, and 'complex ['island'] structure' causes a decrease of, say, 2, combining them should lead to a decrease of 3, not more.)

What Sprouse (2007a) described in great detail, however, was that there was an interaction between the two factors, and a graph like that in Figure 2 (next page), as opposed to the one in Figure 1, obtained: super-additivity when the *long* and *island* levels of the two factors are combined, leading to non-parallel decreasing lines.[16] Put differently, the effect is worse than expected.

The starting point of Sprouse, Wagers, and Phillips's study is that given this defined superadditive effect on acceptability ratings when long dependencies are combined with island structures, it is now possible to articulate a fundamental difference between reductionist accounts like Kluender's and grammar-based theories. As they note, "theories like Kluender interpret the interaction found [in Figure 2] as reflecting a psychological interaction of the two sets of processes represented by the two experimental factors, due to a shared pool of limited processing resources." Grammatical theories, on the

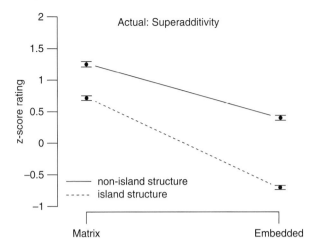

Figure 2   (courtesy of J. Sprouse)

contrary, "attribute the lower-than-expected, superadditive unacceptability of the long, island condition as resulting from a grammatical
constraint that affects only sentences that contain long-distance
dependencies that enter island structures." Crucially, then, the two
theories differ in their account of the source and cause of the interaction: a Kluender-type theory attributes the interaction to a limited
pool of processing resources, and the grammatical theories attribute
the interaction to a grammatical constraint that only targets the
long, island condition.

Sprouse *et al.* stress that the two kinds of theories do not necessarily
differ in their predictions about the acceptability of individual conditions, or even the relative acceptability of pairs of conditions. The two
theories only differ when it comes to the source of the interaction, as
the two theories ascribe different underlying causes to it.

Given this, Sprouse *et al.* reason that by manipulating factors that
affect those underlying causes, one should be able to observe correlated changes in the interaction found in Figure 2. Specifically, under a
theory like Kluender, the strength of the interaction in acceptability
judgments should co-vary with the availability of processing resources,
as Kluender's claim is that it is the limited quantity of processing resources that causes the interaction. Put differently, under a
Kluender-style theory, individuals with larger processing resource capacity should exhibit weaker interactions, and individuals with more
limited processing resource capacity should demonstrate stronger

interactions. Under the grammatical theory, processing resource capacity plays no role in the explanation of the interaction, therefore any individual differences in the strength of island effects that we might see in the population should not correlate with individual differences in processing resource capacity.

The latter state of affairs is exactly what Sprouse *et al.* found. After testing over 300 individuals using two different types of (well-established) working memory measures and two different types of acceptability judgment tasks, Sprouse *et al.* found that the strength of the interaction of the sort depicted in Figure 2 remained constant across subjects.[17] (In fact, the situation is somewhat worse for processing based accounts: for complex NP and subject islands Sprouse *et al.* did not even find evidence of the processing cost of the island structure, contradicting one of the premises of a Kluender-style theory.)

Sprouse *et al.* concluded that their results are consistent with grammatical theories of island effects, which predict no relation between resource capacity and the strength of island effects.

2.4   MERELY INAPPROPRIATE QUESTIONS?

As I pointed out above, processing-based views on islands do not seek a unified theory of islandhood, and although they recognize that "syntactic theories of islandhood have had to recognize a heterogeneity in the universality and rigidity of different island constraints" (Hofmeister and Sag 2010), they do not rely on the subdivisions that syntacticians have advocated in the wake of the breakdown of locality conditions surveyed in Chapter 1. For example, one finds little discussion of the strong vs. weak island distinction from the processing perspective.

On the contrary, those subdivisions are central to the semantico-pragmatic perspective on islands that I would like to discuss in this section.[18] The key distinction here will be that between weak vs. strong islands. As Szabolcsi (2006) points out in her extensive survey of the literature on weak islands, proponents of theories of weak islands typically do not try to extend their accounts to strong islands. As I already indicated in Chapter 1, this stance was made explicit in the very first words of Rizzi (1990), and it remains a basic assumption of those that seek to derive certain island effects (more precisely, the weak island effects) from semantico-pragmatic considerations.

Such accounts took as their starting point the syntactic treatment of a contrast like that in (24) that is the focus of Rizzi (1990).

(24) a. Which glass of wine do you know [whether you should poison __] ?
  b. *How much wine do you know [whether you should poison __]?

The basic idea behind the syntactic account offered by Rizzi is that both examples in (24) illustrate a syntactic prohibition against establishing a movement dependency across a wh-island (extraction out of an embedded question). But the reason (24a) sounds more acceptable than (24b) is due to the nature of the extracted element. Specifically, it is claimed that because *which glass of wine* is more "referential" than *how much wine*, the moved wh-phrase can establish a link between its trace position via a mechanism (long-distance binding) that is not subject to the same locality condition that standard movement is. In doing so, it 'saves' (/'licenses') the gap created by movement, and renders the sentence acceptable.

 Cinque (1990) offered a similar explanation while analyzing a sentence like (25).

(25) How many books do you know [whether you should burn __]?

According to Cinque, this sentence should have two readings, but informants typically find only one of these to be available. As Abrusán (2011a) writes, "the question [in (25)] is licit if the hearer is assumed to have a particular set of books in mind and the speaker wonders about the cardinality of that set. But it cannot be understood as asking whether there is a particular number of books (any books) that the hearer knows whether he should burn." That is to say: "Do you know how many books there are in the pile of books you should burn?" is available in (25) but "Were you told to burn 25, 30, or more books?" is not.

 Cinque relates this fact to examples like (24) discussed by Rizzi and claims that the first reading (the only available one) in (25) can emerge because in this case the *how many* phrase is understood 'referentially,' which allows it to establish a long-distance dependency via binding. By contrast, the second reading, which corresponds to the non-referential reading, can only be obtained by movement, and hence is ruled out syntactically (island violation).

 The main problem with such an account is that the notion of 'referentiality' that is crucial for it to work has proven particularly difficult to make precise.[19] And whatever it may be, referentiality feels more like a semantic notion than a syntactic notion.

 In fact, Kroch (1989) was perhaps the first to argue that the referentiality requirement is a pragmatic one, not a syntactic condition on licensing. Kroch's view is that extraction in both cases in (24) is possible, and well-formed syntactically. But as is the case in (24b), sometimes this kind of extraction produces sentences that are pragmatically odd. For Kroch, the ultimate success of extraction of this type thus boils down to context. Specifically, Kroch follows work by Comorovski (1988) and argues that every question comes with a certain existential presupposition that acts as a requirement on the askability of the question: the speaker must presuppose the corresponding existential sentence in order to use the question felicitously. Bad extractions like (24b) are due to the fact that they lead to an interpretation of the question that clashes with its 'askability.' But if a suitable context can be found that makes this clash go away, the judgment of the relevant sentence improves dramatically.

For example, Abrusán (2011a) observes that in the case of (25), it is quite plausible that there is a particular set of books such that someone can know whether to burn it, and quite plausible to wonder how many books that set contains, but it is less plausible to know about a particular amount whether one should burn that amount of books.

The basic intuition behind semantico-pragmatic accounts of weak islands is that when such extractions sound bad, it's because the most salient reading of the extracted element is the one that is associated with a context of very low plausibility. As Kroch points out, once a more plausible context is constructed, the status of the question improves. Consider (26).

(26) How many points are the judges arguing about [whether to deduct __]?

The sentence is much more acceptable because it is more plausible to imagine a context where there is a certain amount n such that the judges are wondering whether it should be the case that n-many points are deducted.

In the intervening years, Kroch's reasoning was formalized by semanticists. Recently, Fox and Hackl (2007) (relying in part on works by Kuno and Takami 1997 and Rullman 1995) proposed that certain weak island effects, such as negative islands (Ross's 1984 so-called "inner islands," where negation blocks wh-movement, as in *How fast didn't John drive?) arise because in these cases a "maximally informative true answer" cannot be found, which violates the claim made by Dayal (1996) that "questions presuppose that they have a maximally informative true answer in the standard semantic denotation of the question" (a true answer that entails all other true answers). The absence of a "maximally informative true answer" renders the relevant questions illicit.

The condition that there be a maximally true answer, formalized by Fox and Hackl, is very reminiscent of Kroch's 'askability' requirement (the requirement that there be a uniquely identifiable entity of which the property described in the question holds). Abrusán (2007,

2011a, 2011b) has extended Fox and Hackl's account to many other cases of weak islands identified in the literature, and explains why such weak island effects disappear in many situations; compare the cases in (27):

(27) a. *How many children don't you have __?
     b. How many children are you not allowed to have __?
     c. *How fast didn't Bill drive __?
     d. How fast do you hope that Bill didn't drive __?

The account offered by Fox and Hackl/Abrusán is not the only semantic treatment of weak islands: Szabolcsi and Zwarts (1990, 1993, 1997) was the first comprehensive semantic treatment of weak islands, based first on the idea that a certain semantic property of operators (specifically, downward entailingness) caused weak island effects, then subsequently replaced by a treatment in terms of scope (see also Honcoop 1998).

Beck (1996, 2006) proposed yet a different treatment of some weak island effects in terms of focus interpretation, according to which "interveners" (in something like a Relativized Minimality sense) have certain interpretive properties related to focus that lead to ill-formedness (uninterpretability) in certain contexts that correspond to at least some classical weak island configurations.

It does not seem to me to be the place to go into the details of the semantic properties posited in the semantico-pragmatic analyses just mentioned, in part because excellent overviews of this material already exist (see Szabolcsi 2006 and Abrusán 2011a, 2011b in particular). Suffice it to say that many semantic proposals rely on very rich interpretive models whose psychological reality has often been questioned, even within semantic circles (see, e.g., Pietroski in press for a general critique of the excessive richness of models in formal semantics; see also Hinzen 2006, 2007), but the more pragmatic oriented models, such as Abrusán's, extending previous accounts like Fox and Hackl (2007), strike me as very promising alternatives to purely syntactic approaches to weak islands, especially when the latter are forced to appeal to semantically based features like 'referential' or 'specific.'

Whatever their ultimate success, I agree with Szabolcsi that semantico-pragmatic approaches have had the great merit to expand the dataset of interveners and weak islands considerably, from embedded questions to negative markers, affective operators, certain predicates, adverbs, scope and focus markers, and more. Because the morpho-syntactic status of many of these interveners appears to vary cross-linguistically, whereas their 'island'-triggering effects don't,

Szabolcsi 2006 is right to conclude that syntactic attempts would have to be enriched considerably to capture these effects. While this syntactic enrichment would certainly be felt undesirable in current minimalist settings, let me repeat that minimalist desiderata ought to apply equally to semantic models. For this reason, it seems to me that the more we can explain weak islands in terms of pragmatic conditions (along the lines originally suggested by Kroch), the better.

Let me also point out that the expansion of the empirical landscape of weak islands made possible by semanticists has been such that it may not be too realistic to expect a single semantic (or pragmatic) factor to account for them all. As Szabolcsi (2008) points out, it may well be the case that weak islands do not form a natural class, in which case it would be wrong to seek a unified semantico-pragmatic account of them all.

2.5 TAKING STOCK

The repeated attempts to remove island effects from the purview of pure syntax, which were reviewed in this chapter, may yet have to convince syntacticians, but being a syntactician myself I think that such attempts can teach us several important lessons in our quest to capture the nature of the effects discovered by Ross and Chomsky.

Reductionist attempts remind us that if one seeks to simplify the content of Universal Grammar, and carve the human language faculty at its joints, it is important to bear in mind a point made famous by Hauser, Chomsky, and Fitch (2002): that next to that which is specific to language, there are a fair amount of computational properties that belong to the faculty of language in the broad sense, properties that are not specific to language (nor, for that matter, specific to humans), but shape its profile just as well. In recent years, it has become more and more common to find introductory statements such as this (taken from Yang 2011:180):

> How much should we ask of Universal Grammar? Not too little, for there must be a place for our unique ability to acquire a language along with its intricacies and curiosities. But asking for too much won't do either. A theory of Universal Grammar is a statement of human biology, and one needs to be mindful of the limited structural modification that would have been plausible under the extremely brief history of *Homo sapiens* evolution.

This is what Chomsky has in recent years called 'Approaching UG from Below.' Reductionist attempts certainly go in this minimalist direction, although they tend to be skeptical about the specific technical inroads into minimalism adopted by syntacticians. But one should not confuse attempts to operationalize the program with the program itself.

As Chomsky himself has remarked (2007:4):

> Recent inquiry into these questions in the case of language has come to be called "the minimalist program", but there has been so much misunderstanding, even within professional circles, that it is perhaps worth reiterating that it is a *program*, not a *theory*, and a program that is both traditional in its general flavor and pretty much theory-neutral, insofar as the biolinguistic framework is adopted. . . . And whatever one's beliefs about design of language may be, the questions of the research program arise. It may also be worth mentioning that the program can only be pursued, whatever theoretical framework one adopts, insofar as some descriptive account of the phenomena to be explained is reasonably unproblematic, often not the case of course, as expected with any system of at least apparent intricacy.

In other words, there are many alternative minimalist visions one can entertain. As soon as one begins to ask 'why is the language faculty that way?,' like it or not, one is in minimalist territory.

Furthermore, as Frisch (1999:600) pointed out in a different context:

> For the traditional formalist, it is actually desirable for some linguistic patterns, especially those that are gradient, to be explained by [other] principles. The remainder . . . might be a simpler, cleaner, and more accurate picture of the nature of the innate language faculty and its role in delimiting the set of possible human languages.

Reductionist accounts of island effects, even if they fail, serve as useful reminders that it's good to be mindful of interaction effects, that grammar is embedded in larger cognitive systems whose properties are crucial to understanding our knowledge of language.

Reductionist attempts also remind us that as the titles of Ross's and Chomsky's seminal works indicated (cf. the plural marker in con-strain*ts*, condition*s*), island effects may not form a natural class, and that a pluralistic approach may be in order. Although reductionist attempts may fail to capture all island effects, they may be the best explanation we can hope for in at least some cases. The more so if the grammatical theory we favor cannot naturally capture these.

Reductionist attempts also help redirect our attention to factors that lead to island circumvention (a phenomenon I will discuss in more detail in the next chapter under the rubric of 'island repair'). Although Ross already pointed out in his (1967) thesis, and in a later article

(1969), that languages develop various strategies to obviate islands (pied-piping, resumption, ellipsis, etc.), many purely syntactic accounts continue to relegate such phenomena to the periphery. But as several recent works have stressed (see Merchant 2001, 2008, Lasnik 2001, 2005, Boeckx 2003a, 2008a, among others), island obviation may tell us a great deal about the nature of island violations.

Reductionist attempts also remind us that cognitive explanations of the sort advocated by Miller and Chomsky (1963) and Bever (1970), though often mentioned in footnotes, continue to be underutilized by syntacticians. This is very unfortunate, because, far from questioning syntactic analyses, appealing to extra-grammatical, cognitive constraints may help syntacticians avoid the need to posit special rules and conditions that smack of ad hocness. Quick and dirty use of base-generation vs. movement, special licensing conditions and idiosyncratic features may not always be the best way to 'save' the phenomena.

As Hofmeister and Sag (2010) correctly point out, a survey of the syntactic literature on islands quickly reveals that the field has been extremely conservative, especially in the context of islands, in its way of theorizing. I agree with Hofmeister and Sag's assessment that

> [w]hat stands out in the history of research on syntactic islands …
> is the entrenchment of the generalizations that were formed from
> early data sets. Despite … counterexamples, … reassessments of
> the generalizations embodied in the grammatical constraints
> that were first proposed to deal with particular phenomena …
> have been rare. (p. 374)

Kleanthes Grohmann and I concluded our survey of the standard minimalist take on locality (Boeckx and Grohmann 2007) with the same complaint regarding this type of theoretical conservatism. Hofmeister and Sag's assessment also recalls Postal's criticism of the lack of argument for certain standard assumptions regarding islands already mentioned in Chapter 1. Such assessments are not to be understood as general critiques against syntactic accounts, but instead are meant to stress that certain research strategies, e.g., the consistent pattern found in the literature to take islands to ban all kinds of movement and therefore to immediately appeal to base-generation and binding whenever an apparent island violation surfaces, fall well short of explanatory adequacy.

Last, but not least, reductionist accounts remind us of an observation that Ross already made back in 1967, at the very end of his thesis, when he wrote, in a context that I will exploit in Chapter 4:

> [T]he relationship between grammaticality and acceptability must
> become much more abstract than has been assumed. (p. 290)

DISCUSSION QUESTIONS

1. By going through the literature that seeks to treat some islands as non-syntactic effects, identify those islands that they exclude (and view as syntactic). Once you have that list, ask yourself if they form a natural class.
2. Going through Szabolcsi (2006), try to think of ways in which her semantico-pragmatic account could be extended to account for some strong islands.

3 Why the ultimate solution is unlikely to be purely syntactic

> Why should rules which adjoin terms to the right side of a variable be upward bounded, and not those which adjoin to the left of a variable? Why should it be that chopping rules, feature-changing rules, and unidirectional deletion rules share the property of being subject to the constraint, to the exclusion of other rules? Why should there be a difference between unidirectional and bidirectional pronominalization? Why should it be that the constraints are all "downward-oriented" – that is, why should it be that there are phrase-marker configurations that prevent elements indefinitely far below them from undergoing various syntactic operations, whereas there are no configurations which affect elements indefinitely far above them? Why should complex NP's, coordinate nodes, sentential subject clauses, and NP's on the left branches of larger NP's all function the same in defining islands? (Ross 1967:291)

With these questions Ross concluded his seminal study on constraints on variables in syntax. All these questions are facets of the questions many linguists have pondered since then: *Why islands?*, and *Why these islands?*

These are the questions I would like to address in this chapter and the next, the most tentative part of the whole book; the most minimalist oriented as well, given that Ross's questions just quoted are really about the design properties ('why-questions') of the language faculty.

3.1 CONTRASTING TWO GRAMMAR-BASED VIEWS ON ISLANDS

The previous chapter has shown that it seems safe to conclude for the moment that there is some syntactic residue in the domain of islands. It is the superadditive effect that Sprouse *et al.*'s study showed could not be reduced to non-grammatical factors (cf. Figures 1 and 2 on pp. 44–45); it's also the range of (strong) islands that was explicitly left out of semantico-pragmatic accounts.

As Hofmeister and Sag (2010:406) acknowledge, arguments offered in favor of a processing treatment, of the sort reviewed in the previous chapter,

> do not rule out the possibility that the grammar itself is responsible for some of the [island effects, including some of the acceptability variation tied to island violations]. Indeed, it is impossible to prove, given the current state of our knowledge of both grammar and processing, that grammar has no part in creating the observed processing differences.

Accordingly, the questions that will accompany us throughout this and the next chapter are the following: What could be the conditions on transformations that are responsible for (if only a portion of) the observed island effects; and why should they (as opposed to other conditions) have the effects that they do, as opposed to other, equally conceivable effects?

Because of the possibility of accounting for weak islands in non-syntactic terms, I have decided to concentrate on strong islands, which I take to reduce to bans on extraction out of adjoined domains (which covers a whole range of Rossian constraints: relative clauses, sentential subjects, sentential complements to nouns, and others) and out of argument phrases that do not occupy complement positions (e.g., displaced subjects). In other words, my main concern in this and the next chapter will be to account for why (1a) is possible, but (1b) and (1c) are not.

(1) a. Who did you see [pictures of __]?
     b. *Who did [pictures of __] cause Bill to leave the room?
     c. *Who did Bill arrive [after seeing (pictures of) __]?

As several authors have pointed out (see Boeckx 2008b, Hornstein, Lasnik, and Uriagereka 2007), within grammatical theory, one can find two *kinds* of directions to account for this core extraction paradigm (and in general, to answer the why-questions with which we began this chapter). I called these two options 'derivational' and 'representational' in Boeckx (2008b); Hornstein *et al.* referred to them as 'limits on rule application' and 'conditions on the output(s)' of the computational system. The distinction is well captured in the following passage from Phillips (2011):

> Formal grammatical constraints could exert their effects in different ways. On the one hand, a constraint could apply as a *constraint on structure generation*, meaning that the constraint makes it impossible for speakers to construct mental representations that violate the constraint. On the other hand, a constraint could apply as a *filter* on

generated structures, meaning that speakers are able to mentally represent structures that violate the constraint, but that they somehow also encode the fact that those representations are grammatically illicit.

The distinction could also be couched in terms of 'pure syntax' vs. 'interface,' since representational solutions, if they are to gain some traction (explanatory force), must appeal to properties of the external systems with which syntax interacts, and determine which of these properties lead to certain syntactic outputs to be judged illicit. Derivational solutions, by contrast, need not look outside of narrow syntax to rule out the bad outcomes.

Whatever terminology one ends up adopting, readers of this book are likely to be much more familiar with the idea of constraints on structure generation, as they reflect the standard, textbook perspective on islands ('no movement can cross an island'). The idea of filter is somewhat less well represented in the island literature, although interestingly, it goes back to Ross's dissertation. Here is what Ross says about the idea of filter at the end of his work (p. 290):

> Chomsky's A-over-A principle is both too strong and too weak. A far more serious inadequacy in this principle ... is the fact that it cannot be extended in any natural way, as far as I can see, to account for the phenomena which led me to construct a theory of syntactic islands. ... I also gave some evidence that a rather substantial revision in the syntactic component was necessary – that many restrictions previously thought to be best stated as restrictions on particular rules should instead be regarded as static output conditions, with the rules in question being freed of all restrictions. These output conditions effect no change on final derived constituent structures; rather, they lower the acceptability of sentences which are output by the transformational component, if these sentences exhibit certain formal properties which are specified in these conditions.

It's at the end of this reflection that Ross points out that "[t]hus, the relationship between grammaticality and acceptability must become much more abstract than has been assumed," which I quoted in concluding the previous chapter.

In his preface to *Infinite Syntax!*, Postal (1986:xix–xx) noted that "[w]hile the introduction of the notion 'island' is the most important aspect of CVS, it offers many other attractions as well. ... the idea of filters or output constraints ... is introduced here."

Since Ross's thesis, many syntacticians have investigated the possibility that filters may account for several grammatical phenomena, beginning with Perlmutter's seminal dissertation (published in 1971), through Chomsky and Lasnik's (1977) "Filters and control" paper, all the way to the current cartographic trend in syntax, which posits a universal sequence of functional projection and uses it to explain certain observed restrictions on word order and more (see Cinque 1999 and much subsequent work). But perhaps due to the fact that such filters often take the form of blatant stipulations or re-descriptions of the things to be explained ("such and such structure can be generated by our system, but since it appears to make wrong empirical predictions, let us posit a filter that rules out this product," or, simply, "star this structure"), many syntacticians have favored the derivational view (the idea that it is constraints on rule application that are responsible for the cases to be ruled out).[1] And yet, in this and the next chapter, I will argue that on balance, the evidence we currently have appears to favor the filters/representational approach in the context of islands, and that one should seek to add (cognitive) substance to the relevant filters instead of treating them as ad hoc, last-gasp efforts to save the theory. It will be the aim of the next chapter to develop, based on my own work as well as suggestions by others, a particular filter that accounts for the generalization underlying the facts in (1). The aim of this chapter is to present a series of arguments against the more popular, derivational approach to islands.

Because the sort of analysis I will critically examine here is so mainstream, I ask the reader to pay particular attention to the short-comings that I will highlight in the next sections, for even if I am the first to admit that a compelling filter-based approach of the sort I favor remains to be developed (I will review several attempts in the next chapter and sketch what seems to me to be a promising possibility), this should not distract the reader's attention from the numerous, persistent explanatory failures of derivational views that rely solely on properties of narrow syntax.

To prove my point, I will first review the logic of Chomsky's most recent phase-based theory and argue that any account of islands based on such kind of theory seems to be doomed from the start. I will then scrutinize the most detailed phase-based analysis of islands to date (Müller 2010) and show in detail where and why such an analysis fails.

3.2 CREATING ISLANDS ONLY TO ESCAPE FROM THEM, OR OPENING PANDORA'S BOX

Since Chomsky's epoch-making "Conditions on transformations" syntacticians have come to theorize about islands in a very particular way that goes roughly like this: the syntactic component is designed in such a way that operations must take place within a narrow computational window (amounting to the size of the syntactic cycle); in particular, only nice short movements are tolerated. This is what gives rise to the phenomenon of successive cyclic, step-by-step movement. Island effects arise when movement is forced (for one reason or another) to be longer than it should, transgressing the limits imposed by the cycle. This is the reigning idea behind the notion of bounding node, barrier, and, more recently, phase. Minor technical differences aside, all these concepts share the idea that long-distance dependencies are, in a certain sense, a mirage. There is no long-distance dependency, at least in so far as movement is concerned (most theories recognize the existence of mechanism of binding-at-a-(long-)distance, something that I will come back to in this chapter and the next). To repeat, what looks like a long-distance movement rule is in fact the conjunction of small movement steps. It's for this reason that since 1973 islandhood and successive cyclic movement have gone hand in hand in syntactic theory. Back in 1973, and ever since then, the limits Chomsky imposed on the 'window of opportunity' for movement were very stringent: movement could not even cross a clausal boundary (cf. the Tensed-S Condition in Chapter 1). But, as we saw, this limit proved too strong, and Chomsky had to relax this condition, and make room for an escape hatch, right at the edge of the bounding node, to allow for movement to cross clausal boundaries.

In a similar move, Chomsky (1986) developed a system (known as the *Barriers* framework) according to which a large number of categories have a blocking effect on licensing mechanisms (specifically, the then-popular relation of government), ultimately preventing movement (equivalently, preventing the licensing of the trace left by movement). However, due to the large number of blocking categories that Chomsky proposed, he had to introduce a loophole (adjunction to the relevant category) to void unwanted blocking effects, and prevent undergeneration.

And yet again, Chomsky (2000, 2001) had to endow phase heads with extra edge positions to avoid elements being trapped inside the phase, the modern equivalent of the Tensed-S condition.

Because the phase-framework is more recent and has not yet received a standard textbook treatment, let me sketch Chomsky's phase-based approach here and use it as an illustration of the standard derivation account of islands, tied to successive cyclic movement in the following pages. (I hasten to add that the main theoretical points I will make below would remain unaffected if instead of phases I used the

1970s notion of bounding node, or the 1980s notion of barrier; as
Boeckx and Grohmann 2007 showed in some detail, all these notions
resemble each other like identical twins.[2])

Chomsky (2000) argues for a significant departure from the standard
Y-model of grammar inherited from the Extended Standard Theory and
Government-and-Binding eras, where the output of syntactic computations is discharged to the external systems only once (recall 'Surface
Structure'), and proposes instead that syntactic derivations proceed in
incremental chunks, called *phases*. At each phase some portion of the
syntactic structure that has been constructed up to that point is
transferred (spelled-out) to the external systems.

The general idea behind phases is that once these domains have been
built, much of their content is immediately transferred to the interfaces and can therefore be 'set aside' for computational purposes,
thereby alleviating the burden imposed on the system.

Phases, according to Chomsky, subdivide into two domains: a phase
edge, consisting of the head of the phasal projection and everything
above it (specifiers, high adjuncts), and a phase complement, consisting of everything in the complement domain of the phase head, as
shown in (2).

(2)

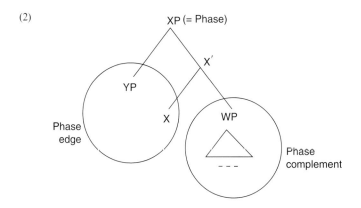

Let us not worry for now about which projections are phasal, and
why only these are. I am well aware that this is a recurrent theme in
the bounding node/barrier/phase-based derivational approaches, and it
is a major source of frustration for many syntacticians because no
satisfactory answer has ever been given in the mainstream literature.
Let me simply say that in the clausal domain Chomsky takes CP and
*v*P (but not, say, TP) to be phasal. (Chomsky is more ambiguous when it

comes to non-clausal categories like PP or DP, although his recent writings suggest that he views these nodes as phasal, as well.)

What I want to highlight here is Chomsky's imposition of a Phase Impenetrability Condition (PIC) on phase-based derivations, given in (3).[3]

(3)   *Phase Impenetrability Condition* (PIC) [Chomsky 2000:108]
      Spell-Out the Complement of Ph(ase) as soon as Ph is completed

According to the PIC,[4] once a phase is completed, the complement domain of the phase becomes opaque, inaccessible to further syntactic computation, and is transferred to the external systems for interpretation.

As Chomsky himself observes, the effect of the PIC yields "a strong form of subjacency" (Chomsky 2000:108).[5] In fact, much like Chomsky's original Tensed-S and Specified Subject conditions, the PIC arguably yields too strong a form of subjacency, for, if nothing else is said, the condition in (3) would have the very negative effect of 'freezing' all the elements inside any phase head complement, making it impossible for, say, standard nominal complements of verbs to move outside their (vP) phase, thus predicting run-of-the-mill *wh*-extraction like $[_{CP}$ *who will John* $[_{vP}$ *see __]]?* to be impossible, since the *wh*-word would be spelled out way before its landing site (SpecCP) is introduced into the derivation.

To avoid this unfortunate effect, Chomsky added a condition to the PIC: before the effect of the PIC kicks in (i.e., before transferring the content of the phase head complement), movement of any element from within the phase head complement to the phase edge is allowed.[6] How? By allowing the phase head to project as many extra specifier positions (intermediate, temporary landing sites) as needed, and endowing it with a generic feature capable of attracting any constituent. Accordingly, $[_{CP}$ *who will John* $[_{vP}$ *see __]]* can be generated as follows:

(4)   a. $[_{vP}$ *[John]* v^0 $[_{VP}$ *see [who]]]*
      b. $[_{vP}$ *who [[John]* v^0 $[_{VP}$ *see [~~what~~]]]]* vP-phase
      c. $[_{TP}$ *John will* $[_{vP}$ *who [[~~John~~]* v^0 $[_{VP}$ *see [~~what~~]]]]]*
      d. $[_{CP}$ *who will* $[_{TP}$ *John ~~will~~* $[_{vP}$ *~~what~~ [[~~John~~]* v^0 $[_{VP}$ *see [~~what~~]]]]]]*   CP-phase

The situation Chomsky faced once he introduced the PIC was identical to the one he faced with his Tensed-S Condition in 1973, and his escape hatch strategy was, again, identical. This time too, long-distance movement dependencies are forced to proceed step-by-step (successive cyclically). But, of course, the explanatory problem for a theory of islands remains the same: once an escape hatch is provided, it becomes necessary to provide a restrictive theory of when this escape hatch can be exploited, for, otherwise, all opacifying (read: island-inducing) effects of the PIC can be voided. Unfortunately, to this day, no such theory is available. In fact, the situation is somewhat worse than in 1973, because back then it was possible to say that if the specifier of a bounding category was already filled prior to the relevant movement, no escape hatch was available (hence, for example, the *wh*-island effect: *what did John ask [who bought __]?*). But in the intervening years, the widely attested existence of multiple specifier constructions (see, e.g., Richards 2001) has made it impossible to restrict (other than by sheer stipulation) the number of edge/specifier positions a given head can have. As a result, it has become impossible, or blatantly stipulative, to prohibit movement to the phase edge even if there is already a filled specifier at the edge of that phase. So, what looked at first like a very restrictive theory (PIC-based derivations, forcing successive cyclic movement) turns out to be far too permissive. As Marc Richards (p.c.) points out, with the unrestricted availability of edge positions, "phases make for lousy islands." Much like the A-over-A condition that Ross took issue with, the PIC is both too strong (if there is no escape hatch provided), and too weak (once such an escape hatch is provided).

The general problem I have just highlighted was recognized by Ceplova (2001) as soon as PIC-based derivations were proposed. Ceplova wrote:

> In the current theory [Chomsky (2001)], all phase-boundary-inducing heads can have P-features [one of the names in the literature for the generic features capable of attracting any element to the edge of the phase – CB]. A head with a P-feature can attract elements with unsatisfied uninterpretable features to its specifier, with the result that the P-feature is checked by the attractee, and the attractee is in a position from which it can move further to satisfy its uninterpretable feature (and thus prevent the derivation from crashing). The *problem* that arises by this proposal is that now *nothing should be an island* if all strong phases allow movement out of them (due to P-features). (emphasis mine)

Faced with such a situation, Ceplova suggested investigating the "possibility of restricting the distribution of P-features that depends on structural position of the category, a possibility reminiscent of L-marking in Chomsky (1986)." Ceplova's suggestion was in fact articulated in recent publications, most explicitly in Müller (2010).[7] Because many syntacticians continue to think that this is the path to follow, I have decided to review Müller's proposal in detail in the next section, but the reader has probably guessed that my assessment will be largely negative.

There is a good reason, I think, to be skeptical about the promises of deriving the CED from the PIC, irrespective of the technical details. (Accordingly, readers not interested in technical details may feel free to skip the next section and move to the next chapter.) As my brief sketch of the phase-based derivations made clear, the PIC turns *comple-ment* domains into islands, but of all syntactic domains, complements are the most transparent. To repeat the relevant data:

(5)   a. Who did you see [pictures of __]?
      b. *Who did [pictures of __] cause Bill to leave the room?
      c. *Who did Bill arrive [after seeing (pictures of) __]?

This is Cattell's (1976) insight, codified in government-terms in Huang (1982), and since then known as the Condition on Extraction Domain (CED). As the CED formulation of strong islands popular in the 1980s captured, it is non-complements (subjects and adjuncts) that must be opacified.[8] The PIC simply gets the CED backward.

3.3   DERIVING THE CED FROM THE PIC: A FAILED ATTEMPT

The focus of this section is what is arguably the most explicitly articu-lated attempt to derive CED-effects from the workings of phases: Müller (2010).[9] Müller claims to provide an account of CED effects said to "follow under minimalist assumptions," dispensing with GB notions like "government, L-marking, and barrier" (p. 35), and making crucial use of phases, specifically, the phase impenetrability condition (PIC). If successful, Müller's proposal would not only be an important step forward in the context of minimalism, it would also vindicate Chomsky's subjacency account. Unfortunately, as I will argue, Müller's work not only suffers from empirical drawbacks, it in fact fails to implicate the PIC, 'deriving' CED effects from other assumptions that are not only independent from phases, but, once examined closely, turn out to be ad hoc and indeed far from 'minimalist.'

I will begin by identifying what I take to be the core traits of Müller's (2010) account of CED effects. Then I will turn to some empirical problems for his proposal, concerning the possibility of extracting from what his account would regard as "last merged" elements: post-verbal subjects in Romance, some shifted objects, and some adjuncts. Finally, I will highlight the stipulative character of Müller's account.

Müller (2010) proposes to derive island effects of the CED sort from a version of the *Phase Impenetrability Condition* (PIC) given in (6), which is essentially Chomsky's (2000) version.

(6)   *Phase Impenetrability Condition* [Müller 2010:36]
      The domain of a head X of a phase XP is not accessible to operations outside XP;
      only X and its edge are accessible to such operations.

Recall that given the PIC, if an element within the complement domain of the phase head is to move to a position outside the phase, it must first move to a domain immune to transfer: what Chomsky calls the *edge* (domain) of the phase.

Müller (2010) departs from Chomsky (2000, 2001) in at least one crucial respect, to which I will return below, but which I want to make clear right away: unlike Chomsky, who takes CP and *v*P to be phases (in contrast to, say, VP or TP), Müller takes all phrases to be phases. As a result, his system is one where transfer of the complement domain of a phase head P_1 takes place when the next phase head P_2 is merged (when P_1 is completed), and P_2's complement domain is transferred when P_3 is merged (when P_2 is completed), and so on, as shown schematically in (7)[10]

(7)   a. Merge $(P_1, X) = [P_1\ X]$
      b. Merge $(P_2, [P_1\ X]) = [P_2, [P_1\ X]] \rightarrow [P_2, [P_1\ \cancel{X}]]$
      c. Merge $(P_3, [P_2\ [P_1\ \cancel{X}]]) = [P_3, [P_2\ [P_1\ \cancel{X}]]] \rightarrow [P_3, [P_2\ \cancel{[P_1\ X]}]]$
      d. . . .

In addition to the PIC, Müller (2010) adopts the following assumptions:

(8)   Müller's (2010:37) assumptions
      a. All syntactic operations are driven by features of lexical items
      b. Those features are ordered on lexical items
      c. So-called Edge features (those features that trigger intermediate movement steps) can be added to the phase head only as long as a phase head is still active

Later on in this section I will critically examine the nature of each of these assumptions, especially that of (8c), which Müller points out at the end of his paper is in fact "the sole indispensable part of the derivation of CED effects from the PIC" (p. 75) — but for now let us see how these assumptions are supposed to work.

Müller (2010) adopts (8a) so that successive cyclic movement (movement to phase edges) can be regarded as feature triggered. In particular, this author invokes Chomsky's (2008) edge feature (henceforth, EF; [•X•] in Müller's notation) in order to account for these steps. Importantly, Müller argues for an *Edge Feature Condition* to make sure that a phase edge is assigned an EF only if successive cyclic movement is to take place:

(9)   *Edge Feature Condition* [from Müller 2010:42]
      An edge feature [•X•] can be assigned to the head γ of a phase only if (a) and (b) hold:
      a. γ has not yet discharged all its structure-building (triggering merge) or probe features (triggering agreement)
      b. [•X•] ends up on top of γ's list of structure-building features

According to Müller (2010), "given [9], phase heads can be assigned additional (i.e., non-inherent) edge features in the course of derivation 'if it has an effect on the outcome', i.e., if that serves to implement intermediate movement steps required by the PIC" (p. 37).[11] Notice that (9) is nothing but a version of (8c), which is required to derive CED effects. Here is why. Without going into too much detail at this point, let me repeat that what needs to be accounted for here is the empirical observation that specifiers and adjuncts (non-governed domains) are islands. Focusing on the first case, we want to derive the impossibility of extracting from, e.g., external arguments, which I take to be base generated in [Spec, v*P] (Chomsky 1995). The scenario we have to consider is depicted in (10): complements are transparent domains, while specifiers are not.

(10) $[_{v*P} [\ldots \alpha \ldots] v^* [_{VP} V [\ldots \beta \ldots]]]$

Now let us assume, with Müller (2010), that all heads have a list of features (either of the Merge or Agreement type, which is marked by the diacritics ● and *, respectively) ordered in a specific way. Let us also assume, again following Müller, that all operations are feature triggered, obeying a *Last Resort* condition, which Müller defines as follows:

(11) *Last Resort* [from Müller 2010:40]
      a. Every syntactic operation must discharge either [●F●] or [*F*]
      b. Only features on the top of a feature list are accessible

In such a system, a transitive v*P is built up by means of the feature lists in (12). In this list, V has a feature [●D●], and v has the feature list [●V●] > [●D●] (where '>' indicates that [●V●], the VP, is merged before [●D●], the external argument). As can be seen, whatever is before > is 'on top' of the feature list.

(12) a. V: [●D●] → $[_{VP} V DP]$
      b. v*: [●V●] > [●D●] → $[_{v*} [_{VP} V DP]] → [_{v*P} DP [_{v*} [_{VP} V DP]]]$

Consider now how the *Subject Condition* (a subject part of the CED) is accounted for. The key assumption of Müller's analysis is that extraction out of a DP depends on a given phase head P having an EF [●X●] before P is *inert*, that is, before P has checked all its features. Take (13), where v* is the phase head P of the phase Γ, λ is V's complement, and β is within the external argument α.

(13) $\Gamma = [_{v*P} [_\alpha \ldots \beta \ldots] \, v^* [_{VP} V \lambda]]$

The gist of Müller's analysis runs as follows: since α is the last merged element in the phase Γ, no EF can be added to the phase head P (as P is already 'inert'), and therefore β cannot be extracted out of α. Notice that the key assumption here is that extraction from α entails movement of β to an outer [Spec, v^*P] position. In particular:

> [I]t is impossible to insert an edge feature for a category α that is merged in Γ (i.e., the maximal projection of a phase head [v^* in (13)]) as the last operation taking place in Γ (because of the condition in [9] – in this case, at the point where α is part of the structure, the head of Γ has no feature left, and has therefore become inert, making edge feature insertion impossible) ... [T]his in turn implies that a moved item β in the edge domain of a category α merged last in a phase Γ is not accessible anymore outside Γ: if α is last-merged, an edge feature cannot be placed on the head of Γ anymore, and a category that is part of α cannot be moved out of α, to an outer specifier of Γ. Therefore, once the derivation proceeds by combining Γ with some new item from the numeration, the PIC renders β in α inaccessible ... [I]t thus follows that extraction from α is predicted to be impossible if α enters a phase as a result of the last operation taking place in that phase, as a consequence of the phase head's features (because of the PIC). (from Müller 2010:43)

If I interpret Müller's account correctly, the *Subject Condition* follows from the impossibility of inserting [•X•] in v^*, which in turn follows from the formulation of (9). If [•X•] were insertable (somehow overriding the inert status of v^*), extraction of β would be okay, and (14) could be formed:[12]

(14) $[_{v*P} [\beta \, [[_\alpha \ldots t_\beta \ldots] \, v^* [_{VP} V \lambda]]]]$

The logic of this does not affect complements (λ in 13), as they are not last-merged in the structure, so insertion of extra EFs is always an option.

Although the specifics of the proposal are clear, what I want to stress here is that it is not at all clear what the role of the PIC is to account for the *Subject Condition*. In particular, I do not see any relevant difference between (14), which cannot be generated in Müller's (2010) system, and (13) when it comes to the PIC. This point will perhaps become clearer in light of (15), where I assume that after the v^*P phase is completed, T (a phase head, for Müller) is merged:

(15) $[_{TP} T [_{v*P} [_\alpha \ldots \beta \ldots] \, v^* [_{VP} V \lambda]]]$

Once T is merged, v*'s complement domain is transferred, which yields (16):

(16) $[_{TP}$ T $[_{v*P}$ $[_{\alpha} \ldots \beta \ldots]$ v* $\overline{[_{VP}$ V λ$]}]]$

The crucial thing now is that, even though VP has been transferred, α and its internal parts are still there, visible to T. Now, what would be wrong with T having an EF that could extract β, yielding (17a)? Once in [Spec, TP], β would be available to C, the next phase head. As far as we can see, Müller (2010) remains silent about this possibility.

(17) a. $[_{TP}$ β T $[_{v*P}$ $[_{\alpha} \ldots t_{\beta} \ldots]$ v* $\overline{[_{VP}$ V λ$]}]]$
      b. $[_{CP}$ C $[_{TP}$ β T $\overline{[_{v*P} [_{\alpha^-} \ldots t_{\beta^-} \ldots]} \overline{v^* [_{VP} V λ]}]]$
      c. $[_{CP}$ β C $[_{TP}$ t$_{β}$ T $\overline{[_{v*P} [_{\alpha^-} \ldots t_{\beta^-} \ldots]} \overline{v^* [_{VP} V λ]}]]$

In brief, unless I missed something in Müller's account, invoking the PIC *alone* cannot account for the *Subject Condition*. For that to be feasible in a PIC-based story, the external argument should be included in the transfer domain, but that would only happen if the v*P in full were transferred upon merger of T, as indicated in (18).

(18) $[_{TP}$ T $\overline{[_{v*P} [_{\alpha^-} \ldots -\beta^- \ldots] v^* [_{VP} V λ]}]]$

What Müller (2010) seems to have in mind, if I interpret him correctly, is a conception of phase theory where the merger of specifiers (inasmuch as they are introduced at the end of the phase) renders phase heads inactive. Since by assumption all operations are triggered by EFs, and EFs cannot be added to phase heads that have already checked all their features (which happens, in the simplest cases, when specifiers are merged), then phase heads cannot trigger any operation that affects external arguments. I find this not only ad hoc (as I will discuss momentarily),[13] but also empirically quite problematic.

So far, I hope to have shown that Müller's (2010) account of CED effects, if it is to go through, must be endowed with highly specific assumptions so that it can be related to the PIC at all. Most notably, for a given element within a phase to be affected by an operation it must be the case that the phase head's list of features has not been exhausted. Once that happens, the phase head becomes inert, and no further operation can take place. This, as noted, does not quite align with the PIC, for elements within a given phase can be affected by processes like movement or agreement involving higher phase heads, as long as they are at the edge. But, for the sake of discussion, let us assume Müller's system, to see where it leads. What I want to argue now is that, even under such a highly specific account of CED effects, there are some cases that would remain unaccounted for: postverbal subjects in some Romance languages, shifted objects, and some adjuncts.

The first case that comes to mind concerns the very *Subject Condition*. Assuming Müller's (2010) proposal, and taking the external argument to be the last merged element within the v^*P phase, then the datum in (19), taken from Uriagereka (1988:118), is unexpected. The key thing to note here is that the subject allows extraction of the wh-phrase if it remains *in situ*.

(19) [$_{CP}$ De qué conferenciantes$_i$ C te   parece   que. . .   [Spanish]
        of what speakers   CL-to-you seem-3.SG that
    a.   . . . (?)[$_{TP}$ T$_S$ me$_z$ van a impresionar$_v$ [$_{v^*P}$ [las propuestas t$_i$] v* t$_z$ t$_v$]]]?
                      CL-to-me go-3.PL to impress-INF   the proposals
    b.   . . . *[$_{TP}$ [las propuestas t$_i$]$_j$ T$_S$ me$_z$ van a impresionar$_v$ [$_{v^*P}$ t$_j$ v* t$_z$ t$_v$]]]?
                      the proposals   CL-to-me go-3.PL to impress-INF
    'Which speakers does it seem to you that the proposals by will impress me?'

Taking the experiencer DP in (19) to be the last element within the v^*P phase (see Gallego 2007, 2010 for discussion), extraction is expected to be impossible under Müller's (2010) account, contrary to fact.

Consider next the case of internal arguments. In some varieties of Spanish, Case marked direct objects (introduced by the dative preposition *a*) have been claimed to be transparent (Demonte 1987:153). If these arguments must raise to [Spec, v^*P], above the external argument, through the last application of Merge within the v^*P phase (see Torrego 1998 for discussion), then the expectation is that they be opaque. However, they are not:

(20) [$_{CP}$ De qué amigo$_i$ C entregaste [a la hija t$_i$]   a la policía]?   [Spanish]
        of what friend   gave-2SG to the daughter to the police
        'What friend did you give the daughter of to the police?'

Finally, let us review the *Adjunct Condition*. Although this CED subcase is cross-linguistically more stable than the *Subject Condition* (Stepanov 2001), as I already pointed out, there are some cases where adjuncts are transparent enough to allow wh-movement. The following data, taken from Truswell (2007:117–118) show this:

(21) a. [$_{CP}$ What$_i$ did you come round [in order to work on t$_i$]]?
      b. [$_{CP}$ What$_i$ did John arrive [whistling t$_i$]]?

Uriagereka (2011:32) reaches a similar conclusion on the basis of data like (22).[14]

(22) a. ? That's the game that he cried (bitterly) [after having lost __]
      b. ?? That's the game that [after having lost __] he cried (bitterly)

If, as Müller (2010:46) argues, adjuncts are last merged (or 'late' merged, as per Stepanov 2001), it is not clear to me how extraction is possible in these and other cases discussed by Truswell (2007) and others.

A stronger piece of evidence that the *Adjunct Condition* can be circumvented can be gathered from Etxepare's (1999) observation that (tensed) conditional clauses are transparent if they occupy a (leftward) specifier position. Since the same effect is found in English (Hornstein 2001), consider (23):[15]

(23)   [Which book$_i$ did you say [that [if Quinn ever read t$_i$] he would abandon linguistics]]?

All in all, it seems that an account like Müller's faces a non-negligible number of empirical problems. But I do not think that the problems just noted are the most worrying aspect of Müller's (2010) account – surely, additional assumptions could be easily added to the list in (8) to cover these facts. What I take to be far more worrying is in fact the set of assumptions reviewed above.

Though perfectly legitimate, these assumptions do not follow from any independent (empirical or theoretical) factors, nor, I contend, do they provide any better understanding of the nature of CED effects. They in fact retain the stipulative character of bounding nodes and barriers.

The first assumption by Müller (2010) is that all syntactic operations are driven by the need to check features encoded in lexical items, therefore adopting a radical interpretation of Chomsky's (1986) *Last Resort* condition. While Müller is certainly not the only one to extend Last Resort in this way, such a view, of course, is only compelling to the extent that it provides a solid motivation for the features involved. In Müller's (2010) paper, features are divided into structure-building features (EFs and subcategorization features) and probe features (responsible for agreement relation), which are distinguished by using the diacritics [•F•] and [∗F∗], respectively. In addition, Müller assumes those features to be *ordered* on lexical items when these enter the syntax. In minimalist terms, this means that not only should the features be motivated, the specific feature-list assumed must be motivated too. As Müller (2010:39ff.) points out, it is a well-known observation that theta roles are distributed in a hierarchical fashion, with agents being higher than themes, and themes being higher than goals (Grimshaw 1990, Marantz 1984, Larson 1988, among others). In order to capture this, Müller (2010) assumes that "Θ-roles are ordered in lexical entries of predicates, and they are mapped onto a list of categorial subcategorization features (i.e., structure-building features: [•F•]) in reverse order, as schematically depicted in [(24)]" (p. 39)

(24) a. Θ-roles:

$\Theta_1 \gg \Theta_2 \gg \Theta_3$ (Agent ≫ Theme ≫ Goal)

    b. Subcategorization features:

[•P•] > [•D•]$_2$ > [•D•]$_1$ [from Müller 2010:39]

Unfortunately, Müller (2010) offers no motivation for the specific features he uses, nor for the hierarchy. This failure is, I think, fatal, for Müller's deduction of CED effects in fact relies, not on the PIC, but on those features and their orderings. This is *very* disappointing in a minimalist context, where the goal is not merely to describe linguistic patterns (after all, these have been described fairly well in previous frameworks), but rather try to understand what they follow from: *why* they are this way.

The third assumption by Müller (2010) has to do with Chomsky's (2000 *et seq.*) framework of phases. In Chomsky's system, only certain categories are the phases. Müller (2010) defends a stronger hypothesis whereby all phrases are phases, the main reason being that all phrases qualify as domains for movement. As Müller (2010) puts it: "it seems to me that the simplest way to bring about highly local successive-cyclic movement via phrase edges is to assume that all phrases are phases; and this is what I will do in what follows. Thus, if every XP is a phase, the PIC forces intermediate movement steps to all phrase edges." (p. 40).[16]

At first glance, a proposal like Müller's (2010) might seem to be the null hypothesis: an application of Merge/a phrase is the smallest syntactic domain that can be considered as a transfer unit. However, there are well-known empirical and conceptual/technical problems with the idea. Empirically, it seems that the interfaces process syntactic outputs in a more punctuated manner than the idea that all phrases are spell-out domains would predict (see Abels 2003, Abels and Bentzen 2009 for arguments based on reconstruction). At the conceptual/technical level, Chomsky has this to say about all phrases being phases:

> Let's consider finally the place of Spell-Out S-O – that is, the choice of phases. We know that S-O cannot apply at each stage of cyclic Merge. Relevant information may not yet be available. Suppose, for example, that Merge has constructed {see, OB}, where the object OB equal *that* or *what*. At this stage we do not know whether OB or *see* is spelled out in situ or whether they move on overtly to be spelled out in a higher position. If they move on (either sometimes or always), then S-O plainly cannot apply at this stage. In a cyclic theory, we do not want to wait too long to determine whether they are spelled out in situ. Ideally, it should be at the next Merge. Suppose further that *see* is a root ... Then the next Merge should also tell us what kind of element it is: the verb *see* or the noun *sight*. In the best case, then, the next Merge should yield {α, {see, OB}}. (from Chomsky 2004:122)

> Problems arise if phases are associated with every operation of
> Merge – e.g., with VP (or RP). One reason is that at VP, information is
> not available as to whether the complement of V will be spelled out in
> situ or raised by Internal Merge, or what its structural Case will
> ultimately be (so that crash at both interfaces is inevitable). Whether
> similar conclusions hold at the Conceptual-Intentional level depends
> on murky questions as to how argument structure is assigned. . . .
> Another line of argument that reaches the same conclusions is based
> on uninterpretable features: structural Case and redundant
> agreement. [from Chomsky 2007:17–18]

Further arguments against collapsing phases and phrases may be
related to the fact that not all phrases have a natural interface characterization, being isolable or semantically/phonologically complete
(Chomsky 2004 *et seq.*). This clearly relates to Chomsky's (2000) claim that
phases are propositional. Chomsky may be wrong, but at least, the idea
that all phrases must be phases must be better motivated, especially
given the fact that it is not necessary for all phrases to be phases in order
for successive cyclic movement to form uniform paths in the syntax (see
Boeckx 2007; see also Chapter 5), which is the result Müller wants.

Let us finally consider the final assumption of Müller's (2010)
account, which he regards as "the most important assumption . . .
needed to derive the CED" (p. 41). In Müller (2010), EFs are inserted in
phase heads (all heads) in order to trigger successive cyclic movement.
Since for extraction to take place in his account of CED effects EFs are
the key – extraction is triggered by EFs –, this assumption is indeed the
most important. Moreover, Müller crucially assumes that EF insertion
takes place before a given phase head has discharged/checked all its
features: if EF insertion took place after, the phase would already be
inert, which Müller wants to avoid. With this much assumed, Müller
postulates an *Edge Feature Condition*, which I repeat for convenience:

(25) *Edge Feature Condition*
     An edge feature [•X•] can be assigned to the head γ of a phase only if (a) and (b) hold:
     a. γ has not yet discharged all its structure-building or probe features
     b. [•X•] ends up on top of γ's list of structure-building features (from Müller 2010:42)

There are two problems with Müller's (2010) view of EFs. The first one is
acknowledged by Müller himself (fn.3, p. 37), and concerns Chomsky's
(1995) *inclusiveness*: feature insertion during the computation would
involve what Chomsky now calls 'tampering' (departure from what
the lexicon provides). Müller (2010) dismisses this objection, assuming
that *inclusiveness* can be violated, unlike *Last Resort*: since every operation is feature triggered (given Müller's interpretation of *Last Resort*),
EF insertion is necessary to capture successive cyclic movement.

I have already made the point that Müller's (2010) interpretation of *Last Resort* is at least not innocent, and requires motivation of the features used. Here I would like to concentrate on a second problem that Müller (2010) does not refer to. Roughly put, the problem is that Müller's interpretation of EFs is quite distinct from the one Chomsky attributes to EFs, the one that Chomsky sees to be better grounded conceptually (hence the one that a minimalist should adopt). In Chomsky (2007, 2008), EFs are not bona fide features, but a way of formalizing the idea that Merge is unbounded or free.[17] As Chomsky puts it: "EF permits free Merge to the edge, infinitely. That yields a certain subcategory of recursive systems: with embedding, a pervasive feature of human language" (Chomsky 2008:144). The following quote expresses the same idea:

> The property of unbounded Merge reduces to the statement that LIs have EF. The property has to be stated somehow, and this seems an optimal way. So far, then, the only syntactic properties of UG are that it contains Merge and LIs with undeletable EF, and that expressions generated must satisfy interface conditions. (from Chomsky 2007:11)

Technically, there are several properties of EFs that make them differ from other features (Case, number, gender, etc.) in Chomsky's system:

(26) a. EFs do not involve Match
      b. EFs do not involve Valuation
      c. EFs do not delete
      d. EFs do not provide any interface (PF or LF) instruction

Perhaps the last property is the one that more clearly indicates the theory internal nature of EFs, which is precisely Chomsky's point: EFs are a way of capturing the unbounded nature of Merge, not a feature that enters in, say, agreement/feature-checking. As for the other properties, they have also been discussed by Chomsky: (26a) is related to the fact that EF is indiscriminate, it can match anything (Chomsky 2008:151); (26b) speaks for itself, as there is no obvious value one could relate to EF; and (26c) is also pointed out by Chomsky, explicitly.

> If EF is always deleted when satisfied, then all expressions will be of the form LI-complement; in intuitive terms, they branch unidirectionally. If EF is not deletable, then the elements of expressions can have indefinitely many specifiers … Variation among LIs with regard to deletability of EF would be a departure from SMT, so we assume that for all LIs, one or the other property holds. There is no obvious principled way to choose between them on computational grounds, but there does appear to be good empirical evidence – perhaps

reducible to CI interface conditions – that restriction to complements only is too strong. We therefore tentatively assume that EF is undeletable, a property of UG. (from Chomsky 2007:11)

If EFs are undeletable, then notice that the backbone of Müller's analysis collapses: EFs do not have to be inserted on phase heads for (successive cyclic) movement to take place. Since all lexical items have a permanent EF, no extra EFs are needed. From all these observations, one should recognize that EFs are not just features, but a way to capture the nature of Merge.

Yet again, Chomsky could be wrong, and Müller right about edge features, but for this to be the case, Müller needs to provide a justification for these features. I seriously doubt this can be done, but at least for the time being, it seems clear to me that the analysis rests on stipulations that are no better than those used in a Barriers-based framework. In other words, I disagree with Müller's (2010) claim that his proposal provides an account of CED effects that dispenses with GB-era concepts, like government, L-marking, etc. The clearest conclusion that can be drawn from Müller's (2010) approach is that the PIC is not directly related to CED effects. If this is so, it seems to me that the skepticism about the role of phases in the context of locality expressed in the previous section of this chapter is vindicated. To repeat, this should not come as a surprise: the CED intends to capture the fact that non-complements are more opaque than complements, whereas the PIC expresses the idea that complements become opaque (impenetrable), while non-complements serve as escape hatch. This is a tension that has been with us since the subjacency account in the 1970s; it's a tension that shows no sign of disappearing in the mainstream literature.

3.4   CONCLUSION: THE CED AND THE PIC ARE NOT MADE FOR ONE ANOTHER

Coupled with the consistent lack of a satisfactory answer for why some nodes are phases (equivalently: bounding nodes, blocking categories, barriers, etc.) while some others are not, though prima facie they could perfectly well be, the repeated failure to constrain cyclic derivations (in a natural, non-stipulative way) once escape hatches are allowed on purely empirical grounds is the perfect illustration of the "entrenchment of the generalizations that were formed from early data sets" criticized by Hofmeister and Sag (2010) (a statement already quoted in the previous chapter).

At the end of my brief survey of the history of syntactic treatments of islands in Boeckx (2008b), I wrote that

> Looking back at the dominant analyses of islands, it is impossible not to be struck by how conservative the field has remained ever since Chomsky 1973 outlined one possible approach to conditions on transformations. It may well be that the degree of restrictiveness achieved there was already such that only a few options can be entertained, or it may be that we have not been willing to explore too many options. The future will tell us if we have been right to hold to consensus views for so long. (pp. 162–163)

As I will show in the next chapter, I think that there are in fact quite a few options left open to us; in fact, I think that explanatory demands of the sort emphasized in the context of linguistic minimalism more and more point to the inadequacy of the standard derivational view on islandhood, and urge us to explore (interface-based) alternatives.

DISCUSSION QUESTIONS

1. Despite my claims to the contrary, can you think of avoiding Ceplova's conclusion discussed in the context of Chomsky's phase-based proposal?
2. Building on Boeckx and Grohmann (2007), try to find more parallels between phases, barriers, and bounding nodes.

4 Priority to the interfaces

The previous chapter revealed the serious explanatory limitations of (currently available) accounts of (strong) islands couched in purely syntactic terms. Although phase-based analyses tend to resort ultimately to more general, non-syntactic considerations to motivate the existence of phases (e.g., computational efficiency), I was at pains to show that phases in and of themselves do not impose conditions that can account for islands, if only because the periodic 'forgetting' (opacification) that phase-based derivations impose on the syntactic computation applies to the most transparent domains (complements) in the island landscape. As a result, phase-based analyses, like previous bounding nodes/barriers-inspired attempts, are forced to resort to syntax-internal, lexical properties like 'L(exical)-marking,' or 'edge features' and formulate constraints on the basis of these (proper government, edge feature condition, and the like) to prevent the generation of island-violating structures.

It goes without saying that such accounts are compelling only insofar as these lexical properties and the conditions imposed on them can be given a natural explanation. To date (after close to 40 years of trying), this is not the case. For this reason alone I think that it is worth looking outside pure, narrow syntax to seek properties of the external (mental) systems with which syntax interacts that could explain why certain structures generated by the syntactic component are judged less acceptable than others. Put differently, I am suggesting we exploit the sort of interface-based accounts that linguistic minimalism favors because such accounts tend to maximize the cognitive resources independently made available by the external systems of thought and sound/sign, leaving the content of narrow syntax maximally minimal and simple (hence, easier to rationalize a priori).

Interface-based accounts are the minimalist versions of filter-based explanations that Ross already explored in his thesis and that I contrasted with derivational accounts at the beginning of Chapter 3. In this chapter I will try to highlight the merits of such filter-based explanations, particularly those that do not limit themselves to positing the relevant filters, but seek to endow them with cognitive substance derived from the external systems. A big part of my case in favor of such explanations will come from a range of phenomena known as 'island repair strategies' that show how 'island-violating' structures generated by the syntactic component do not necessarily lead to unacceptability, as long as the external systems 'read' (or 'handle') them in a particular way, to be detailed below.

I will begin this chapter with reviewing an account proposed by Uriagereka (1999a) that provides a perfect transition between this and the previous chapters, as it combines components of purely syntactic explanations of (strong) island effects ('no movement structures can be generated across islands') and components of interface-based explanations (suggesting that requirements imposed by the external systems shape the course of syntactic derivations, rather than filtering them).

4.1 LOCKING ISLANDS: TOO SOON

Uriagereka's (1999a) account shares with phase-based theories of (strong) island effects the idea that domain opacity (islandhood) is the result of early transfer of portions of the syntactic computation to the external system, which prevents movement from taking place across certain domains. But the key difference between Uriagereka's early spell-out and Chomsky's cyclic spell-out proposals is that those domains that Uriagereka claims undergo early spell-out (hence opacification) are precisely non-complements. As a result, no (ad hoc) escape hatch apparatus must be developed to let extraction from complements take place.

Uriagereka's original proposal is couched in terms of linearization.[1] The rough idea goes as follows: as long as the syntactic structure is built by expanding right branches (complement domains), hierarchical structure can be mapped straightforwardly onto linear order: if A dominates B, A precedes B. Proceeding bottom up, every element added to the existing structure will come to precede said structure at the point of linearization, as represented schematically here in (1)–(2):

(1) Step 1: combine {A, B}: [$_{AP}$ A B]
     Step 2: combine {C, {A, B}}: [$_{CP}$ C [$_{AP}$ A B]]
     Step 3: combine {D, {C, {A, B}}}: [$_{DP}$ D [$_{CP}$ C [$_{AP}$ A B]]]
     Etc.

(2) Linear order: D > C > A > B

Uriagereka takes this to be the key insight behind Kayne's (1994) Linear Correspondence Axiom. Unfortunately, the language faculty we have, like the world we live in, is more complex than the situation just sketched. In particular, there are good empirical reasons to allow for complex left-branches in syntax, as well as for complex adjuncts. These units prevent syntactic derivations from being strictly monotonic (i.e., derivations where each element would be introduced one step at a time): In addition to tall, vertical, 'skinny' syntactic trees like (3), we also must recognize flatter, 'bushier' trees like (4).

(3)

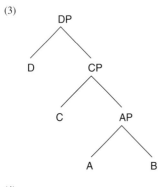

(4)

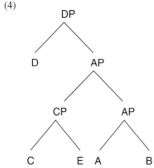

Trees like (4) are typically produced by having C and E combine in a separate derivational space, in parallel to A and B, and only the resulting unit 'CP' being integrated monotonically, as a single unit.

Uriagereka's insight is that this way of introducing units that would otherwise disrupt strict monotonicity into the syntactic spine – as a single, elementary, simplified unit – could be used to account for island effects. Specifically, Uriagereka (1999a) proposed that precisely because they complicate the simplest linearization procedure – the core idea behind Kayne's Linear Correspondence Axiom – that rests on a perfect match between hierarchical structure and linear order (in particular, E in (4) never really combines with AP directly, it does not dominate AP directly, but nevertheless it precedes AP), complex left branches and adjuncts will have to be linearized early. Concretely, such complex units will be built in a separate syntactic workspace and will then be sent to the external system responsible for linearization. This system will 'compactify'[2] the complex unit and return it to the syntax as if it were a single, atomic, lexical element, where it will be introduced strictly monotonically into the main spine of the tree. For Uriagereka, it is this operation of early spell-out and linearization that leads to the opacification of the relevant units, and to strong island effects: once linearized, the elements inside the complex units are frozen in place, they can no longer be (sub)extracted, leading to the CED effects illustrated in (2) above.

Unlike Chomsky's phase-based model, discussed in the previous chapter, which spells out complement domains early, Uriagereka's approach makes exactly the right first cut to capture CED-effects, since it affects non-complement domains. Unfortunately, the approach suffers from a number of serious drawbacks.

The first is downright empirical: as I already pointed out in Chapter 1 (I will return to some examples in the following sections), not all non-complement domains have turned out to be islands cross-linguistically, or even internal to one and the same language. (5) provides two relevant examples, with licit extraction from a complex specifier (5a) and from a complex adjunct (5b).[3]

(5)   a. Which candidates were there [posters of __] displayed all over town?
      b. What did John arrive [whistling __]?

But in virtue of being non-complements, the logic of Uriagereka's approach forces all such domains to undergo early compactification, hence opacification.[4] Like he did in the context of Chomsky's A-over-A condition, Ross would say that Uriagereka's proposal is not "modifiable enough": it makes a very strong prediction (all non-complements are islands), which is a very good thing for a theory, but it's too rigid to accommodate the now well-established selectivity and permeability of island domains, which, to repeat, goes beyond classic weak island cases, and also affects strong islands.

Another, more conceptual, problem for Uriagereka is that his approach requires a fair amount of 'look-ahead.' What is essential under his (1999a) system is early linearization ('atomization') to retain the monotonic character of derivations. There are, of course, many ways to integrate complex left-branches monotonically. For example, as the following quote from Chomsky (2007) makes clear, labels achieve this in the standard account since labels allow for complex units to be treated as atomic lexical items.

> If an element Z (lexical or constructed) enters into further computations, then some information about it is relevant to this option: at the very least, a property that states that Z can be merged, but presumably more, it is commonly assumed. The optimal assumption is that this information is provided by a designated minimal element of Z, a lexical item W, which is detectable by a simple algorithm; the *label* of Z, the head projected in X-bar theories. (Chomsky 2007:9)

Uriagereka's innovation lies in the fact that by not resorting to labeling and instead forcing these complex units to be linearized early (fixing the linear order of these units' contents), he turns them into islands. But why should syntactic derivations mind linearization requirements so much as to force early spell-out? Why couldn't syntax let extraction out of complex left-branches happen, and let the linearization rules get more complicated? In fact, why couldn't syntax 'solve' the linearization problem by forcing massive extraction out of initially complex left-branches, only to leave a single atomic unit to be linearized (everything else being gaps left by movement)? True, this would make wrong empirical predictions, but nothing appears to exclude this scenario under Uriagereka's account.

Alternatively, why couldn't the system spell-out (atomize) the main spine of the tree and integrate it to the (unatomized) complex specifier or the (unatomized) complex adjunct? This would predict 'reverse-CED' effects, but it is something that the system seems to make available.[5]

To my mind, the most severe problem Uriagereka's solution to (strong) island effects faces is a phenomenon that I have already alluded to above (as well as in previous chapters) and that I will discuss at length in the next section: island 'repair.' As Ross already noted in 1967, languages exhibit a range of contexts in which even the strongest of island effects 'disappear.' I am not here talking about the sort of selectivity that many linguists point to in order to question the existence of syntactic islands and that I reviewed in Chapter 2. Rather, I have in mind situations where a domain that would typically lead to a robust island effect allows for licit extraction if the island domain is subsequently elided, or if instead of a gap, a resumptive proform appears. Empirical details will be given in the next section.

Right now, I just want to concentrate on the logic of the phenomenon in relation to Uriagereka's proposal.

Repair phenomena appear to be very robust cross-linguistically, and at least some of them have been shown to require an analysis where extraction from within the island domain takes place,[6] only for the island violation that would otherwise arise to be covered up by a subsequent computational, post-syntactic step (e.g., deletion for ellipsis or (partial) copy pronunciation of the gap left by movement for resumption).

Island repair poses a serious problem for derivational approaches to islandhood, not only for purely syntactic accounts such as those discussed in the previous chapter, but also for those accounts like Uriagereka's[7] that let interface considerations influence the course of syntactic derivations, for the two types of accounts are designed to prevent the island-violating extraction from taking place. It is thus a very serious puzzle for such approaches if it indeed turns out that the relevant extraction can be shown to have taken place, only to be legitimized by a subsequent, post-syntactic operation. How can something be repaired if it was never constructed in the first place? How can something be legitimized in certain contexts if it is predicted never to happen in any context?

It is phenomena like island repair that seem to me to tip the balance in favor of representational, filter-based accounts of island effects, according to which, instead of banning the application of certain rules outright, certain outputs of perfectly possible syntactic operations are eventually deemed illicit. (I will expand on this point in the next section because this is one of the most important lessons that I want readers to draw from this chapter.)

Incidentally, the term 'repair' may not be the most fortunate lexical choice to capture the phenomenon under discussion, for it seems to imply that movement across an island leads to a violation that can subsequently be erased or fixed. While this appears to be the treatment that some syntacticians favor (see Lasnik 2001), the relevant class of phenomena may instead be construed as circumventing, via ellipsis or resumption, what would otherwise turn out to be an illicit structure post-syntactically, with no syntactic violation in the first place. My treatment of island repair to follow in fact favors this latter interpretation, and for this reason I will sometimes use the more neutral term 'island circumvention,' as opposed to the more standard 'repair,' but since the latter has become so standard in the literature (reflecting the derivational bias of theoretical analyses of islands), I think we are sort of stuck with this term, which I will then also use.

Before exploring the topic of island circumvention further, let me point out that Uriagereka has attempted to come to grips with the problematic empirical predictions of his original approach (transparency of some non-complement domains, island repair) in several publications (see Hornstein, Lasnik, and Uriagereka 2007, Uriagereka 2011).[8] For example, in the context of island repair, specifically ellipsis, Uriagereka has pointed out that relevant elements need not be linearized early since they will subsequently undergo deletion, thereby predicting extraction out of them to be licit, given that, under his (1999a) account, it is the need for early linearization that induces islandhood. Although intriguing, such an approach highlights the look-ahead problem I pointed to above (how does syntax know if a complex left-branch will eventually be elided?), but it also faces another, perhaps more serious problem: it appears to confuse linearization and spell-out (or early linearization and early spell-out). There are good reasons to keep the two separate, and to take spell-out to be necessary even if linearization is ultimately not required. For one thing, spell-out feeds not just the external system ultimately responsible for externalization, but also the system responsible for (semantic) interpretation. Since elided domains are interpreted much like non-elided domains are, they have to be spelled-out, hence ought to undergo compactification if they are complex left-branches/adjuncts. Second, a variety of frameworks, most prominently Distributed Morphology (see Halle and Marantz 1993, Harley and Noyer 1999, Embick and Noyer 2001, 2007), provide several arguments for numerous post-spell-out, but pre-linearization, morphological operations, which crucially involve elements that will turn out to be phonetically null (the textbook *wanna*-contraction example nicely illustrates the role of phonetically null elements in the domain of morpho-phonology). If these approaches are right (and Uriagereka's model is sympathetic to Distributed Morphology), elided constituents would have to be spelled-out early, even if they are not linearized at a later stage, rendering their non-opaque status mysterious.

Thirdly, Uriagereka has attempted to account for the fact that some complex left-branches are not islands in terms of base-generation, an old strategy, as readers of this book will now know (cf. Chomsky 1977). But as I will argue below, base-generation should no longer strike us as such a good way out, now that syntacticians are gradually reducing all construal rules to movement and its component parts (see Hornstein 2001, Reuland 2011, Kayne 2002, Boeckx 2003a, and many others).

For all these reasons I am led to conclude that Uriagereka's early-spell-out approach as of yet does not provide a satisfactory answer to why islands exist, although his paying attention to properties of the external systems with which syntax interacts is certainly a step in the right direction.

4.2   IF IT WAS REPAIRED, IT MEANS IT MUST HAVE BEEN CONSTRUCTED IN THE FIRST PLACE

As I have acknowledged in numerous places in this book, Ross's dissertation not only provided an empirically adequate characterization of domains that block movement, he also stressed that no domain blocks absolutely all kinds of dependencies, and exploited the existence of a class of phenomena that now goes under the name of island repair to make his point. In so doing he gave us, I think, a key ingredient to help us understand the nature of islandhood – one that did not figure much during the heydays of locality (the *Government-and-Binding* era), but that has played a much more central role with the advent of minimalism, perhaps because thinking about 'repair' goes hand in hand with thinking about the influence on grammatical structures of the external systems with which syntax interacts – a focus of minimalist inquiry.[9]

4.2.1   Repair contexts

The first class of island circumvention identified by Ross falls under the rubric of *resumption*. As has been widely documented in numerous languages, the presence of a resumptive pronoun where we expect a gap leads to an improvement in island contexts. Contrast the pair in (6)–(7), from English, where the use of a resumptive pronoun is usually regarded as substandard, and certainly not as natural as in languages with extensive resumption such as, say, Modern Irish or Hebrew. But this will do for purposes of illustration.

(6)   *Which woman did John started laughing [after __ kissed Bill]?
(7)   (Tell me again:) which woman was it that John started laughing [after *she* kissed Bill]?

The second class of island circumvention, again discussed by Ross in his thesis, goes by the name of *pied-piping*. Ross noted that taking the island domain along with the moving element renders the relevant (in this case, *wh-*) dependency possible.

(8)   a.   *Whose did you buy [__ book]?
      b.   [Whose book] did you buy ?

The third class of island circumvention was also discussed by Ross, not in his thesis, but in a famous (1969) paper where he introduced the phenomenon of *sluicing* (IP-ellipsis). Ross noted that including the island as part of the *ellipsis* site increases acceptability, as shown in (10).

(9)   *Who did John refute [the claim that Peter saw __]?
(10) John refuted the claim that Peter saw someone, but I can't remember who
      [elided: <John refuted the claim that Peter saw __>]

Perhaps the least surprising instance of island circumvention from the point of view of the mainstream, derivational account of islands is pied-piping, since, by taking the island structure along with the moving element, no movement dependency is established across the island, so no island effect is expected. By contrast, depending on how one analyzes resumption and ellipsis, islands may turn out to be domains out of which extraction can take place after all, provided a subsequent operation (resumption/ellipsis) 'hides' this fact from the eyes of the external systems looking at the syntactic representation. Suppose we can establish that movement takes place out of the ellipsis site in (10), or in the context of resumption in (7), it would then follow that islands cannot be seen as domains that categorically block movement processes (the leitmotiv of mainstream accounts). In other words, if movement can be shown to take place in cases like (7) or (10), one would no longer be able to maintain, at least not in its simplest form, the view that treats islands as bans on rule application (a notion introduced at the beginning of the previous chapter). At the minimum, proponents of a derivational account of islands would have to posit a rule that can reach into islands to account for the dependencies found in the repair contexts (cf. Ross's copying rule mentioned in Chapter 1, or base-generation of the *wh*-phrase followed by 'binding'/licensing-at-a-distance). But in a theoretical climate like the current one, where minimalism dominates, Occam's razor should make us look at the proliferation of such rules with suspicion. What other rule could be responsible for the dependencies in (7) or (10), if not movement (i.e., 'internal' merge, as Chomsky 2004 calls it)?

Let me stress this, because I think it is an important point that has not figured prominently in the existing literature: within minimalism, the default position should be that dependencies are formed in terms of movement (i.e., merge). That is to say, when faced with situations of island repair, the thing to demonstrate is that movement did not take place (i.e., to argue in favor of an extra syntactic operation like binding, or some such), not that it did, because movement is what one ought to expect. The reason that proponents of movement-accounts in the context of sluicing and resumption (Merchant 2001, Boeckx 2003a, and others) have had to argue *in favor of* movement taking place in these situations is because mainstream syntactic theory equates islands with the impossibility of movement, ignoring Ross's careful reflections. This has logic backwards. The movement hypothesis ought to be the one to be defended only if we had a strong theoretical reason to ban movement out of islands. But we don't have this, what we have is a habit of thinking that island effects arise when movement crosses certain nodes.

My impression from the literature is that apart from forcing us to drop the idea that islands block movement, there are no good arguments *against* allowing movement in island (repair) contexts. And, in fact, positing movement in such contexts not only accounts for the dependencies we find there (which is, after all, the basic thing to capture), but also allows us to explain what would otherwise be anomalies, such as the existence of superiority effects in the domain of resumption (Aoun and Li 2003, Boeckx 2003a), which are traditionally understood as movement effects (Move the closest *wh*) or the presence of lexically governed case-marking on *wh*-remnants in sluicing, which, as Merchant (2001) argued, strongly suggests that the *wh*-remnant occupied at one point in the derivation a position close to the verb assigning the relevant case, which is part of the ellipsis site. Both phenomena are illustrated in (11)–(12).

(11) (data from Lebanese Arabic; Aoun and Li 2003)
    a. miin ʔənbasatto laʔinno saami ʕarraf-o   ʕa-miin
      who pleased.2pl because Sami introduced-him to-whom
      'who were you pleased because Sami introduced (him) to whom'
    b. *miin ʔənbasatto laʔinno saami ʕarraf   miin ʕəl-e
      who   pleased.2pl because Sami introduced whom to-him
      'who were you pleased because Sami introduced who to him'

(12) (data from German; Merchant 2001)
    a. Er will jemandem schmeicheln, aber sie wissen nicht,
      he wants someone.DAT flatter   but they know   not,
      *wer/   *wen/   wem
      who.NOM who.ACC who.DAT
      'He wants to flatter someone, but they don't know who'
    b. Er will   jemanden loben, aber sie wissen nicht,
      he wants someone.ACC praise but they know not,
      wer/   wen/   wem
      who.NOM who.ACC who.DAT
      'He wants to praise someone, but they don't know who'

Perhaps because such facts receive a straightforward account under a movement analysis, or perhaps indeed because there is little reason to rule out movement in contexts of island repair, the view that treats islands as conditions on outputs has gained adherents in the context of minimalism:[10] if movement can take place out of islands, the unacceptable structures known as island effects must be due, not to movement, but to some properties of the external systems with which syntax interacts which cause the outputs of movement across islands to be judged illicit, unless some operation takes place to 'cover' up what would otherwise be an offending structure (resumption, ellipsis).

But, of course, the plausibility of output-oriented treatments of island effects ultimately depends on how convincing the 'filter' meant to capture island effects (the property of the external systems responsible for decreased acceptability) really is – it's not enough to just say "star this structure". This is the issue I turn to now.

4.2.2 A matter of phonology?

At present, the most popular treatment of island repair takes the phenomenon to indicate that the cause of island effects is to be traced back to properties of the phonological component of the grammar. Following Ross's idea that chopping rules – those that the reader will recall are among the rules that are island sensitive – involve reordering operations followed by deletion (the silent 'gap' left by movement), and taking into account that there is no gap inside the island under repair, either because it appears to be filled by a proform (resumption), or because the only relevant gap is the one created by movement of the entire island-domain, not one inside the island (pied-piping), or because the entire island is left unpronounced (ellipsis of the sluicing kind), many authors (see especially Merchant 2001; Lasnik 2001, 2005; Hornstein, Lasnik, and Uriagereka 2007, Fox and Pesetsky 2005) have suggested that islands boil down to a filter pertaining to the presence of gaps inside certain domains.

The obvious question is what that filter is precisely, and why it should hold. After all, it can't be the mere presence of a phonetically empty element inside a certain domain that causes the island effect, for classic island domains readily allow for phonetically null elements (e.g., the object of ate in Mary left [after Bill ate], or the parasitic gap in What did you read __ [before filing __]?, or indeed the subject of filing in the example just given).[11] Aware of this issue, the literature arguing in favor of a PF treatment of island effects often insists on the fact that the problematic gaps are those that are related (by movement) to an element outside the island. But note right away that if this is the relevant generalization, it is far more 'syntacticy' than merely a phonological statement about null elements inside certain domains: it is a statement about how such elements were formed syntactically. But does phonology have access to this information?; and even if it does, why should it care?

As a matter of fact, we appear to be facing the very same problem that processing-based reductionist accounts face and which I raised in Chapter 2: why is it that a gap inside an island causes much more trouble than the mere conjunction of a filler gap dependency and an island domain would lead us to expect?

Furthermore, for those who take the problem to be 'phonological' in nature, it still remains to be seen how this line of reasoning singles out those domains that are islands, for not any gaps (related to an antecedent by movement) inside any domains cause problems.

I do not know of any detailed answer to these questions in the existing literature. It seems to me that much of the literature on repair simply bets on a phonological solution because silence (ellipsis) or extra pronunciation (resumption) are the most salient properties of repair contexts. Since these refer to aspects of pronunciation, researchers tend to assume that islands will turn out to be 'PF'-effects. Whereas some (Lasnik 2001, Merchant 2001, 2008) merely state that operations like ellipsis have the capacity to remove the 'uninterpretable' PF-feature that is associated with the mere fact of crossing an island, which I take to be nothing more than a redescription of the island effect, others have tried to be more specific. As stated above, following Uriagereka (1999a), the intuition that many have explored is that islands are at bottom a linearization problem. Recognizing the problems faced by Uriagereka's original proposal, Hornstein, Lasnik, and Uriagereka (2007) made a suggestion building on Fox and Pesetsky's (2005) framework, where linear order is fixed cyclically, phase-by-phase. Since Fox and Pesetsky's analysis acknowledges the need to pay attention to interface properties, while at the same time preserving elements of the traditional, subjacency-style vision on locality, I think it deserves a brief digression.

According to Fox and Pesetsky, movement is forced to take place successive cyclically because (and this is their major proposal) the linear order of elements is fixed once and for all at the completion of each phase. In particular, if an element x (say, the complement of the verb in a typically SVO language like English) is to move long-distance, it could not do so in one fell swoop (from its base position directly to its final landing site), for if it did, the phonological component would get contradictory instructions: within the verbal phase,[12] PF would be told that the verb precedes the object, but subsequently, in a higher CP phase would be told that the object precedes elements that precede all

the elements of the Verbal phase, including the Verb, as sketched in
the sample derivation in (13).

(13) a. VP Phase: [Subj *v* V Obj]
           Spell-Out ➜ linear order: Subj > *v* > V > Obj   (> indicates precedence)
      b. CP Phase (after movement of Obj in one fell swoop): [Obj C T *v*P]
           Spell-Out ➜ linear order: Obj > C > T > *v*P
           Total linear order (contradictory): Obj > C > T > Subj > *v* > V > Obj
                                                  ! Obj > V and V > Obj

To avoid contradictions of this kind, Fox and Pesetsky resort to successive cyclic movement, allowing for movement internal to each phase to
alter the linear order of the elements within the phase. In the toy
example at hand, movement of Obj to the edge of the VP phase will
yield an instruction to the effect that Obj precedes V (in that phase), an
instruction that no subsequent movement of Obj will contradict, as
shown in (14).

(14) a. VP Phase: [Subj *v* V Obj]
      b. movement of Obj to the edge of the phase
           Spell-Out ➜ linear order: Obj > Subj > *v* > V
      c. CP Phase (after movement of Obj): [Obj C T *v*P]
           Spell-Out ➜ linear order: Obj > C > T > *v*P
           Total linear order: Obj > C > T > Subj > *v* > V
                               Obj > V at both the VP and the CP phase

In presentations based on their (2005) article, Fox and Pesetsky have
suggested that locality conditions on movement (such as (certain)
island effects) may be understood within their framework as situations
where movement to the edge of a given phase is for some reason
unavailable, resulting ultimately in contradictory linearization
instructions.

The intuition, then, remains the same as in Chomsky (1973): island
effects arise when successive cyclic movement fails; the difference
between Chomsky's original account and Fox and Pesetsky's is that
the consequence of this failure is detected not in syntax per se, but in
the phonological component responsible for linearization.

Fox and Pesetsky point out that their suggestion concerning islands
may account for why ellipsis repairs what would otherwise be island
violations: since there is no need to linearize what will not be pronounced, ellipsis essentially hides any conflicting linearization
instructions. In a similar vein, Hornstein, Lasnik, and Uriagereka
(2007) suggest that the introduction of a resumptive element avoids
linearization conflicts: instead of having to deal with situations where,
say, an Object *wh*-phrase is said to both precede and follow a Verb, the
presence of a resumptive pronoun co-indexed with the *wh*-phrase gives

rise to non-contradictory statements like V precedes the resumptive pronoun, whereas the *wh*-phrase precedes V.

Hornstein, Lasnik, and Uriagereka adopt Uriagereka's (1999a) claim that those domains corresponding to strong islands must be linearized early,[13] but I fail to see why, once having adopted Fox and Pesetsky's analysis, they can account for the islands. In particular, I fail to see why the need to linearize CED-domains early leads to contradictory linearization statements. For Fox and Pesetsky, problems arise when the edge of a given phase (domain undergoing cyclic/early spell-out) ceases to be available. Early linearization per se is not (indeed, cannot be) the problem. We are thus back to the old problem discussed extensively in the previous chapter: why are the edges of island domains inaccessible? I fail to see how this could be a phonological problem. Thus, whereas in a framework like Fox and Pesetsky's, properties of the phonological system (contradiction in the linearization instructions) lead to unacceptability, the cause of this contradiction remains a mysterious syntactic fact.

It may be a good place for me to remind the reader that Ross's rules that were subject to island constraints did not all involve key phonological properties: chopping rules and unidirectional rules of deletion certainly did, but feature-changing rules (e.g., according to Ross, the rule responsible for the distribution of negative polarity items, for example), mentioned in Chapter 1, did not, so perhaps insisting on the presence of a phonetically null element (gap) may not be the most promising way to go. Although obviously, if it's not that, what is it, then?

I will review some suggestions that have been made in this regard in the next two sections of this chapter, but before I leave the topic of island repair, I would like to discuss a few more important topics that arise in the context of island circumvention. (I urge the reader not to skip ahead to the next sections, for the remarks to follow are worth bearing in mind in subsequent sections of this chapter.)

4.2.3 Further remarks on repair

The first remark I would like to make concerns the potential existence of a fourth kind of island circumvention, which Ross did not identify, and which I am perhaps one of the few syntacticians so far to treat as a case of island repair/circumvention. The phenomenon I have in mind is *wh*-in-situ. Cross-linguistic research (spearheaded by Huang 1982 and Lasnik and Saito 1984) revealed that leaving a wh-phrase in situ (an option made available in some languages such as Chinese and Japanese) in interrogative contexts does not give rise to island effects, despite the fact that some kind of dependency crossing the island appears to be necessary to capture the relevant scope of the wh-phrase and understand the sentence as a question. Perhaps here, too, Ross's intuition that islands constrain only some types of dependency, but not all, may prove correct (see Tsai 1994 and Reinhart 1998 for specific suggestions regarding how in-situ wh-phrases can be licensed, even across islands).[14]

(15) Ni   xiangxin Lisi   mai-le   sheme   de   shuofa
     You   believe   Lisa   bought   what   DE   claim
     'You believe the claim that Lisa bought what?'

The wh-in-situ data prove even more interesting, once we take into account the fact, first noted by Huang (1982), that some wh-in-situ (most robustly, adjunct wh-phrases equivalent to *why*) give rise to island effects.

(16) *Ni   xiangxin Lisi   weisheme lai   de   shuofa
     You   believe   Lisa   why   came   DE   claim
     'You believe the claim that Lisa came why?'

It's data of this sort that led to the idea in the GB-literature that wh-phrases in situ (at least those that are island-sensitive) undergo covert, invisible movement, and are therefore expected to behave on a par with wh-phrases that move overtly, as they do in English. But let me stress again that in a minimalist context, the default position should be that all the relevant dependencies are formed by movement (merge), so that the contrast between (15) and (16) must be explained in some other way (perhaps a semantico-pragmatic treatment of (16) is necessary; but see my third remark in this section below regarding the possibility of assimilating in-situ wh-questions to resumptive strategies, which may account for the contrast given the lack of resumption with adjuncts).

Be that as it may, my point is that the lack of island effect with wh-in-situ may be part of the bigger family of phenomena here called island circumvention (one that may still lead us to think of islands as PF-phenomena, given that here too there is no silent gap in the island domain).

The second remark I would like to make will be obvious, but is worth stressing: the theoretical weight of island repair phenomena in the context of the debate on the nature of islands depends on how phenomena like ellipsis, resumption, pied-piping/phrasal movement, and wh-in-situ are treated in general (i.e., outside of island domains). Although several works have devoted many pages to arguing that at least some of these phenomena involve movement crossing islands, hence argue directly against derivational theories of islands that do not allow any movement across island boundaries (see, among many others, Merchant 2001, Lasnik 2001, 2005, Boeckx 2003a, 2008a), it goes without saying that the phenomena we are dealing with here are very complex, much more so than the brief overview offered here suggests. Moreover, much of that complexity remains to be understood. By bringing up the issue of island repair in this chapter I merely wanted to point out, once again following Ross's theoretical flair, that island circumvention data can provide a rich source of insights into the nature of islandhood. My intention is certainly not to settle the issue here, nor to discuss all the intricacies of each phenomenon providing the repair context. As a matter of fact, I think that the relevant phenomena – resumption, ellipsis, phrasal movement, and wh-in-situ – each deserve a book-length survey of their own. If such surveys don't exist yet, it's simply because the dust has not settled sufficiently for theoreticians to see through the maze of possibilities that are currently entertained in the literature, and the nuances that each new study focusing on one of these phenomena uncovers.

I should perhaps point out that although the capacity to 'repair' islands of certain processes like ellipsis has been known since the late 1960s, it is only recently that linguists have gone back and examined repair phenomena in detail. I suspect that the resurgent interest is due to the fact that the island repair phenomena require one to look at the interaction among various components of the grammar to be understood, hence this becomes an area of great interest in the context of minimalism, which puts a premium on interface explanations. I also suspect that island repair was ignored for such a long time because it offers such a powerful argument against the standard, derivational view on islands, especially once we dismiss the all-too-easy strategy of base-generation whenever an island appears to have been crossed.

The reader of this section should bear in mind that although I have referred to repair phenomena like resumption, ellipsis, etc. as if they were uniform phenomena, this is, to judge from the growing literature on these topics, far from certain. All the four types of repair contexts mentioned in this section appear to be subject to a massive degree of cross-linguistic variation. While it is fairly well established that some kind of ellipsis, resumption, wh-in-situ, etc. alleviate some islands in some languages, it is also clear that some instances of what has been called ellipsis, resumption, and wh-in-situ, don't.[15]

It is only fair to acknowledge the fact that theoretically speaking much remains to be understood regarding all the phenomena involved in island repair. While this is virtually always true of any phenomena in science, and certainly in linguistics, there are certain phenomena that have 'stabilized,' theoretically speaking, over the years, and about which one can therefore put forth certain conclusions with some confidence. This is not the case for the contexts of island repair quite yet. But in part I think that this is due to the fact that such phenomena have always been inextricably linked with islands. This has had a most unfortunate result that the standard take on islands ('no movement can cross island boundaries') has seen a movement analysis, for example, of resumption ruled out, simply because of the lack of island-effects in the presence of resumption.[16] As a consequence, even some of the most basic questions that a movement account would entail have not been asked, or have only been raised so recently that no conclusive answer is available yet. For instance, our knowledge of the availability and range of reconstruction effects (effects typically used as a movement test) in resumptive environments remains very primitive, even in languages whose resumptive patterns have been extensively investigated.[17] Saying that there is thus much groundwork to be done is a euphemism.

The clearest evidence of the need for deeper understanding of the repair environments arguably comes from pied-piping. Although its discovery is now over 40 years old, we still lack a satisfactory account of how a phrasal unit x containing a key element y can, under movement, act as a surrogate for y (doing virtually all the things that y would typically do in isolation), even if x itself, taken in isolation, would be incapable of satisfying the requirements that it does when it pied-pipes y: think of the A-bar movement of a prepositional phrase containing a wh-element, as in *[with whom] did you see this movie?*. What accounts for this transfer of 'syntactic potential'?

As reviewed by Heck (2008) and Cable (2010), most analyses of pied-piping have explored several variants of a single idea: x can act as a surrogate for y in pied-piping contexts because x and y have entered into a syntactic relation that has transferred the key syntactic features of y to x, enabling x to 'act' as y. Two of the most popular candidates for this syntactic relation are agreement between, say, the preposition and its complement and feature projection (percolation) from the complement of P to the dominating PP node. Unfortunately, there is little *independent* evidence for such a relation, which makes pied-piping stand out in the theory like a sore thumb, the more so given the extensive cross-linguistic variation in this domain, which does not sit very well with the expected universality of the mechanism underlying pied-piping typically appealed to. (Later on in this section I will sketch

Cable's proposal, which seems to me to offer some insight into the nature of the phenomenon.)

Until recently, the contours of the landscape surrounding island repair were perhaps clearest in the context of ellipsis. Resuscitating the earliest account of sluicing (roughly, TP-ellipsis) due to Ross (1969) and the idea that deletion removes the offending material (island violation) from the output being evaluated for well-formedness (in addition to Ross 1969, see Chomsky 1972), Merchant (2001) and Lasnik (2001) provided compelling arguments for a movement + deletion account of island repair under ellipsis, and against non-movement alternatives such as Chung, Ladusaw, and McCloskey 1995. Not only did Merchant's and Lasnik's works provide a rather strong case for allowing movement out of islands, and therefore, against standard derivational treatments of island effects,[18] they also helped clarify certain properties of islands (assuming, of course, the correctness of their analyses). First, they provided evidence, based on the different 'repair' capacity of VP-ellipsis vs. sluicing (TP-ellipsis) that not any instance of ellipsis leads to island-circumvention; specifically, on the basis of contrasts like that between (17) and (18), Fox and Lasnik (2003), Merchant (2008) drew the conclusion that all intermediate steps taken by the movement that crossed the island should be contained in the ellipsis side for ellipsis to have its repair effect. (The idea is that in (18), there is enough syntactic room around "they do" for the *wh*-phrase to leave an intermediate phrase and form a chain, in contrast to (17).)

(17) They want to hire someone who speaks a Balkan language, but I don't know which language (deleted CP: [they want to hire someone who speaks __])

(18) *They want to hire someone who speaks a Balkan language, but I don't know which language they do (deleted VP: [want to hire someone who speaks __])

However, I should point out that Fox, Lasnik, and Merchant all observe that VP-ellipsis imposes constraints on wh-movement that extend beyond island contexts, suggesting that (18) may not tell us as much about island repair. Thus, these authors note that certain otherwise licit examples of movement give rise to degraded results in VP-ellipsis contexts, as the following examples (taken from Merchant 2008) illustrate:

(19) They said they heard about a Balkan language, but I don't know
    a. which (language) they said they heard about   *no ellipsis*
    b. which (language) [deleted: they said they heard about]   *sluicing*
    c. *which (language) they did [deleted: say they heard about]   *VP-ellipsis*

Merchant and Lasnik also pointed out that whereas ellipsis can repair islands, it does not seem to be capable of repairing all kinds of constraints on movement. In particular, superiority effects and violation of the ban on preposition-stranding (both phenomena introduced in Chapter 1) appear to be immune to the alleviating properties of sluicing:

(20) (data from Serbo-Croatian; Boeckx and Lasnik 2006)
A: Somebody bought something, but
B: a. Ivan i   Marko ne znaju ko   šta
          Ivan and Marko neg know who what
        b. *Ivan i   Marko   ne znaju šta   ko
          Ivan and Marko   neg know what who
          'but Ivan and Marko don't know who what'

(21) (data from Greek; Merchant 2001)
         I   Anna milise me   kapjon, alla dhe ksero *pjon/me pjon
         the Anna spoke with someone but not I.know who/with who
         'Anna spoke with someone, but I don't know who'

Data of this sort led Boeckx and Lasnik (2006) to argue that these unrepairable constraints are better analyzed as derivational, rigid conditions according to which no movement is allowed to violate them in the first place, and so the opportunity to 'repair' them never arises. In other words, these conditions on transformations, though traditionally lumped together with classic island conditions, may be of a very different kind, which would reinforce the idea that locality is not a homogenous domain in language (yet another blow to the dream of a unified theory of locality at the heart of Chomsky (1973), discussed in Chapter 1), and also reinforce the arguments in this chapter in favor of a representational account of island effects.[19]

To wrap up this brief survey of the recent literature on repair by ellipsis, I would like to point out that despite its success, the Merchant/Lasnik view on island repair by ellipsis is not the only possible analysis, although the alternative I am about to mention retains the idea that movement takes place across islands, hence preserves most of the implications for the nature of islands of the Merchant/Lasnik view discussed so far. But it has desirable implications for the nature of islandhood that the more popular Merchant/Lasnik account lacks, and which I will pursue in the remainder of this section.

The view I am about to sketch – which takes resumption to be implicated in sluicing contexts – has a long history in the generative literature, but traditionally it has been thought of as a non-movement alternative to the movement approach pioneered by Ross and adopted by Merchant and Lasnik (as a matter of fact, I suspect it was devised to avoid the conclusion that islands can be violated).[20] For this reason,

Merchant (2001) sought to discard it. But I would like to suggest that if we consider a version of the alternative that makes room for move-ment, as a few authors have done recently, it is no longer as easy to discard it as Merchant claimed. In fact, it may turn out to be superior on empirical and conceptual grounds to the now standard Merchant/Lasnik account.

The resumptive strategy was revived by Wang (2007) and, building on him, Boeckx (2008a). Both Wang and Boeckx agree with Merchant and Lasnik concerning the presence of the island domain in the ellipsis side, but instead of the standard movement account, they argue that inside the elided island domain there is a resumptive proform, as illustrated in (22).

(22)   John countered the claim that Fido bit someone, but I didn't hear who
         (deleted: John countered the claim that Fido bit *pro*)

The theoretically important point Wang and Boeckx seek to make is that if (22) is the correct representation of the relevant example, it is not ellipsis per se that leads to island repair, but rather, it is resumption. According to these authors, the role of ellipsis regarding island repair would be reduced to something more indirect: the licensing of a resumptive proform being facilitated (in English-type languages, where resumptive pronouns are not so readily available as in, say, Hebrew or Irish) under ellipsis because of the presence of an antecedent in the clause licensing ellipsis ("someone" in (22), licensing *pro*).[21]

Crucially, for present purposes, Wang and Boeckx do not deny the basic fact that there is movement crossing the island in sluicing contexts, for they assume, following Boeckx (2003a), that resumptive dependencies are not only compatible with, but are in fact better analyzed in terms of, movement. So, the relevant sluicing data still point to the need for allowing movement across island structures. What is affected, however, is the idea that island violations are due to a phonological filter. If it is indeed ellipsis, understood as deletion, that repairs island violations, the idea of a phonological filter is quite plausible (even if, as we saw, the exact nature of the filter remains to be articulated), but if it is in fact a resumptive proform that saves the island violation, the phonological filter perhaps loses its initial plausi-bility,[22] depending, of course, on how resumption is analyzed, a ques-tion that will be discussed in the remainder of this section and in the next one.

It is in fact on the basis of this possible extension of the resumptive strategy to cases of island repair under ellipsis that Boeckx 2008a suggests a unified, resumption-based perspective on island repair, and this is the third and final remark that I would like to make in this subsection.

To better understand the nature of the proposal made in Boeckx (2008a), I should stress that by resumption Boeckx (2008a) means something slightly different from the textbook definition of resumption.

There are, in fact, two textbook views on resumption: one that takes the presence of a resumptive pronoun to indicate that there was no relevant movement of the A-bar element binding the resumptive pronoun (the base-generation view), and the other that takes the resumptive pronoun to be the phonological realization of the gap left by movement. There is, however, a third possibility, argued for extensively in Boeckx (2003a) and adopted in Boeckx (2008a), according to which the resumptive pronoun is present in syntax, and combines with its antecedent, which subsequently moves in the course of the derivation, 'stranding' its resumptive companion, as schematized in (23).

(23) Wh-element [... [... [resumptive pronoun [~~wh-element~~]] ...] ...]

The derivation in (23) combines properties of the base-generation view (the resumptive pronoun has an independent syntactic life) and of the movement account (the antecedent of the resumptive pronoun leaves a gap). In so doing, the stranding accounts can straightforwardly accommodate the evidence in favor of movement in resumptive contexts (such as the superiority effects in (11) above), as well as the syntactic (and semantic) effects of resumptive pronouns (reviewed in Boeckx 2003a).[23] In the context of islands, the stranding view allows one to make a difference between 'regular' movement and movement whose gap is complemented by – and therefore potentially licensed by – the presence of a resumptive pronoun.[24] This is an issue that I will expand on in the next section. For now, I want to sketch the possibility that all instances of island repair abstractly look like (23), and point out that a stranding analysis casts doubt on the phonological treatments of islands, especially on those suggestions that blame the presence of a gap created by movement in island domains.

Aside from positing resumptive elements in ellipsis contexts (of the sluicing type), as I just discussed, Boeckx (2008a) claims that wh-in-situ patterns could in fact be profitably regarded as cases of 'reverse resumption,' with the wh-element in situ playing the role of a resumptive element, filling a position where we would otherwise expect a gap.[25] Following Watanabe (1992) and much subsequent work (see especially Hagstrom 1998 and Cable 2010), Boeckx takes the wh-in-situ

element to be bound by a phonetically null operator that ends up
occupying a high position in the left periphery of the relevant clause.
Wh-in-situ would then look abstractly like this:

(24) Wh-operator$_{null}$ [... [... ["resumptive element" [~~wh-operator~~]] ...] ...]

Boeckx points out that a resumptive analysis of wh-in-situ would
straightforwardly capture the special (i.e., island sensitive) behavior
of true adjunct wh-phrases in situ (the equivalent of English *why*),
illustrated in (16) above. Given the cross-linguistically well-established
absence of resumptive proforms for adjunct phrases, no resumptive
pattern can underlie cases of adjunct wh-phrases in situ, hence their
island sensitivity, given the idea (to be developed in the next section)
that only movement chains combined with resumptive elements can
cross island boundaries without leading to unacceptability.

   The remaining case of island repair not covered so far by the
resumptive pattern is pied-piping. However, recently, Cable (2010)
has assimilated pied-piping configurations to wh-in-situ by arguing
that pied-piping has so far been misanalyzed. Instead of corresponding to a situation where properties of an element must percolate up
the tree (or enter into a special agreement relationship) to endow the
bigger constituent being moved to act as a surrogate, pied-piping,
according to Cable, boils down to the merger of a (possibly phonetically null) Q-element (precisely the null operator of Watanabe's 1992
analysis just referred to above) at the top of the pied-piped unit. It
is this Q-element that is the relevant 'wh-element'/operator moving,
and not, say, the wh-sounding element inside the phrase being
pied-piped.[26] Put differently, Cable suggested that the puzzle about
pied-piping was due to the fact that most syntacticians took the
target of movement to be the element embedded inside the bigger
unit moving. This problem[27] disappears if we take this embedded
element to be like a wh-phrase in situ, i.e., a variable, or a resumptive
proform. Once we do so, pied-piping reduces to regular phrasal movement (the problem of how XP can act as a surrogate for *wh* disappears
once we take an element merged with XP to be the real target of
movement).[28]

   The representations in (25)–(26) provide schematic views of the traditional approach to pied-piping and Cable's alternative, respectively.

(25) [[$_{XP}$ ... [*wh*]] ... [... ~~[$_{XP}$...[*wh*]]~~ ...] ...]
      , with *wh* being the ultimate target of movement
(26) [[$_{QP}$ Q [$_{XP}$ ... [*wh*]]] ... [... ~~[$_{QP}$ Q [$_{XP}$...[*wh*]]]~~ ...] ...]
      , with Q being the ultimate target of movement

If something like (26) is the right schema for pied-piping, the latter can then be assimilated to a resumptive pattern, via the link with wh-in-situ. The parallelism with wh-in-situ could even be made stronger by having the Q-element merge with the wh-unit and move away from it, reprojecting (as in movement analyses of relative clauses), as shown in (27)).[29]

(27) $[[_{QP} Q [_{XP} \ldots [Q [wh]]]] \ldots [\ldots [_{QP} Q [_{XP} \ldots [Q [wh]]]] \ldots] \ldots]$

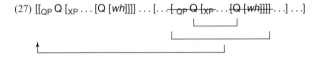

If the structures in (22), (23), (24), and (26/27) prove tenable, we would be in a position to entertain a unified representation for island repair contexts. We still need, of course, to understand what it is about resumption that alleviates island effects (to repeat, if the resumptive pronoun is not merely a phonetic realization of a gap, it can't be a matter of pure phonology), something that I will address in the next two sections, but I would like to point out for now that the possibility of a unified configuration of island repair suggests that there ought to be an underlying unity to (strong) islands. Wouldn't it indeed be really puzzling if genuinely different conditions on transformations could be uniformly repaired by a single strategy? It seems much more plausible to assume that the reason that generalized resumption works to circumvent all strong islands is because these all have something in common. Chomsky's dream of a unified theory may still live on after all. This, then, would be the great theoretical benefit of unifying repair contexts, and a genuinely new argument in favor of a unified treatment of islandhood.

Let me repeat in concluding this section on island repair that everything I have said remains very tentative. Although my remarks in this section were based on works that have provided detailed empirical analyses of individual repair contexts, I cannot stress enough the fact that we need to understand better the nature of all the situations leading to island repair before we can be sure that our interpretation of the remarkable phenomenon of island alleviation can be said to be on the right track. My current assessment is that the case in favor of movement is very strong indeed (recall that the theoretical cost of base-generation is very high indeed: it must recognize a licensing operation other than merge), and that repair contexts provide one of the most powerful arguments against the mainstream account of islands as domains banning any kind of movement.

4.3 ISLAND SENSITIVITY AND THE COMPONENTS OF MOVEMENT

What is it about movement, absent resumption, that makes the operation sensitive to islands? Ross already knew in 1967 that it can't be the length of the dependency established, since well-formed dependencies that are longer than those violating islands can be constructed. And it can't be movement (the presence of a gap) as such that is the problem if, as I have suggested in this chapter (building on previous work of mine, Boeckx 2003a and references cited there, especially Ross's own work), resumptive structures are coupled with movement. So, what is it about movement that is not associated with a proform that triggers island effects?

In the context of the minimalist program, which scrutinizes the nature of every grammatical operation posited, a few syntacticians have explored the possibility that it may be a component of movement that is sensitive to islands, and that in cases where island effects are not felt, this component is allowed to be missing, or somehow suppressed, or taken care of by the resumptive element. This is the line of research I will discuss in this section.

Building on the early minimalist attention to the reconstruction effects associated with movement (see Chomsky 1993), Johnson (2008) suggested that perhaps it is the reconstruction aspect of movement that is subject to islands. In other words, it's ok for an element to cross island boundaries, but such a movement for some reason cannot reconstruct, which one may reasonably expect will lead to ill-formedness when the output of syntax is inspected for matters of interpretation, if reconstruction is, at bottom, interpretation of the copy left by movement. Such interpretation is required for proper theta-role assignment, for example. If reconstruction is blocked, theta-assignment may fail, leading to unacceptability.

Johnson's suggestion[30] should not come as a surprise to those who are familiar with the minimalist literature: it's often been suggested that reconstruction effects arise because movement is the result of a copying operation (see Chomsky 1993), and that what we call reconstruction is in fact interpretation of the original, in-situ element that was copied ('the gap'). Thus, reconstruction is to the semantic component what copy-deletion is to the phonological component: both systems interfacing with the syntactic component must deal with the sets of copies produced by movement. It's quite natural to suggest, like Johnson did, that island effects reduce to constraints on reconstruction (interpretation of the low copy); after all, the suggestion is the semantic counterpart of the more popular – though I believe

ultimately wrong – idea that islands are effects caused by the problematic nature of the low copy that is deleted (the 'gap') in the phonological component.

The problem with Johnson's suggestion is also reminiscent of the
treatment of islands as phonological effects. Much as it remains to be
made precise what exactly is the phonological problem with gaps, it is
not clear what is the problem with reconstruction in island contexts.
In other words, the idea that reconstruction is to blame is a logical
possibility, and, to be sure, an interesting avenue to explore, but before
we can adopt it, much work remains to be done, and many basic
questions answered. And I suspect it won't be easy because it's now
quite clear that the link between movement and reconstruction is
more indirect than often assumed by syntacticians, even outside island
contexts. As Boeckx and Hornstein (2008) discuss, reconstruction under
movement is not automatic: there are numerous instances of movement where reconstruction effects are blocked (see, e.g., Lasnik 2003
for extensive discussion). Witness (28), which cannot mean something
like 'it is certain that no one will solve the problem' (the reading that
would obtain if reconstruction/interpretation of the low copy left by
raising the subject were possible)

(28) No one is certain to solve the problem.

Given that lack of reconstruction is found independently of the presence of islands or other locality constraints on movement ((28) is a run-
of-the-mill raising structure), we need a theory of when reconstruction
is allowed to take place before we can test Johnson's suggestion
regarding the cause of islandhood. Unfortunately, no such theory is
currently available.[31] But let me stress that Johnson's suggestion has
the merit of forcing us to think about the semantic side of the grammar, redirecting our attention away from the currently more popular
intuition that islands are due to properties of the phonological
component.

An alternative answer to the question 'what is it about movement
(unaccompanied by resumption) that makes it subject to islands?' was
offered by Boeckx (2003a), building on independent proposals by
Chomsky (2000) and Richards (2001).

From Chomsky (2000), Boeckx (2003a) took the hypothesis that what
we call 'movement' is in fact a complex operation consisting of at least
three suboperations. According to Chomsky (2000), for 'movement'
to happen, some featural relation must be established between the
element to be moved and the host (/head of the phrase providing the
landing site) even prior to movement. The element to be moved and

the host must first establish a *matching* relation of features (i.e., they must have at least one feature in common). Second, once features have been matched, an *agreement/valuation* operation must take place that will transfer the value of the matching feature(s) from the element to be moved onto the host (e.g., C will become [+interrogative] once it combines with a *wh*-phrase). Crucially, Chomsky claims that such agreement operation can take place in the absence of movement (as evidenced from the numerous cases of long-distance agreement found cross-linguistically; see Boeckx (2008c) for a collection of this phenomenon, which includes existential constructions like *there seem to be three men in the room*, where the indefinite *three men* manages to trigger agreement on the finite verb in the higher clause without moving into that clause). Finally, 'movement' per se happens, in the sense that once agreement has taken place, the element that valued the features of the host is copied, and the copy is *remerged* in the appropriate landing site. To sum up: according to Chomsky (2000), movement consists of:

  (i) match,
 (ii) agreement, and
(iii) copy + remerge.

Boeckx (2003a) suggested that perhaps one of these ingredients is the culprit for island effects. Boeckx furthermore reasoned that (i) given that we have empirical reasons to believe that some dependencies can cross islands (as the island repair data indicate), and (ii) given that we have conceptual (minimalist) reasons to want to reduce all long-distance dependencies to movement (cf. Hornstein 2001 for a spirited defense of this idea),[32] we could entertain the idea that not all of the suboperations just listed are necessary for movement to be said to have taken place, and exploit this possibility to allow for movement to take place across islands in some, but not in all contexts. Put differently, Boeckx (2003a) suggested we distinguish between those suboperations underlying movement that are necessary for movement to take place, and those that are not, and blame islands on the operation that is presumably missing when movement is allowed to cross islands (e.g., in the context of resumption).

Put yet another way: if we want to blame islandhood on a property of movement, and at the same time allow movement to cross islands (cf. repair contexts), we'd better find a property of movement that does not always (have to) obtain (and blame islandhood on that property), because otherwise island effects will be expected to always obtain in the context of movement.

Following this reasoning, Boeckx claimed that of the three operations identified by Chomsky, Match and Copy/Remerge are plausibly necessary components of all movement operations, but the agreement component does not appear to be so necessary – the idea being that it is sufficient for two elements to share a feature for them to (re)merge, even if neither of these elements needs to be valued. Perhaps then, island effects are to be reduced to the presence vs. absence of agreement under movement. But why should agreement matter so much in the realm of islands? After all, since Chomsky (1977) we have learned to distinguish between A- and A-bar movement, and agreement seems to be relevant to A-, but not A-bar type dependencies, whereas islands primarily pertain to A-bar dependencies, since A-dependencies have even stricter locality restrictions; cf. the discussion of Chomsky 1973, 1977 in Chapter 1.

Although implicating agreement in a domain where it is usually deemed irrelevant appears far-fetched at first, Boeckx (2003a) adduced a series of arguments that taken as a whole suggest that we should not dismiss the hypothesis too quickly. Let me review these briefly here.

First, Boeckx points out that it is quite telling that what is often called long-distance agreement (agreement in the absence of movement) cannot take place from anywhere. Much like in the domain of islands, distance does not appear to be what constrains long-distance agreement; the constraints appear to be more structural. In fact, like A-bar movement, agreement-at-a-distance appears to be constrained by islands: I know of no agreement dependency that is capable of reaching across a strong island boundary (inside an adjunct or inside a displaced argument like a raised subject). In addition, agreement-at-a-distance is subject to Relativized Minimality, like movement is: no agreement can take place if the elements trying to agree are separated by an element that has features that are capable of entering into agreement relations (see Boeckx 2008c for extensive discussion, examples, and references). So the locality conditions on agreement appear to match pretty closely those of typical movement. This would not be surprising if, as Chomsky (2000) argues, agreement underlies movement: any constraint on the former will be inherited by the latter. This very conclusion opens up an interesting theoretical possibility: if agreement could somehow be suspended or suppressed, movement may be free of locality constraints.

Second, Boeckx observes that resumptive elements are typically bundles of agreement features (pronouns). This may not be a coincidence: perhaps the fact that resumption alleviates islands is to be understood as indicating that once an extra element (proform) that has all (and only?) those properties that enter into agreement relations can actually take care of some agreement relation, movement (of its associate) is island-free.

Third, Boeckx gathered evidence from a variety of languages that shows that agreement has a freezing effect, blocking otherwise legitimate extraction (equivalently, lack of agreement rendering otherwise illegitimate extraction possible). Put differently, agreement induces islandhood the same way that displacement and adjunction do.[33]

Let me provide a few examples of this freezing effect for the sake of illustration.

Consider the following examples from Fiorentino (original data due to Brandi and Cordin 1989).

(29) a. La Maria l' è venuta
        The Maria she is come
        'Maria came'
     b. Gli è venuto la Maria
        It is come the Maria
        'Maria came'
     c. Quante   ragazze gli è venuto con te?
        How.many girls   it is come with you
        'How many girls came with you?'
     d. *Quante   ragazze le   sono venute con te?
        How.many girls   they are   come   with you

(29a) shows that in this language preverbal subjects relate to clitics matching in features (3rd fem. sg). By contrast, post-verbal subjects don't (29b), the clitic bearing default morphology. The contrast between (29c) and (29d) indicates that subject extraction requires the use of a non-agreeing clitic. Based on (29c), we could conclude, as Rizzi (1982) did, that in standard Italian examples like (30), subject extraction takes place from a post-verbal position related to a silent non-agreeing clitic (*pro*), which obviates the ban on subject-extraction from embedded clauses (the so-called [*that*-trace] effect of Chomsky and Lasnik 1977). In other words, lack of agreement renders extraction possible.

(30) Chi hai detto che e partito?
     Who has said that is left
     'Who did he say that left?'

Boeckx also mentions the fact that objects are islands for standard wh-extraction in languages with object agreement, like Basque (31), and takes this to suggest that agreement turns an otherwise transparent domain (object) into an island. (Datum from Uriagereka 1998.)

(31) *Nori buruzko sortu zitusten aurreko asteko istiluek zurrumurruak?
     Who about-of create scandals last   week   scandals rumors
     'Who have last week's scandals caused [rumors about __]?'

In languages like English, objects show no verbal agreement, and are therefore transparent. By contrast, subjects agree, hence are islands (cf. the subject condition).

Finally, Boeckx (2003a) also took data showing lack of agreement between a resumptive pronoun and its antecedent, of the sort given in (32),[34] to suggest that when the antecedent of the resumptive pronoun is not required to enter into any agreement relation inside the island, its movement is not subject to island constraints. I should point out that agreement mismatch between the resumptive pronoun and its antecedent is certainly not a pre-requisite for movement to be island-free; presence of a resumptive element suffices in the general case. After all, the fact that the resumptive pronouns match the features of its antecedent is not evidence that agreement between the two took place. The two elements may have been independently introduced into the derivation with matching features. What is more important is the lack of agreement relation between the moving element and any clausal predicate inside the island domain, which the lack of agreement between the moving element and the resumptive pronoun, which agrees with clausal predicates, can be taken to provide indirect evidence for.

(To keep the level of complexity of the examples down, the following sentences focus on the lack of agreement between the resumptive and its antecedent, and do not involve island structures. For data with islands, see Boeckx 2003a.)

(32) a. Lack-of-Person Agreement
        A   Alec, tusa a   bhfuil an Béarla aige ...   [Irish]
        Hey Alec you aN is   the English at-him
        'Hey Alec you that know(s) English ...'
      b. Lack-of-Number Agreement
        Na daoine a chuirfeadh   isteach ar an phost sin   [Irish]
        The men C put-cond-3sg in   for the job that
        'The men that would apply for that job'
      c. Lack-of-Gender Agreement
        Dè   a'mhàileid   a chuir thu am peann ann   [Sc. Gaelic]
        Which the.bag-Fem C put   you the pen   in-3-Masc
        'Which bag did you put the pen in'
      d. Lack-of-Case Agreement
        (i) Bha thu a'geàrradh na craoibhe   [Sc. Gaelic]
            Be-pst you cutting the three-Gen
            'You were cutting the tree'
        (ii) Dè a'chraobh   a bha   thu a'geàrradh
            Which tree.Nom C be-pst you cutting
            'Which tree were you cutting'

Boeckx (2003a) took all of these facts to be quite suggestive, and set out to explain the freezing role of agreement relations: why should a movement operation that includes an agreement step be subject to islands, and a movement operation that does not be island-free?

Boeckx pursued an approach inspired by a proposal in Richards (2001), which I am about to sketch.[35] But let me say upfront that I don't think that the specific answer given in Boeckx (2003a) and that I am about to state is definitive. But I think that it has the merit of pointing towards a better solution, which will be the subject of the next section of this chapter. But before we get there, let me review Richards's and Boeckx's proposals briefly.

According to Richards (2001), Universal Grammar imposes a ban on chains (i.e., products of movement) that are "too strong," or, put differently, on moving elements that "try to do too many things." According to Richards, certain (crucially, not all) feature-checking relations make a chain 'strong'[36] or 'heavy'; too many of these relations cause the chain to break, and this is what Richards suggests we have called locality conditions on movement. That is, locality conditions such as islands are contexts where a given element is forced to enter into too many strong checking relations, causing its chain to break.

To be more specific, Richards claims that the breaking point arises not in syntax per se, but at the interface between syntax and morpho-phonology (he does so to allow for island repair effects of the ellipsis type). For him, a strong feature-checking relation is actually an instruction to help morpho-phonology linearize the chain created by movement; essentially, strong feature-checking relations serve as a flag to linearize the relevant element at that checking site. If the chain enters into too many strong feature-checking relations (more than one such relation appears to be too much), morpho-phonology will be at a loss, for it will receive conflicting instructions: it can only linearize the moved units once, and cannot receive instructions like "place it here and also there," which is the effect entering into multiple strong feature-checking relations would have, according to Richards.

To capture the island-inducing role of agreement discussed above, Boeckx (2003a) hypothesized that the establishment of certain case/agreement feature-checking relations is among the things that make a chain strong (in Richards's sense). Accordingly, establishing an agreement relation of the strong type and then trying to extract the element that has entered into that agreement relation beyond its 'agreement' site will lead to a chain that would be too strong for the morpho-phonology to handle.

Boeckx captured the 'rescuing' role of resumption by saying that the presence of a resumptive pronoun frees up the moving element from the freezing effect of agreement because the resumptive pronoun can

take care of a strong feature-checking relation like agreement and
the moving element can dedicate itself to establishing a relation with
an A-bar head, as the following schematic representations ((33)–(34))
illustrate.

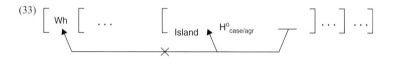

(33)

(34)

OK

Resumption, then, is essentially a way of balancing, or splitting into
two, those chains that would be otherwise too strong.

Although we may have moved closer to understanding the role of
resumption in the context of islands by claiming that its presence
allows for the moving element to dedicate itself to establishing the
relevant A-bar relation, the account presented so far does not yet
capture strong island effects. All it says is that once an element has
entered into a certain type of case/agreement relation, it cannot
extend its chain any further. But CED effects are not about extraction
(of, say, agreeing subjects), they are about subextraction (extraction of
elements contained inside, say, agreeing subjects). It seems that what
we need is something like the following generalization:

(35) The (sub)extraction/agreement generalization
      Units that have entered into a strong agreement relation, such as English-type raised
      subjects, can no longer be moved (extracted), *nor can the elements that these contain be
      moved (subextracted)*

Metaphorically speaking, one could say that those domains that are
islands are those domains that have exhausted their 'featural potential,' and have become deactivated (opaque) as a result. It's as if syntactic units came with features that give them a certain life span: once
exhausted, this life span cannot be extended. Islands are precisely
domains that have reached their 'limits.'

But this is a metaphor, and (35) needs to be looked at more closely.
The generalization in (35) points to a connection between elements
that are hard to move (such as raised subjects) and those domains that

are hard to move from, which I believe is interesting and deserves further discussion. But I must first address an obvious criticism often raised at (35), made most explicit by Richards (2011). Richards correctly points out that

> Just because the head of the moved XP [has established a strong feature-checking relation], [and is] thus inactive for further [operation], this does not in and of itself imply that its internal constituents must themselves become frozen. That's an extra assumption, simply asserted as fact in Chomsky (2008):
>
> "EF [the edge feature driving A-bar movement] of C cannot extract the PP complement from within SPEC-T: if it could, the subject-condition effects would be obviated. It must be, then, that the SPEC-T position is impenetrable to EF, and a far more natural principle is that it is simply invisible to EF [. . .]. That principle generalizes the inactivity condition of earlier work, which takes the head of an A-chain (which always has any uninterpretable features valued) to be invisible to Agree. A reasonable principle, then, is that an A-chain becomes invisible to further computation when its uninterpretable features are valued. That will incorporate the effects of the earlier inactivity condition, restated in terms of phases." (Chomsky 2008: p.16 of 2005 ms.)

Richards points out that none of this seems to have the ring of necessity about it. It appears to be simply stipulated on the basis of the empirical observation. Richards notes that it is just as plausible or "reasonable" that only the head of the A-chain is deactivated, and its internal constituents remain active.

While Richards's point is well taken, I think that it misses an important property of the analysis under discussion (inherited from Richards 2001), i.e. its chain-based character. As Boeckx (2003a) pointed out, the transitivity effect (from head of chain to elements internal to the chain) that Richards regards as a 'leap of logic' is to be expected in a chain-based context. Specifically, it is to be expected under Chomsky's (1995) contention that the movement chains that the external systems process are to be defined in terms of their contexts, and concretely in terms of their sisters. So, the chain formed by the object complement of a verb is to be defined in terms of that verb. If so, we expect the transitivity effect in (35), for an element trying to move out of a subject that has established a strong featural relation will have its chain defined in terms of that element, and will inherit the constraints imposed on it. In particular, if the latter is subject to freezing effects because its chain is strong once it has entered into an agreement relation, the elements that it dominates will be frozen as well – all this, of course, from the perspective of the morpho-phonological component, which reads off chains (structures created by movement) on the basis of their structural contexts.

Put differently, while Richards's (2011) point makes a lot of sense in a derivational context, it does not in a representational, chain-based approach.

But having said this, I want to repeat that I don't think that the analysis just sketched is the ultimate solution to the problem of strong islands, and I want to end this section by pointing out some real, major problems an approach like Boeckx (2003a) faces.

First, the solution is highly dependent on feature-checking relations, and which ones count as 'strong.' This renders the explanation feature-based, and thus inevitably quite fragile: we do not have a good theory of features in syntax, let alone one that provides non-ad hoc character-izations of why a given feature-checking relation is strong (see Boeckx 2010a, 2011b for an extensive critique of feature-based syntactic ana-lyses in general).

Second, the solution crucially depends on movement being a com-posite operation. It thus departs from what is arguably the simplest analysis of movement as just another instance of merge (Chomsky's 2004 idea that movement is 'internal merge': merger of an element that is already part of the tree). If movement is just merge, there is no need of an agreement relation underlying it. If so, blaming a con-straint of movement on agreement relations established prior to move-ment becomes conceptually problematic.

Third, the analysis as sketched here works best for the 'subject' part of the CED. It can be extended to the adjunct part (Boeckx 2003a hypothesized that the adjunction relation amounts to the establish-ment of a strong feature-checking relation, and therefore prevents subsequent (sub)extraction), but this is clearly stipulative. Apart from capturing the facts, there is no reason to take adjunction to establish a strong feature-checking relation.

Still, for all its problems, the approach reviewed in this section has certain properties that I regard as desirable and worth preserving, which is why I devoted close to a section to them. Let me highlight them here.

First, in order to understand the freezing role of agreement, Boeckx (2003a) exploited an idea of Richards (2001) ("chains that are too strong"), which is chain-based, and interface-based, and this is a prop-erty of the explanation that I want to capitalize on in the next section.

Second, Boeckx's analysis is very reminiscent of Ross's idea that it is not movement per se that island domains block; rather, it is particular operations, among which Ross included feature-changing rules – whose nature is close to agreement (at bottom, a feature-valuing rule) – that cause islandhood. This continues to strike me as correct.

Finally, I'd like to point out that by identifying agreement (if Chomsky 2000 is right, crucially a non-movement operation) as the cause of certain locality effects, Boeckx (2003a) reverses the logic of Chomsky's (1977) account of locality effects, where locality was inextricably tied to movement. As Adger and Ramchand (2005) have independently observed, this result is inevitable, once one recognizes the existence of non-movement operations like Agree (Chomsky 2000). Since such non-movement operations also obey locality conditions, these conditions become inevitably divorced from movement per se. It is interesting that certain treatments of locality, most explicitly Koster (1978a, 1987), had already anticipated that movement per se was not what islands were constraining. (Koster came to this conclusion by highlighting the fact that under the trace theory popular in Government-and-Binding, locality conditions had become licensing conditions on traces, but once traces were treated like anaphors, locality conditions reduced to binding conditions, not conditions on movement per se.)

4.4 ISLAND SENSITIVITY AND THE PRODUCT OF MOVEMENT

Although I have pointed out on several occasions that the vast majority of syntactic theories of islands retain a derivational character, which not only continues to influence current accounts of island effects but also influences the type of questions asked of theories of islands or the criticisms raised at existing accounts (witness my comments concerning Richards 2011 in the previous section, as well as my comments on Hornstein's skepticism regarding filters within minimalism in note 1 of the previous chapter), representational accounts of islands have been developed in the minimalist literature, and I want to review some of them here, before proposing a new representational account of my own that hopefully avoids the problems faced by existing ones, or at least goes a bit further in answering Ross's questions: "Why islands? Why these islands?"

Perhaps the earliest representational account of islands in the minimalist literature is the one developed by Takahashi (1994). Takahashi adopts Chomsky's (1993) idea that movement is the result of copy + (re-)merge, and seeks to derive some (crucially, not all) locality conditions on chains by taking the notion of copy very seriously. Specifically,

Takahashi claims that the ban on extraction out of displaced elements (the 'subject' part of the CED) is due to the fact that movement proceeds successive cyclically. Now, if extraction is to take place out of a given domain, Takahashi assumes that the moving element must first go through an intermediate landing site at the edge of the extraction domain (an idea that the reader will recall goes back to Chomsky 1973). But if that domain is itself the result of movement, such an intermediate step to the edge is bound to be ruled out, Takahashi contends, because this movement will inevitably create a difference between the (displaced) copy of the extraction domain and the original copy (in the in-situ position), as depicted in (36). (Unpronounced copies are enclosed in angled brackets.)

(36) a. *Who did [pictures of __] seem to Bill __ to be nice?
     b. Who did [<who> [pictures of <who>]] seem to Bill <[pictures of who]> to be nice?

According to Takahashi, the ban on extraction out of displaced elements thus reduces to a condition that copies created by movement should be identical. Syntactic outputs violating this condition are filtered out post-syntactically, although it is not clear what portion of the grammar rules it out (that is to say, it is not clear what part of the grammar dictates that copies be identical, as opposed to, say, nondistinct).

A different representational analysis of some island effects is offered by Rizzi 2006 and Rizzi and Shlonsky (2007). According to these authors, certain syntactic positions are associated with a requirement, not unlike the more popular minimalist operation of feature-checking, that they characterize as a *criterion*. A criterion demands that a given syntactic position be filled (in this sense, the requirement that is known as the Extended Projection Principle boils down to a Subject criterion demanding that SpecIP be filled). Each chain is defined by a lower bound and an upper bound, each associated with a criterion. The lower bound corresponds to the site into which the moved element was introduced (for arguments, think of the theta-criterion), and is relatively unproblematic.[37] Problems arise concerning the upper bound. Rizzi and Shlonsky take positions like 'Subject position' or SpecCP to be associated each with a criterion. Now, because a chain formed by movement cannot have more than one upper bound, no element can satisfy both the subject and wh-criterion.[38] This accounts for the subject freezing principle (and, as Rizzi 2006 contemplates, the subject part of the CED, by the sort of chain-based transitivity discussed in the context of (35) at the end of the previous section).

Rizzi and Shlonsky's explanation is not too different from Richards's (2001) ban on chains that are too strong, for the positions Richards takes to be strong coincide with those that Rizzi and Shlonsky take to be criterial. Presumably, having more than one upper bound is as confusing for the external systems interpreting chains as too many instructions associated with strong feature-checking sites.

The problem for such analyses lies in finding a non-stipulative characterization of what counts as a strong or criterial position. In addition, much like Takahashi's analysis, Rizzi's or Richards's analysis has only limited scope: whereas it offers an account of the ban on extraction out of displaced elements (since such elements will be part of chains that are too strong), it does not extend naturally to the other part of the CED, the ban on extraction out of adjuncts. (One could, of course, say that all positions in adjuncts are strong or criterial, but the question, of course, is why.)

Stepanov (2001, 2007) took this limitation to be an argument in favor of Takahashi's analysis, since he claimed that the CED should not receive a unified treatment, but as I pointed out in Chapters 1 and 2, the evidence offered by Stepanov in favor of such a heterogeneous treatment of the CED is rather weak.

Boeckx (2008a) sought to rescue an analysis like Rizzi's (or Richards's), i.e. extend it to the other part of the CED, by relying on Chomsky's (1995) idea that members of a movement chain are to be defined in terms of their sisters, already mentioned in the context of (35). Boeckx (2008a) pointed out that such a 'contextual' definition of chains is reminiscent of Chomsky's (1994) treatment of phrase structure, where levels of projection like XP, X′, and X^0 are defined contextually, in terms of their sisters (X^0 is the occurrence of X that is the sister of the complement, X′ is the occurrence of X that is the sister of the specifier, etc.). On the basis of this analogy, Boeckx proposed that chains be thought of as projections of sort (superprojections, if you wish; projections defined on the basis of projections), and proposed that chains should then be subject to well-formedness conditions (filters) known to hold of regular projections.[39] This would immediately account for Rizzi's condition concerning the need for a unique lower bound and a unique upper bound on chains: given a suitably defined X-bar theory, there can only be one X^0 and one XP (see Chomsky 1970, Kayne 1994).

Boeckx (2008a) pointed out that if we take members of chains to be defined in terms of their sisters, it is quite natural to demand (i.e., have the grammar impose a well-formedness condition to that effect) that members of a chain must be defined in terms of elements that can be members of uniform projections. That is to say, if one seeks to group

chain members together into a single chain, the sister-elements defining these chain members should themselves be well-connected.[40] This
condition would immediately account for the ban on chains crossing
adjunct domains, for by definition, adjuncts are not connected to the
main branch of the tree.[41] Accordingly, the chain members defined in
terms of these adjuncts cannot be integrated into chains belonging to/
defined in terms of the main part of the tree.

However, while it incorporates the adjunct condition, Boeckx's
(2008a) treatment suffers from a series of shortcomings that it ultimately shares with analyses like Rizzi's and Richards's, the main one[42]
being that it has no good (i.e., non-stipulative) answer for why 'A-'
positions associated with case/agreement, criteria or strong feature-
checking relations cannot be part of A-bar chains, while A-projections
can be embedded inside A-bar projections (e.g., TP embedded inside
CP). Put differently, why are chains (superprojections) that contain A-
and A-bar relations too strong, but A-bar projections containing
A-projections ok?

I am the first one to recognize that no natural answer to this
question is forthcoming, but I think that even if they ultimately turn
out to be flawed (as I think they are, which is the reason why I have not
gone into the details of their technical implementations, much as
I have avoided going into the details of proper government relations
at the heart of the productive GB period), the analyses reviewed above
can nevertheless teach us several valuable lessons regarding the nature
of (strong) islands, lessons which taken together may direct us towards
a more satisfactory solution, like the one I will outline in the remainder of this section (see also Boeckx 2008d, 2009, 2010a, 2011c). Here are
the lessons I have in mind:

First, and to my mind foremost, the idea that locality problems arise
not when certain nodes are crossed but because chains are too strong,
or too contradictory, or too heavy, or not well-connected, suggests that
islands are not environments that block movement of any element
attempting to cross them, but rather islands, even strong islands, are
relativized environments, or (to borrow a term from the ethology literature) *umwelts*: it is the extracting element that, in virtue of entering
into certain relations (certain checking relations that are 'strong') or
reaching certain criterial positions, creates its own island, for itself
and for the elements it contains/pied-pipes, but not for elements that
are, say, adjacent to it.

The idea that islands have to be relativized to properties of the
extracting element is already familiar from the literature on weak
islands, but the accounts reviewed in the previous section add a

further twist to this story: islands not only have to be relativized to the lexical (/semantic) properties of the extracting element (say, D-linking), they also have to be relativized to the syntactic action of the extracting element (the relations that this element establishes): a given CP may become an island domain for a subject because the subject of that clause enters into a special relation with C, whereas that same CP need not be an island for, say, an object that does not enter into a special relation with C. Islands, in other words, are to be understood dynamically.

Put yet another way, conditions of transformations cannot be defined along the schema introduced in Chomsky (1973) ("No rule is allowed to cross such and such domain") because the appropriate characterization of the domain depends not so much on the type of rule (assuming the minimalist guideline that there is only one kind of rule: merge), but on the derivational history of the element undergoing that rule. To repeat, if the works above are on the right track, islands are formed by the elements that cross them, they are not 'predefined' lexically as bounding nodes (phase-heads, barriers, etc.).[43]

I take the old data point known as the *that*-trace effect (Chomsky and Lasnik 1977) to illustrate just this idea: a complementizer position lexicalized by *that* blocks movement of the subject it contains (37), but not the object (38). In such cases, it is impossible to say something along the lines that no movement can cross a finite clause headed by *that*. Some instances of movement are not possible, but some are.

(37) *Who did you say [that __ bought a book]

(38) What did you say [that Bill bought __]

The second lesson I draw from the representational accounts of islands discussed so far is that it was wrong to view islands as only relevant to the A-bar system, as Chomsky (1977) did (departing from what I think is the more accurate perspective defended in Chomsky 1973). It turns out that A-relations matter a lot for whether an A-bar chain will be island-sensitive. I like to think of this as the 'resumptive' lesson. A resumptive element is a prototypical A-element. As has often been pointed out, it's the minimal nominal unit that can enter into case/agreement ('A'-type) relations. The fact that such an element frees up A-bar movement suggests that at least some constraints on A-bar movement arise because of certain A-relations that are established by the extracting element before undergoing A-bar movement.

Clearly, it cannot be just any kind of A-relation that impedes A-bar chain formation, for the most transparent domains (complements;

e.g., objects) also enter into A-relations. And ideally, we want to avoid resorting to diacritics or ad hoc notions to identify which A-relations pose a problem: we don't want to resort to qualifications like 'strong' or 'criterial.'

In the paragraphs that follow, I will turn my attention to which A-relations cause problems. This will lead me to propose a new account of the 'subject' part of the CED, which, unlike the representational accounts reviewed so far, I will ultimately be able to extend to the other, 'adjunct' part of the CED.

The key contrast, I think, is (37)–(38), repeated here as (39)–(40), and the CED-contrast in (41)–(42):

(39) *Who did you say [that __ bought a book]?

(40) What did you say [that Bill bought __]?

(41) *Who did [pictures of __] cause a riot?

(42) Who did John see [pictures of __]?

In recent years, and inspired by the representational accounts reviewed so far, I have come to defend a view (see Boeckx 2008d, 2009, 2010a, 2011c) that rests on the idea that the source of the problem in (39)/(41) is that the A-relations established by subjects require A-movement (raising to SpecIP), whereas those established by objects don't. Once a movement has taken place to meet A-requirements, the element that was forced to undergo movement (and, by transitivity, the elements it contains and whose chains the head of the A-chain defines) does not seem to be able to go on and form a legitimate A-bar chain anymore, whereas elements that were not forced to form an A-chain have no problem undergoing A-bar movement.[44] Put differently, the constraint we are dealing with in (39)/(41) is intimately related in the forced presence of an A-chain.

But why should this be? And whatever it is that makes this true, how can it be extended to the realm of adjuncts?

This is the question I would like to address now.

Several researchers (Chomsky 2007, 2008; Richards 2007; Epstein, Kitahara, and Seely 2010; Boeckx 2010a) have independently argued that the structure surrounding the A-relation established by moving the subject is quite complex, and quite difficult to deal with for the external systems that inspect the syntactic derivation. (I will return momentarily to the hypothesized nature of said complexity.) In order to simplify the structure, thereby alleviating the burden to be borne by the external systems and allowing the syntactic derivation to proceed in an efficient manner, it's been claimed that the relevant portion of the syntactic tree must be spelled-out (transferred to the external systems to be digested, as it were) as soon as it has been completed.

The claim I would like to make is that this obligatory step of spell-out *indirectly* leads to the (strong) island effects that we have been dealing with in this chapter. Specifically, I claim that if the portion of the tree being spelled-out contains a unit that can be regarded as independent and 'complete,' such as a complete A-chain, or an adjunct phrase, such a unit will be processed and considered 'closed' by the external systems interacting with syntax, leading to its opacification. If at a later stage in the processing of the syntactic derivation the external systems receive a portion of structure that demands reprocessing of the structure that was considered closed, an island effect will result. To put it concisely: early closure, induced by early spell-out, leads to islandhood.

The basic intuition having been stated, let me now return to why the formation of an A-chain or adjunction triggers immediate spell-out, why this leads to CED-effects, and why this does not affect complement-domains.

Perhaps the most straightforward situation is that of adjunction. According to Chomsky 2004, adjunction[45] leads to a labeled structure that is more complex than regular merge. Chomsky speaks of the difference between Pair-Merge (adjunction) vs. Set-Merge (complementation). Whereas combining A and B by Set-Merge yields the simple set {A,B}, or perhaps the labeled set {A {A,B}} ([$_A$ A B]), Pair-Merge yields a complex label: {<A,B> {A,B}}, which serves as an instruction to the external systems that adjunction is an asymmetric process: it is B that adjoins to A (and not vice versa).

Because adjunction gives rise to this complex label, spell-out must take place immediately upon adjunction to 'simplify' the label (see Chomsky 2004, Boeckx 2010a, Narita 2011; see also Johnson 2009, who speaks of the doubly rooted nature of structures associated with adjunction). This immediate spell-out operation returns a structure akin to that of set-merge. This is achieved by transferring the entire content of the adjoined phrase to the external systems (if the adjoined phrase is taken to be a phase, this means that both the phase complement and the phase edge which together constitute the entire adjunct must be spelled-out, as was first pointed out to my knowledge by Raposo 2002). This, I claim, is what leads to the adjunct island: once spelled-out, the adjunct domain and all the elements it contains are 'frozen' – adjuncts being edgeless domains.[46] In the absence of a phase edge that would create a connection between what is spelled-out and what remains syntactically active, it is as if adjuncts were treated like independent clauses; closed units, hence islands from the perspective of the external systems.

When it comes to the relation between immediate spell-out and A-chain formation, two answers have been pursued in the literature.[47] Both build on the idea recently stressed by Chomsky that the source of 'A-'features (case, agreement) associated with (obligatory) raising of the subject are originally associated with the head C (the complementizer), and not with the head of the phrase to which the subject ultimately raises, i.e. I(nfl). According to Chomsky, Infl comes to be the host of the subject A-relation as a result of a process he calls Feature Inheritance, whereby the A-type features that originated C are inherited by its complement I(nfl). Chomsky 2007, 2008 (see also Richards 2007) ties this process of inheritance to spell-out: once inherited, the features on Infl must be spelled-out as they are being valued by the subject. This is so, according to Chomsky, because delaying spell-out would prevent the external systems from knowing that the features on Infl should not be assigned a semantic interpretation (according to Chomsky, only valued features should be assigned an interpretation; seeing features being valued is still good enough for the semantics not to interpret them, but seeing them after valuation would lead to them being wrongly assigned an interpretation). Chomsky's reasoning is quite complex, and it is enough for present purposes to stick to the idea that the presence of A-type features on Infl dominated by C induces immediate spell-out.[48] Spelling out the complement of C will have the effect of spelling out the entire A-chain formed by raising of the subject phrase. This, I claim, is what turns the latter into an island. Like adjoined structures, A-chains are complete enough for the external systems to process as independent units (like an independent projection, if chains are (super)projections, as I argued in Boeckx 2008a), closing them as soon as they are processed, thereby turning them into islands.

Epstein, Kitahara, and Seely (2010) offer a different implementation of the idea that the portion of the tree associated with subject raising undergoes immediate spell-out. Epstein, Kitahara, and Seely adopt Chomsky's idea that A-type features on Infl are inherited from C, but they reject the idea that in such a situation, the subject raises to SpecIP dominated by C (the standard structure that Chomsky assumes). According to them, such a movement would not target the root of the tree, and would therefore violate the idea that movement must always target the root and not be counter-cyclic (an idea that Chomsky 1993 called the Extension Condition). To avoid this counter-cyclic movement step, Epstein, Kitahara, and Seely propose that the structure formed by Feature-Inheritance is a doubly rooted structure where C and T stand side-by-side as it were, with T(P) hosting the raised subject, as shown in (43):

(43)

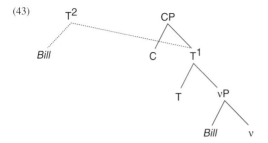

Epstein, Kitahara, and Seely go on to claim that the complexity of such a doubly rooted structure leads to immediate spell-out of TP. This, again, will have the effect of trapping the subject chain into the portion of the tree being spelled-out, leading to the subject island. In fact, the doubly rooted structure amounts to an adjunction structure. Spelling it out amounts to trapping the A-chain inside an adjunct (as I pointed out above, Johnson (2009) claims that adjunction also gives rise to a doubly rooted structure, which makes his argument for immediate spell-out exactly parallel to the one provided by Epstein, Kitahara, and Seely). Because it is the formation of the A-chain that caused the doubly rooted structure, one can say that the A-chain participated in the creation of its own island, much like phrases become islands when they adjoin.

On the basis of the discussion so far, we can thus formulate the following generalization, covering both the 'subject' and the 'adjunct' aspects of the original CED:

(44) Structures that induce immediate spell-out (e.g., doubly rooted, adjoined structures)
      are islands for those elements (and the elements that these properly contain) that led
      to the construction of such structures and to which the external systems can assign
      independent, autonomous, complete status (A-chains, adjoined phrases).

The claim being made here is that trying to integrate an A-bar chain into one of the structures that the external systems have already processed and considered closed would give rise to a species of garden path: a unit that the external systems had previously closed would have to be re-opened to accommodate an extension (the A-bar chain), causing the external systems to 'gag.'

Importantly, regular complements are immune to this problem, because, as is well-established, unlike subjects, they need not form

A-chains to establish the relevant A-dependencies (case/agreement) – there is no obligatory EPP with objects, no Object criterion. In fact, when they have to undergo movement, as in so-called Exceptional Case Marking contexts, objects become islands, just like subjects:[49]

(45) *Who did John believe [pictures of __] to have caused the riot?

Incidentally, the hypothesized difference between subjects and objects does not disappear even if we adopt Chomsky's claim that just like the A-type features associated with Infl are inherited from C(omp), the A-type features hosted by V and responsible for object case marking are also inherited from the phase head *v* (inducing spell-out). As the following representations (46a,b) make clear, whereas the spelled-out portion of the tree contains an A-chain in the case of subjects, it does not in the case of object. As I have argued in Boeckx (2010a), I think that this is in fact the reason why there is a subject-EPP/criterion but not an object-EPP/criterion: the recipient of features from the phase head is not a sister of the subject phrase, whereas it is in the case of (direct) objects, forcing the formation of an A-chain in the former, but not in the latter.[50] Because no A-chain need be formed in the case of direct objects, no doubly rooted structure of the sort we saw in (43) is formed, hence, according to Epstein *et al.*, no immediate spell-out needs to take place. Since spell-out does not take place at that point, no early closure leading to islandhood will ensue.[51]

(46)   (a) Subject   (b) Object

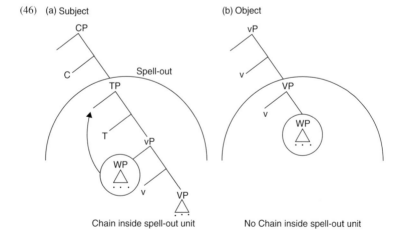

Chain inside spell-out unit   No Chain inside spell-out unit

If the idea proposed here is on the right track, several remarks are in order.

First, note that I have not said that the problem of embedding a chain inside an already closed/processed unit only pertains to the phonological interface: it arises on both the phonological side and the semantic side. It's therefore compatible with the idea that the problem with chains inside islands is due to the presence of a gap (the phonological answer; cf. Hornstein, Lasnik, and Uriagereka 2007), or due to the fact that islands block reconstruction (Johnson 2008), or other hypotheses not reviewed in the preceding pages (e.g., the claim that island structures lead to disjointed denotations and cause the semantic computation to crash (Johnson 2009), or violate the single event condition imposed on chains by the semantic system (Truswell 2007)). For me, it's a problem coming from both sides of the grammar.

Second, although the account of CED-effects just proposed retains certain elements of previous chain-based analyses reviewed in this chapter, it is less feature-dependent than these other accounts: it need not resort to strength, or criteria, or types of features involved: it simply requires (in the case of subjects) a process of Feature-inheritance (nothing more about the nature of the features involved is necessary). I take this to be a point in favor of this proposal.

Third, the proposed analysis predicts that in-situ subjects[52] will be as transparent to extraction as objects. Likewise, the account predicts that if there is an option for adjuncts not to create a Pair-Merge structure, as several authors have argued (see Hornstein and Nunes 2008, Boeckx 2008a, Narita 2011), extraction out of adjuncts would be possible.[53] Interestingly, Truswell (2007) argues that extraction out of adjoined phrases is licit only when the adjunct does not create its own event substructure and denote a single event with the main predicate. If correct, this generalization could be made to follow from the possibility for those adjuncts not to undergo early, independent spell-out (leading to the formation of an independent subevent representation), by not creating a Pair-Merge option.

Fourth, the account of CED effects just offered can accommodate the 'repair' (or better said, the circumvention) effect of islands via resumption (which, recall, I take to generalize to situations of ellipsis, pied-piping, and wh-in-situ). The intuition is this: the presence of a resumptive element essentially frees its antecedent from participating in the sort of relations that would trap them inside spelled-out portions of the tree, and fall inside islands as per (44). The situation is on a par with what obtains in the context of ellipsis. As many textbooks point out to illustrate the difference between complementation and adjunction, whereas complements must go silent if the head of a nominal phrase is replaced by *one* (47), adjuncts need not (48).

(47) *John met the member of Congress, and Bill met the one of Parliament.

(48) John met the student from Chicago, and Bill the one from Boston.

Thanks to the resumptive element, the antecedent essentially functions as a free 'unit' that can be attached to a higher portion of the tree,[54] retaining an anchor to the extraction site via the resumptive pronoun, but crucially not forming part of the structure that the external systems deem complete or closed.

Put differently, thanks to the presence of a resumptive pronoun, to which the moving element is adjoined, the latter is spelled-out independently of the domain that forms an island: it is not included in the A-chain (which is formed by the resumptive pronoun), nor is it properly contained inside the bigger adjunct (island), hence it is immune to the island status of the latter.

Fifth, I believe that the type of solution sketched here could dovetail with reductionist accounts of island effects based on processing factors discussed in Chapter 2. It strikes me as quite plausible indeed to entertain the idea that doubly rooted structures that pose problems for chain-formation create on-line processing problems, problems that may be alleviated in certain circumstances if the parser can find an alternative parse or can resort to a heuristic strategy to recover the intended meaning (giving rise to the sort of fluctuating judgments that proponents of reductionist accounts take as crucial). Crucially, though, as the formulation of CED-effects in (44) makes clear, the definition of what counts as an island structure cannot be dissociated from the dependency being established, an interconnection which I take to be the source of the superadditive effect that was discussed in Chapter 2.

Sixth, the solution suggested here, being chain-based, is of the representational kind, but it incorporates a key element of the more standard derivational perspective on syntactic islands, i.e., cyclicity. Like Chomsky (1973) and Uriagereka (1999a), it somehow reaches the conclusion that the cyclic character of derivations (in our case, cyclic spell-out) required for purposes of efficient computation (here, the need to eliminate doubly rooted trees as soon as they arise) has the indirect effect of producing structures at the interfaces that contain units (A-chains, adjuncts) that can no longer be reopened for further chain integration, as the external systems regard them as closed. Where the present solution departs most sharply from Chomsky's (1973) subjacency-based analysis is in the context of successive cyclic movement. Recall that for Chomsky it was failure to take nice, short successive cyclic movement steps that led to island effects. For me, the formation of intermediate movement steps is completely orthogonal to the issue of islands.[55] According to the solution offered here, only members of chains entering into certain feature-based relations like agreement ('A-chains') will cause freezing; chains that are not feature-associated (such as those formed by intermediate movement steps, or those associated with a resumptive) will not, because such chains have no special identity (no label, as it were), hence are not regarded as complete/closed by the external systems.[56] Cyclicity is only relevant in so far as it forces early spell-out of certain units. If early spell-out did not exist, chains could presumably be embedded in other, bigger, chains because the external systems would have access to the entire representation, much like the parser would not be subject to garden-path effects if it could inspect the entire sentence at once, as opposed to being presented with words one at a time.

Finally, I find it interesting that the claim made here that no chain headed by a given element x can embed another chain headed by that same element x (no A-chain inside an A-bar chain) may receive independent support from a condition proposed by Arsenijević and Hinzen (to appear), who have reached the conclusion that no phrase of type x can immediately contain another phrase of the same type (no CP immediately embedded inside CP, no TP immediately embedded inside TP, etc.).

I interpret this restriction as showing that the external systems ban 'X-within-X' structures (CP-within-CP, chain-within-chain, etc.), perhaps because the two units of the same kind would be so close as to be indistinguishable, a point I return to in the concluding section of this chapter.

4.5 CONCLUSION

Let us take stock. The empirical focus of this chapter has been relatively narrow. I am well aware of the fact that I have relegated to footnotes, or not mentioned at all, a great many details that the vast literature on islands has uncovered. I have preferred to focus on the core generalization concerning strong islands: displaced arguments and adjoined structures block subextraction, which I have sought to unify with the observation that in GB days fell under the purview of the Empty Category Principle: the very same displaced arguments and adjuncts are themselves subject to stricter locality conditions than those affecting in-situ arguments like direct objects.

I have shown in the previous chapter that the still popular derivational attempts to account for this core generalization are unlikely to be on the right track: to avoid blocking legitimate instances of extraction, they open the door to numerous unwanted derivations, which can only be ruled out in a stipulative fashion. Uriagereka's (1999a) alternative derivational account in terms of multiple spell-out appears to fare better at first, but quickly proves too rigid to handle the broad range of attested extraction possibilities. Perhaps the most salient problem for derivational accounts arises in the context of island repair, where otherwise illicit extractions turn out to be possible, if only a subsequent, post-syntactic operation licenses them.

The phenomenon of island repair has played a major role in this chapter. It not only allowed me to cast doubt on derivational treatments of islands and favor more representational, filter-based analyses, it also led me to examine, and reject, a variety of morphophonological filters put forth to capture major island effects.

Based on the possible underlying unity of island repair phenomena under the rubric of resumption, I have examined the role of resumptive elements in licensing otherwise impossible extractions. This led me to pursue the possibility that it is certain relations established inside what is traditionally called the island domain that lead to the island effect, as opposed to the movement itself that crosses the island. To understand the freezing effect of these relations, and avoid resorting to too many features (and feature types), I have resorted to the idea that certain relations (adjunction, A-chain formation) cause the formation of structures that must be immediately spelled-out, whose effect when it comes to the external systems processing syntactic structures is to turn these into islands.

If I am correct, islands are inevitable side-effects of a grammatical system that is designed in such a way as to ensure, via cyclicity, an efficient computation – one that seeks to reduce computational bottlenecks such as multiple roots as soon as they arise. A side-effect of immediately spelling out certain structures is that certain elements within these see their fates being sealed 'too early.' Although nothing in syntax prevents these elements from moving, the external systems that receive early information about them take that information to be complete, and set these elements aside, effectively turning them into islands.

This would then be my answer to the minimalist why-question that Ross asked at the end of his dissertation, and that has gained prominence in the context of linguistic minimalism. The syntactic residue of islandhood, the source of the superadditivity discussed in Chapter 2 is a bit like a grammatical conspiracy. For an island effect to obtain, a variety of factors have to come into play. Islands can no longer be regarded as structures headed by lexically predefined bounding nodes. They cannot be dissociated from the process that constructs them. That is to say, islands are dynamic, emergent entities.

Readers might feel that the various analyses reviewed in the last two sections of this chapter are all variants of the same basic idea, and they might be right, but I think that attempting several formulations of the same basic idea can have its benefits. As physicist Richard Feynman once pointed out,

> [i]n the particular case I am talking about [theories of gravity] the theories are *exactly* equivalent.... Psychologically they are different because they are completely unequivalent when you are trying to guess new laws. (Feynman 1965:47)

By reviewing accounts that view the solution to islands to lie in chains being too strong, or too heavy, or too ambiguous, etc. I have tried to find a formulation that makes it easier for us to identify the properties of the external systems that induce islands, and thereby help us understand the nature of islands themselves.

Although we have come a long way from the original A-over-A condition, and Ross's island typology, I find it pleasing that certain elements of the earliest approaches to islands remain as part of the explanations being offered today, including the one made in this chapter. Recall that the A-over-A condition was based on the idea that "transformations must be unambiguous," and Chomsky (1973) suggested that conditions like his Specified Subject Condition have the effect of "reducing ambiguity." Ambiguity is a concept that Kayne (1984) also incorporated into his path-based theory of islands (cf. his notion of "ambiguous path"). Likewise, Rizzi (1990) pointed out that "the functional correlate of this formal principle [Relativized Minimality] is the reduction of ambiguity in government relations." Finally, it is worth pointing out that Chomsky's earliest generative treatment of syntax (Chomsky 1955/1975:309) contained the following remark: "[t]he first requirement of grammatical transformations is that the result of a transformation must be unambiguous."

In a certain sense, the solution developed above extends this theme, by suggesting that no element can head both an A- and an A-bar chain: no chain can be both. The present solution also incorporates the spirit of Chomsky's A-over-A condition in a different way: much like I have suggested that no A-bar chain can contain an A-chain, likewise, the A-over-A condition can be said to boil down to a statement to the effect that no unit of type A can contain a chain headed by a smaller unit of type A if the bigger unit could itself form such a chain.

The solution I have offered also incorporates another early insight of Chomsky's. Discussing the greater unacceptability of self-embedding, Chomsky (1965: 14) states that

> [w]e might assume, for example, that the perceptual device has a stock of analytic procedures available to it, one corresponding to each kind of phrase, and that it is organized in such a way that it is unable (or finds it difficult) to utilize a procedure φ while it is in the course of executing φ.

I don't think it's too far-fetched to see in this passage an antecedent of (44). It indeed appears to be the case that the external systems do not tolerate syntactic outputs where elements that are too similar end up too close to one another, or embedded inside one another. This cyclically evaluated Anti-locality, Distinctness Condition, or Identity-Avoidance Condition, as it has been called (see Grohmann 2003, Richards 2010, van Riemsdijk 2008, respectively), may well be what underlies the perception of grammatical islands, and what unifies locality effects. For although the solution offered in this chapter is limited to strong islands, it shares a family resemblance with the standard Relativized Minimality treatment of weak islands (those that remain once semantico-pragmatic issues have been factored out; cf. Chapter 2). Relativized Minimality rests on an anti-similarity defined over c-command relations, while my chain-based approach to strong islands rests on an anti-similarity (no chain inside a chain) defined over embedding (dominance). If, as has occasionally been suggested (see Boeckx 2003a, Fukui 1997, and especially Hornstein 2009), conditions based on c-command and dominance can (and should) be unified, the old dream of a unified theory of locality may not be completely out of reach, even if what counts as 'similar' in the context of anti-similarity constraints may appeal to different properties of syntactic objects (chains, features, etc.).

But if this chapter has shown how some early insights concerning islands remain valid, even when couched in very different theoretical idioms, it has also shown, together with the other chapters, that certain standard opinions regarding islands ought to be abandoned, even if they continue to dominate grammatical theorizing. It seems fair to say that whatever they are, islands are *not* domains that block movement. We have seen that it is possible to 'repair' island violations, so it is possible to construct them, i.e., it is possible to move across islands. We have also seen that no domain is an absolute island. That is, there is no condition on transformation of the sort "No [movement] rule can cross a domain of type *x*." All islands are relativized, to different grammatical properties and objects, which gives rise to the strong/weak island distinction.

In addition to the empirical evidence against the standard position, I think that it is fair to say that minimalism (as a program) seems to lead inevitably to the same conclusion: if there really is no such special operation called movement (if there are no traces, if move is just (internal) merge, indeed if everything is merge (cf. Boeckx 2010a), then the fact, taken for granted by everyone, that some type of dependency can be formed across islands means that some type of (internal) merge (i.e., move) dependency can be formed across islands. Resorting to base-generation, long-distance binding and the like won't do. It's not minimalist/explanatory enough.

In general, the idea of a minimally specified grammatical system (the essence of minimalism) leads to an architecture where the grammar does not have all the resources to rule out all the unacceptable cases. It 'overgenerates' (see Chomsky 2004:111; Boeckx 2010a; Ott 2010). For islands, this means that the syntax contributes to, but does not fully determine the effects we call 'islands.' Put differently, islands retain an irreducibly grammatical aspect, but islandhood is seriously underdetermined by syntax.

Finally, I would like to point out that minimalism also demands that we be as precise as possible when it comes to saying what exactly the problem with island violations is: it won't do to speak of *-marks that can be eliminated under deletion; if movement can cross islands, we seem forced into representational solutions. These will take the form of interface conditions, which, if they can be made precise enough, may lead to a more fruitful interaction with grounded and reductionist accounts of island effects (cf. Chapter 2).[57] Everyone should be delighted to abandon a portion of their explanatory claim on islands and look forward to such interactions in years to come.

DISCUSSION QUESTIONS

1. If you are familiar with the minimalist literature, try to find illustrations of the difference between modular thinking (characteristic of the Government-and-Binding model) and the interface thinking that minimalism favors.

2. In footnote 57, I wrote "one might seek to relate the analysis of strong islands offered here to the structure of memory and the limited number of elements that can be included in the 'focus of attention' during processing (see Wagers 2008)". Can you think of concrete ways of establishing this relation?

5   A tribute to Ross

'Haj' Ross was right not to ignore Chomsky's seemingly innocent remark concerning what came to be called the A-over-A condition, which at first looked like just another example of disappearance of an otherwise expected ambiguity following a transformation. Ross's issues with the A-over-A condition changed linguistic theory.

I do not know if Ross realized that the constraint he saw as not "modifiable enough" would turn out to open up so complex an area of research, but the final remarks he wrote in 1967 still apply with equal force to the present work:

> All the proposals I have made should be regarded as being extremely tentative, for our present knowledge of syntax is ridiculously small. This work has raised far more questions than it has attempted to answer. (p. 291)

As I hope to have shown in the preceding pages, Ross was right about many more things concerning islands, not the least of which was his claim that not all instances of extraction are banned across islands. It has taken syntacticians over forty years to recognize that this, as so many other suggestions he made, was fundamentally on the right track, although many continue to resist this conclusion in the existing literature.

Ross was also aware that once the notion of island got established empirically, *why*-questions would inevitably arise. To quote again the final lines of his thesis (p. 291):

> Why should rules which adjoin terms to the right side of a variable be upward bounded, and not those which adjoin to the left of a variable? Why should it be that chopping rules, feature-changing rules, and unidirectional deletion rules share the property of being subject to the constraint, to the exclusion of other rules? Why should there be a difference between unidirectional and bidirectional pronominalization? Why should it be that the constraints are all "downward-oriented" – that is, why should it be that there are

phrase-marker configurations that prevent elements indefinitely far below them from undergoing various syntactic operations, whereas there are no configurations which affect elements indefinitely far above them? Why should complex NP's, coordinate nodes, sentential subject clauses, and NP's on the left branches of larger NP's all function the same in defining islands? Can islands be shown to behave like psycholinguistic entities?

These why-questions are at the heart of current minimalist investigations; they have motivated Chomsky's (1973) subjacency account and all subsequent attempts to develop a comprehensive explanatory theory of islands, not only those using the transformational tools that Ross used (witness the attempts of Sag 2010, Levine and Hukari 2006, Postal 1997, 1998, using frameworks like Head-Driven Phrase Structure Grammar, Construction Grammar, and Arc-Pair Grammar). These why-questions animate all (narrowly) syntactic, semantic, pragmatic, reductionist, grounded, derivational, and representational views on islands reviewed in this book.

Syntacticians have come to realize that although it is tempting when you are a hammer to treat everything as a nail, not all islands are likely to be syntactic, but I think it would be wrong to conclude from this that there is nothing syntactic about islands. I have made some original suggestions at the end of Chapter 4 regarding what I think is the syntactic residue of islands but I am under no illusion that these will be the final words on the topic.

As Epstein (1999) writes, citing philosopher of science Alfred Hall, "the explanation of phenomena at one level is the description of phenomena at a more fundamental level": Ross put forth island conditions to account for the phenomena (not) covered by the A-over-A condition, then Chomsky formulated the subjacency condition to capture the island facts covered by Ross's constraints, then linguists of all persuasions have tried to explain subjacency effects by positing higher-order principles, and so on, and so on, until now and into the future. But Ross knew this too, for he began his thesis with the following anecdote, told of William James.

> *After a lecture on cosmology and the structure of the solar system, James was accosted by a little old lady.*
>
> *"Your theory that the sun is the center of the solar system, and that the earth is a ball which rotates around it, has a very convincing ring to it, Mr. James, but it's wrong. I've got a better theory," said the little old lady.*
>
> *"And what is that, madam?" inquired James politely.*
>
> *"That we live on a crust of earth which is on the back of a giant turtle."*

Not wishing to demolish this absurd little theory by bringing to bear the masses of scientific evidence he had at his command, James decided to gently dissuade his opponent by making her see some of the inadequacies of her position.

"If your theory is correct, madam," he asked, "what does this turtle stand on?"

"You're a very clever man, Mr. James, and that's a very good question," replied the old lady, "but I have an answer to it. And it's this: the first turtle stands on the back of a second, far larger, turtle, who stands directly behind him."

"But what does this second turtle stand on?" persisted James patiently.

To this, the little old lady crowed triumphantly,

"It's no use, Mr. James – it's turtles all the way down!"

Appendix: On the robustness of the freezing-effect of chains

Given that both Chapters 3 and 4 take the CED generalization to be what requires a syntax-based analysis (the syntactic residue of islands, as I have called it), I feel that I should dispel a few doubts cast in the recent literature on the correctness of the CED-generalization, which are distinct from Stepanov's critique already discussed (and dismissed) in the main text (cf. Chapters 1 and 2).[1]

In particular, Chomsky (2008) has argued that some instances of extraction out of A-chains are licit. Likewise, Rizzi (2006), in part building on original observations by Esther Torrego, has argued that extraction out of A-bar chains is sometimes licit. Both Chomsky's and Rizzi's arguments threaten the generalization put forth at the end of Chapter 4, according to which no chain can embed another chain. For this reason, I want to examine both types of situations, and show that the counterexamples to the original CED are only apparent. There will thus be no need to qualify the account of (sub)extraction possibilities defended in the main text.

Let us consider Chomsky's (2008) cases first. Chomsky focuses on the paradigm in (1). (The judgments are Chomsky's. CAPS are meant to indicate that the relevant elements are (contrastively) focused. I should note that many speakers consulted regard (1b-b′) as degraded.)

(1) a. It was the CAR (not the TRUCK) of which they found [the driver *t*].
     a′. Of which car did they find [the driver *t*]?
     b. It was the CAR (and not the TRUCK) of which [the driver *t*] was found.
     b′. Of which car was [the driver *t*] awarded a prize?
     c. *It was the CAR (and not the TRUCK) of which [the driver *t*] caused a scandal.
     c′. *Of which car did [the driver *t*] cause a scandal?

Chomsky takes the facts in (1), especially (1b-b′) to suggest that extraction out of derived internal arguments is possible, and goes on to develop an intricate phase-based account of the contrast between (1b-b′) and (1c-c′) in terms of minimal search, simultaneous probing, and feature inheritance. I will not summarize his account here (see Broekhuis 2006 for an excellent summary), since it is framed in terms that I have not discussed extensively in this book. What is more, there are several empirical arguments against Chomsky's empirical generalization, and therefore against his technical analysis.

For Chomsky, the key conclusion to draw from the paradigm in (1) is that extraction is possible from subjects that were raised from the complement position (internal argument position) of the relevant predicates, but not from those subjects that began their derivational lives from the external position of the relevant predicates. Since the 'No-chain-within-chain' generalization does not make room for such a distinction (both types of subjects form A-chains, hence should be opaque), Chomsky's empirical claim must be shown to be incorrect if my account is to be preserved.

Fortunately for me, Broekhuis (2006) in particular has provided three arguments from Dutch that argue against Chomsky's view that extraction out of derived complements is possible. Let me reproduce the essence of Broekhuis's arguments here.

First, as Broekhuis notes, the Dutch counterparts of the constructions in (1) are of a very restricted sort in the sense that the allegedly extracted PP can only be headed by a limited set of prepositions. In Dutch this set is exhausted by *van* 'of' and *over* 'about'; PPs headed by, e.g., clearly locational prepositions are never extracted from DP. This is illustrated in (2) for extraction from object; (2b) is acceptable when the PP is construed as a locational adverbial phrase but not on its intended reading as a modifier of the noun *huis* 'house.' It is not at all clear how (2b) is to be excluded under Chomsky's account.

(2) a. Jan heeft het huis op de hoek gekocht   [Dutch]
     Jan has the house on the corner bought
     'Jan has bought the house on the corner'
  b. *[Op de hoek]$_i$ heeft Jan [het huis t_i] gekocht

Second, it is not so clear whether the *van*-PP in (3a) (which corresponds closely to Chomsky's crucial example) is really extracted from the object. Under the right contextual and pragmatic conditions the object *de eigenaar* 'owner' can be replaced by a pronoun. Since pronouns normally resist modification, this suggests that the preposed *van*-PP does not function as a complement or a modifier of the noun, but rather as an independent adverbial phrase (as Broekhuis had suggested in independent work). Note in passing that the preposed *van*-PP in (3) triggers a contrastive reading, and that apparently the same holds for Chomsky's examples in (3).

(3) a. Van DEZE auto hebben ze de eigenaar nog niet gevonden (van DIE wel) [Dutch]
     of this car have they the owner yet not found   of that yes
     'Of which car did they not find the owner yet?'
  b. Van DEZE auto hebben ze hem nog niet gevonden (van DIE wel)
     From this car have they him yet not found   of that yes
     'Of which car did they not find him yet?'

Another piece of evidence in favor of the claim that the preposed *van*-PP is an independent adverbial phrase is that the preposed *van*-PP can be modified by a focus particle, whereas a postnominal *van*-PP cannot; if the preposed *van*-PP in (4a) originates from within the object DP, the unacceptability of (4b) would be very surprising.

(4) a. Alleen van deze auto hebben ze   de eigenaar nog niet gevonden
        only of this car   have they the owner yet not found
           'Of only this car did they not find the owner yet'
     b. *Ze hebben de eigenaar alleen van deze auto nog niet gevonden
        they have   the owner only of this car   yet not found
           'They haven't found the owner of only this car yet'

As a final argument against Chomsky's conclusion, Broekhuis notes that even if we were to maintain that the extracted PP really did originate in the displaced subject, the Dutch facts in (5) show that Chomsky's contrast between subjects that were internal arguments and subjects that were external arguments does not always obtain.

(5) a. Van deze fabriek hebben de werknemers gisteren   het werk onderbroken
        of this factory have   the employees yesterday the work interrupted
           'Of this factory, the employees interrupted their work yesterday'
     b. Van deze school   hebben alle leerlingen verleden jaar de marathon gelopen
        of this school   have   all pupils   last   year the marathon run
           'Of this school, all the pupils ran the marathon last year.'

It seems to me that Broekhuis's arguments show that something special, other than direct extraction out of displaced subjects, is going on in (1).

As a matter of fact, the claim that sentences like (1b) require a special treatment goes back to Kuno 1973. Discussing examples similar to (1) (already reported in Ross 1967), Kuno notes that the judgments of such sentences greatly vary among speakers. He goes on to note that for all speakers, subextraction with pied-piping of the preposition is considerably better than subextraction without pied-piping. Contrast (1b-b') with (6a-a'). (Chomsky 2008 also notes this fact.)

(6) a. *It was the CAR (and not the TRUCK) which [the driver of <which>] was found
     a'. *Which car was [the driver of <which car>] awarded a prize?

Kayne (1984:189) reports a similar contrast, reproduced in (7).

(7) a. ?Of which words is learning [the spellings <of which words>] difficult?
     b. *Which words is learning [the spellings of <which words>] difficult?

I take the role of pied-piping to point to the correctness of Broekhuis's claim that the extracted PPs are modifying adjuncts (which are known to resist P-stranding more than arguments;[2] see, e.g., Hornstein and Weinberg 1981).[3]

I conclude from these remarks that the ban on extraction out of displaced subjects is robust.

This does not entail that extraction out of subjects is impossible.

That such extraction is possible goes back to Rizzi's 1982 seminal work on postverbal subjects in *pro*-drop languages briefly discussed in the main text. In-situ subjects are known to behave on a par with complements in terms of extraction. The same is true for subextraction. Facts like (8) and (9) from English, already mentioned in the main text, illustrate this.

(8) which candidate were there [posters of *t*] all over the town?

(9) *which candidate were [posters of *t*] all over the town?

A similar contrast obtains in Dutch (data from Broekhuis 2006).

(10) a. Wat hebben   er [*t* voor mensen] je moeder bezocht?   [Dutch]
        What have-3PL there for people your mother visited
        'What sort of people have visited your mother?'
     b. *Wat hebben [*t* voor mensen] je   moeder bezocht?
        What have-3PL for people your mother visited
        'What sort of people have visited your mother?'

Finally, the same preverbal/postverbal asymmetry can be seen in Spanish. (The data are taken from Uriagereka 1988, but I should point out that the data base was greatly expanded in Gallego 2007, who has shown in detail that subextraction is only possible from non-displaced subjects).[4]

(11) De qué conferenciantes te parece   que...   [Spanish]
     Of what speakers   you seem-3SG that...
     a. ... (?)me van   a   impresionar [las propuestas *t*]?
            me go-3PL   to   impress-INF the proposals
     b. ... *[las propuestas *t*] me van   a impresionar?
            the proposals   me go-3PL to impress-INF
     'Which speakers does it seem to you that the proposals by will impress me?'

Let me now turn to Rizzi's 2006 alleged cases of extraction out of A-bar chains, beginning with Torrego's (1985:31) observation that cases like (12) are acceptable in Spanish.[5]

(12) [De qué autora] no sabes   [qué traducciones *t*] han   ganado premios
     of what author not know-2SG what translations   have-3PL won   awards
     internacionales?
     international
     'Which author don't you know what translated books have won international awards?'

Rizzi (2006:114) reports similar facts for Italian (13), as do Chomsky (1986) and Lasnik and Saito (1992) for English.[6] (I should note that, just as in the case of Chomsky's examples in (1), the status of the example in (12) varies greatly from speaker to speaker.)

(13) ?[Di quale autore] ti domandi   [quanti   libri *t*] siano
     of which author you wonder-2SG how-many books   be-3PL
     stati censurati   [Italian]
     been censored
     'Which author do you wonder how many books by have been censored?'

(14) ??Of which author do you wonder [how many books *t*] Bill read

Such facts led Rizzi to claim that only the head of a displaced constituent is frozen in place. Rizzi's characterization goes against the treatment of subextraction defended in the text, according to which the entire phrase pied-piped by the subject is rendered opaque by chain-formation.

Fortunately again for the account presented in Chapter 4, there are reasons to doubt Rizzi's claim. As Gallego 2007 and Gallego and Uriagereka 2007b show in detail, Rizzi's characterization is not correct. Specifically, they argue that the subextracted element in (12) is best ana-lyzed as an aboutness phrase base-generated outside the A-bar chain headed by *qué traducciones*. In other words, subextraction does not take place in (12) (and, by extension, in (13)–(14)).

Gallego and Uriagereka provide several empirical arguments in favor of treating the 'subextracted' element in (12) as an aboutness phrase. First, they note that the verb used by Torrego (*saber* 'know') readily makes room for such an aboutness phrase.

(15) Juan sabe   de María que fuma   [Spanish]
      Juan knows of María that smokes
      'About María, Juan knows that she smokes'

They also point out that the addition of an aboutness phrase in (12) renders the example unacceptable, as shown in (16).

(16) a. Juan sabe   [de María] [[qué novelas de Cortázar] ha   leído]
         Juan know-3SG of María   what novels by Cortázar have-3SG read
         'About María, Juan knows which novels by Cortázar she has read'

      b. *[De qué escritor*i*] sabe   Juan [de María] [[qué novelas *t*] ha   leído]
         of what writer   know-3SG Juan of María   what novels   have-3SG read
         'By which writer does Juan know about María which novels she has read?'

Gallego and Uriagereka argue that the presence of an additional aboutness phrase forces subextraction (as it prevents the extracting element from functioning as an aboutness phrase). Since this leads to unacceptability, it seems safe to conclude that subextraction in (12) is only apparent.

In sum, subextraction possibilities appear to be limited to cases of extraction out of non-displaced (theta-marked) elements, as the approach defended in Chapter 4 predicts.

Suggestions for further study and recommended readings

As I wrote at the beginning of this book, I expect readers to already have some amount of background in syntactic theory. Most of the notions that I use can be found in good introductory texts to syntactic theory such as Adger 2003 (*Core Syntax*. Oxford University Press), Carnie 2006 (*Syntax: A Generative Introduction (2nd edition)*. Malden: Wiley-Blackwell), Haegeman 1991 (*An Introduction to Government-and-Binding Theory (2nd edition)*. Malden: Wiley-Blackwell), among others. For more advanced minimalist concepts, I recommend Hornstein, Nunes, and Grohmann 2006 (*Understanding Minimalism*. Cambridge University Press).

Readers who want to read more on specific issues touched on in this book are encouraged to turn to the primary literature, for which there is no substitute. With the exception of Postal 1997 (a New York University manuscript, access to which was kindly provided to me by Howard Lasnik), which regrettably remains unpublished, all the other works on islands cited in the book should be easy to locate in libraries or online sources.

I would encourage interested readers to go through Ross's 1967 MIT dissertation "Constraints on variables in syntax" (or the 1986 book version of it: *Infinite Syntax!* Norwood, NJ: Ablex). Although I have already quoted from it extensively in the text, there is still so much more in it than I had space for. Chomsky 1973 ("Conditions on transformations." In *A Festschrift for Morris Halle*, ed. S. Anderson and P. Kiparsky, 232–286. New York: Holt, Rinehart, and Winston) is more challenging, but I feel, well worth the trouble, as it provided the point of departure for much theorizing about islands.

Given the theoretical importance of Relativized Minimality effects, I also think it worthwhile to examine proposals like M. Starke 2001 Ph.D. thesis (University of Geneva) more closely.

Outside the immediate realm of syntax, I recommend Szabolcsi's 2006 overview of semantico-pragmatic treatments ("Weak and strong islands." In *The Syntax Companion*, ed. M. Everaert and H. van Riemsdijk, 479–531. Oxford: Blackwell), and Kluender's work cited in the reference section for what is to date the most detailed reductionist attempt to capture island effects.

As I stressed on several occasions in the text my main aim in this book is to provide readers with ingredients that point to a better understanding of island effects. It goes without saying that much remains to be clarified and understood at this point concerning islands. The material discussed in Chapters 3 and 4, as well as in the Appendix, provides what I think is a good overview of where we now stand. Those readers that want to try to take our understanding of islands further are encouraged to reconsider my claim that derivational accounts of the subjacency-type are unlikely to be able to capture (strong) island effects by seeking alternatives to Müller's (2010) account (On deriving CED effects from the PIC. *Linguistic Inquiry* 41:35–82). They should also examine the nature of 'island repair' contexts further. Phenomena like resumption, ellipsis, pied-piping, and wh-in-situ are so complex, so cross-linguistically varied, and so rich in subtleties that they are bound to tell us much more about islands than what I have been able to assert here. The references that I have given in the footnotes should provide good starting points for those brave readers that want to venture into the primary literature. Finally, I urge readers to critically examine the proposal I made at the end of Chapter 4, judge for themselves if my claim concerning the robustness of CED-effects in the Appendix is valid, and if they believe that my proposal has a fighting chance of making the right cut, consider how it could cover phenomena that I have left aside, like parasitic gaps, extraction from indirect objects, inherently case-marked arguments, and much, much more.

Glossary

A-movement: Movement type typically associated with case-agreement relations.

A-bar movement: Movement type typically associated with quantificational relations, targeting the left-periphery of the clause.

Across-the-Board (ATB) movement: Movement that extracts elements of a conjoined structure in parallel (i.e., from both conjuncts at the same time).

Adjunct condition: Constraint that takes adjoined structures to be islands.

Anti-locality: Ban on movement that is 'too short' (typically, movement that fails to cross an entire phrasal domain).

A-over-A principle: Principle that dictates that if a given syntactic rule potentially targets either A or B, and B is contained in/dominated by A, A should be targeted.

Base-generation: Non-movement alternative to establishing a long-distance dependency (typically coupled with binding at a distance).

C-command: An element X is said to c-command an element Y if the syntactic unit X combines with contains Y.

Chain: Product of movement. More precisely, unit of syntactic computation that groups in a set all the grammatical relations that a given element is involved in. For example, *who* in *who is leaving?* is the *agent* of the action expressed by the verb, is the element that triggers *agreement* on the auxiliary verb, and is the *interrogative* word. Syntacticians assume that no element can express multiple relations in a single position. If an element A relates to several other elements B, C, and D in the structure, element A must occupy three different positions (in the vicinity of B, C, and D, respectively). A chain keeps a record of all the positions occupied by a given element within a structure.

Chopping rule: Movement rule that leaves a gap (as opposed to a copying rule, which leaves a copy of the moved element in its original location).

Clause-boundedness: Constraint that limits the application of syntactic rules to a single clause.

Complement: Immediate sister of the head of a phrase.

Complex Noun Phrase Constraint: Condition that takes a Noun Phrase modified by a relative clause or a sentential complement to be an island.

Condition on Extraction Domain (CED): Generalization that groups together the adjunction condition and the subject condition, and captures the fact that non-complement domains are islands.

Construal (rule): Non-movement/post-syntactic rule establishing a dependency between two (typically non-adjacent) elements.

Coordinate Structure Constraint: Condition that takes conjoined structures to be islands.

Copy: Operation that duplicates an element A to allow A to occupy several positions in a given syntactic structure.

Cyclicity: Hypothesis that syntactic computations are divided into domains of applicability ('cycles') which stand in a subset-superset relation with one another, such that a given syntactic process A can no longer apply in a domain D if D is already contained in a larger domain D'.

Derivation: Conception of syntactic computation that crucially involves strict ordering/timing of syntactic processes/rules.

D(iscourse)-linking: Property of certain interrogative words that limits the range of possible answers to a discourse salient set of elements.

Domination: Containment, which the head of a projection achieves via labeling.

Downward entailment: Property of quantification elements indicating the direction of entailment relation from superset to subset (e.g., if it is true that *no* dog barked, it follows that *no* small dog barked).

Ellipsis: Deletion of structural elements (equivalently: lack of pronunciation of syntactic elements).

Extended Projection Principle (EPP): Requirement that clauses with a finite verb contain a subject.

Extension Condition: Requirement that displacement of a syntactic element always targets a higher position in the structure (i.e., expands the syntactic structure upward).

Feature: Minimal unit of syntactic computation; a word is typically seen as a collection of phonetic, semantic, and syntactic features (i.e., properties).

Head: Necessary and most important element in a syntactic group (*phrase*).

Improper movement: Illicit instance of a movement operation displacing an element from an A-type position to an A-bar-type position and back to an A-type position.

Inclusiveness: Restriction of syntactic computation that forbids syntax from adding to or removing properties from lexical items in the course of a derivation.

Inner island: Constraint preventing the establishment of certain dependencies across clausal modifiers like negation.

Island: Domain that once formed becomes inaccessible to certain grammatical computations. The island is said to be *weak* if it nevertheless allows certain elements to be accessible to these grammatical computations; *strong*, otherwise.

Left branch condition: Constraint that takes the modifiers of a Noun Phrase located on the 'left' of the Noun (roughly, specifier position) to form islands.

Linear Correspondence Axiom (LCA): Specific mechanism used to convert a syntactic structure onto a linear string by assuming a one-to-one mapping between asymmetric c-command relations within syntax and asymmetric linear order, such that if A c-commands B (i.e., A syntactically combines with X which contains B), A precedes B.

Linearization: Process by which syntactic structures are converted into a linear string, as required by the sensori-motor systems.

Locality: Area of syntactic theory that focuses on the lower bound and upper bound imposed by Universal Grammar on movement of elements, and on the distance that may separate two elements that enter into a syntactic relation.

Magnitude estimation: Experimental technique used to determine how much of a given sensation (e.g., acceptability) a person is having. In a magnitude estimation experiment subjects are presented with a standard stimulus and are told that the stimulus has a certain magnitude (say, 10). The subjects are then presented with a series of stimuli that vary in intensity and are asked to assign each of the stimuli a number relative to the standard stimulus.

Merge: Basic structure building mechanism. Merge takes two elements A and B and forms a two-membered set labeled C. C can then be merged with another element. Merge is said to be *external* if A and B are previously unconnected elements. Merge is said to be *internal* if A combines with B and B contains D with which A had previously combined.

Minimality (Relativized): Condition that states that A and B can be related syntactically if and only if there is no C such that C is of the same syntactic category as A and B, and C combines with an element D that contains B.

Negative Polarity Item (NPI): Element that is licensed in the vicinity of negative markers (e.g., English *any*, as opposed to *some*).

Parasitic gap: Construction where a typically illicit configuration (movement across a domain that cannot be moved out of) is made licit if the moved element also appears to move from a domain out of which movement is licit.

Phase: Recent term for *cycle*, and currently taken to correspond to points of spell-out. Phases divide into two domains: a complement domain that is the sister of the designated phase head, and the phase edge (the head of the phase and everything 'above' it within the phase projection: specifiers and adjuncts).

Phase Impenetrability Condition: Constraint that renders a portion of a given phase (specifically, the complement domain) inaccessible to operations outside the phase.

Poverty of Stimulus: Refers to the fact that the linguistic data available to the child are not enough to infer the mature linguistic knowledge of an adult.

Projection: Operation which labels the set formed by the combination of two elements A and B by repeating or copying A and B, thereby designating one element as the container of the other.

Reconstruction: Situations where an element is interpreted in a position distinct from where it is pronounced, i.e., a position that the element occupied before movement.

Representation: Outcome of a syntactic derivation that can be subject to specific grammatical conditions; structure created by the application of syntactic rules.

Right-roof Constraint: Constraint that limits the application of rightward movement rules to a single clause.

Satiation: Report of improved acceptability upon repeated exposure.

Scope: Set relations among quantificational elements.

Self-paced reading task: Task that allows readers to use button presses to control the exposure duration for each word of a text they read (e.g., on a screen), and used to identify cognitive expectations.

Sentential Subject Condition: Condition that takes clausal subjects to be islands.

Sluicing: Construction where the interrogative word is the only word pronounced in an interrogative clause (the rest of the clause is deleted and its content recovered from the preceding sentence in discourse).

Small clause: Relation established between a subject and a non-verbal, non-tensed predicate.

Specifier: Sister of intermediate projections of the head of a phrase.

Spell-Out: Point in the syntactic derivation at which syntactic information is transferred to the sound and meaning interfaces.

Subjacency: Constraint on movement that has the effect of forcing long-distance dependencies to be formed by combining a series of smaller movement steps, proceeding from the lowest cycle to the next higher cycle, and so on until reaching the final landing site.

Subject condition: Constraint that takes subjects (especially, displaced subjects) to be islands.

Successive Cyclic Movement: Hypothesis that long-distance dependencies are composed of shorter dependencies that are established within larger and larger syntactic domains, and ultimately combine into one.

Superiority: Condition that states that if a transformation can be applied to more than one constituent, it must be applied to the superior one, i.e., the one that is structurally higher in a given syntactic representation.

VP-internal subject hypothesis: Claim to the effect that the subject of a clause typically starts within the verbal domain/phrase and typically raises to its surface position in the course of the derivation.

Wh-island: Constraint that prevents certain dependencies from being formed across interrogative clauses.

Notes

Notes on Preface

1 Here are two representative opinions:

> Foremost among these [enduring contributions of the entire transformational framework to the understanding of the nature of language], in my opinion, will be the discovery of the island phenomenon. (Postal 1986:xix)

> the one area in which generative grammar really shone. What I have in mind are the constraints on what was called "secondary computation" above. The most important of these are known as "locality principles." (Koster 2010:8)

Ross was, characteristically, rather modest when he stated in the preface to *Infinite Syntax!* (p. xv):

> what I regard as one of the most important concepts developed in this [thesis] – the concept of *islands*.

Notes on Chapter 1

1 I say 'relevant' because there is a third reading of the sentence where Mary saw the boy as *she* was walking toward the railroad station (cf. the well-known ambiguity of *John shot the elephant in his pajamas* or *Mary hit the man with an umbrella*).

2 For an excellent introduction to early transformational analyses, see Lasnik (2000).

3 I am indebted to a presentation by Howard Lasnik (LSA Institute, July 29, 2005) for making me aware of this very early discussion of locality in Chomsky's *opus*.

4 True, there has been a shift of focus back on to individual constructions in frameworks like Construction Grammar and on to properties of specific lexical elements in the context of microparameters in recent years, but even in such works, concerns with general conditions, with *theory*, are not completely absent.

5 Most of these quotes are taken from Postal (1997:1–2), whose reflections on islands I will return to in this work.

6 This condition is now known as the ban on improper movement.

7 The qualification of the (c) condition "and α is a tensed S" is important, for as Ross had already observed, movement across a non-tensed S is possible even in the presence of a filled COMP:

(i) What do you wonder [how to eat __]

8 For an excellent survey of the cycle, see Lasnik (2006).

9 Chomsky went back to his (1955) observation (cf. example (1) in this chapter) about the difficulty of extracting out of subjects (not just out of sentential subjects), and incorporated this (generalized) subject condition into the formulation of subjacency.

10 For attempts to unify both conditions, see Boeckx (2003a), Fukui (1997), and Hornstein (2009).

11 For an excellent collection surveying the properties of parasitic gaps, see Culicover and Postal (2001).

12 As I pointed out above, although Postal is certainly correct in claiming that most syntacticians approach categories as non-islands by default, in practice many syntacticians ascribe to many categories the key property that turns them into islands (most categories these days have been said to be bounding nodes, blocking categories, phases, etc., inducing successive cyclicity through virtually all categories (see Boeckx 2007 for a survey).

I should also point out that Postal's suggestion is not without antecedent. Both Cinque (1978) and Gazdar (1981), from different theoretical perspectives, essentially took syntactic domains to be islands by default.

13 See Rosenbaum's (1970) Minimal Distance Principle, Chomsky's (1973) Superiority Condition, as well as the proposals in Wilkins (1977, 1980), and Koster (1978a). Chomsky (1986) also proposed a minimality principle, but one that proved too rigid, as it failed to be relativized to the type of dependency being established.

14 Ross called these "inner island" effects.

15 Rizzi also discussed intervention effects in the context of head-movement, a third type of movement not recognized in Chomsky (1977), but well established at the time Rizzi wrote his monograph.

16 Flexibility was in fact Rizzi's goal, as he tried to amend the minimality principle proposed by Chomsky (1986), which was deemed "too rigid" (much as his A-over-A principle was found "not modifiable enough" by Ross in (1967), as Ross recounts in the final pages of the (1986) book version of his thesis).

17 See Boeckx (2003: Chapter 3) for a specific claim along these lines, synthesizing many independent proposals about individual island cases.

18 An early alternative account was proposed by Kuno (1973). Kuno put forth a 'Clause Non-final Incomplete Constituent Constraint,' which states that it is not possible to extract any element out of a bigger element of category N or C that occupies a clause non-final position. Kuno pointed out that his condition subsumed Ross's Sentential Subject Condition. Accordingly, for Kuno, movement is not the issue; rather, it is the fact that the domains out of which extraction takes place are not clause-final. Though intriguing, Kuno's explanation suffers from numerous counterexamples, such as those in (i), and for this reason did not gain wide acceptance.

(i) a. Who did you buy [a picture of __] from Mary?
     b. Which man did you find [photos of __] on the lawn?

(Kuno suggested that examples like (i) are ok because the elements following the extraction sites are generally optional items. But it is not clear why this should make a difference.)

19 I do not know if Stepanov was the first one to make this argument based on cross-linguistic considerations in print, but I can say that the argument was quite commonly heard in classes when I was a student.

20 Stepanov also points out that the subject condition and the adjunct condition behave differently when it comes to satiation effects (gradual decrease of the feeling of unacceptability upon repeated exposure), an issue that I come back to in the next chapter.

Notes on Chapter 2

1 But see Sprouse (2007a,b, 2011), and Sprouse and Almeida (2011) for a radically different assessment.

2 I owe the terms 'grounded' vs. 'reductionist' theories to Phillips (2011).

3 As such, grounded accounts are immune to many of the problems that reductionist accounts may face. As Phillips (2011) correctly points out:

> Evidence against reductionist accounts of a given phenomenon may still be compatible with grounded accounts. Grounded accounts of syntactic constraints are not direct claims about the form of the constraints in the minds of speakers, but rather are claims about how the constraints arose in human language. They argue that certain types of constraints are more natural or more adaptive, because of their benefits for language processing. But unlike reductionist accounts, grounded accounts continue to maintain that the constraints are genuine formal restrictions.

4 See, e.g., Cinque (1993), Zubizarreta (1998), Reinhart (2006), Irurtzun (2007); see already Jackendoff (1972). For a more ambitious attempt to reduce interpretive structures to grammatical structures, see Hinzen (2006, 2007).

5 The best counter-empirical argument against an approach like the one advocated by Goldberg that I was able to come across is due to Benjamin Bruening, who writes the following in a 2010 blog entry (http://lingcomm.blogspot.com/2010/11/information-structure-approaches-to.html):

> There is a strand of research that tries to explain island constraints on movement entirely in information-structural, or discourse, terms. Goldberg (2006) and Erteschik-Shir (2007) are recent examples of this. Both point to some phenomena that they claim are non-syntactic and yet are sensitive to islands, and conclude from this sensitivity that island constraints are not syntactic.
>
> Citing Morgan (1975), Goldberg (2006, 132–133) claims that direct replies to questions are sensitive to islands. In all of the following, try to understand the answer to be "she is dating someone new." This is possible when that phrase does not occur inside an island, but not when it does:

(1) Q: Why was Laura so happy?
    a. The woman who lives next door thought she was dating someone new.
    b. #The woman who thought she was dating someone new lives next door.
    c. #That she's dating someone new is likely.
    d. It's likely that she's dating someone new.
    e. #John shouted that she was dating someone new.
    f. John said that she was dating someone new.
    g. #John was hysterical 'cause she was dating someone new.
    h. John left Manhattan in order that she could date someone new.

> However, as Goldberg herself notes in footnote 3, this phenomenon is not fully general. Direct replies can occur inside complex NPs; example (2) is from Goldberg's foonote, and I add example (3). They can also occur inside initial *if*-clauses, which are very strong islands (4):

(2) Q: Why was Laura so happy?
    A: I heard [a rumor that she was dating someone new].

(3) Q: Why was Laura so happy?
    A: I talked to someone who said she was dating someone new.
      (cf. *Who did you talk to [someone who said she was dating –]?)

(4) Q: Why was Laura so happy?
    A: If she was dating someone new, I would have heard about it.
      (cf. *Who did you say that [if she was dating –] you would have heard
      about it?)

It is therefore simply false that direct replies are sensitive to the same
island constraints as movement.
   Citing James (1972), Goldberg (2006, 133–134) also claims that
exclamatives are sensitive to islands. Again, in all of the following try to
take what is being remarked upon to be "Laura/she is dating someone
new." This is possible if that phrase is not inside an island, but impossible
if it is:

(5) a. Ah! The woman who lives next door thought Laura was dating someone
     new!
   b. *Ah! The woman who thought Laura was dating someone new lives
     next door!

(6) a. Ah! It is likely that she was dating someone new!
   b. *Ah! That she is dating someone new is likely!

(7) a. Ah! John said she was dating someone new!
   b. *Ah! John shouted that she was dating someone new!

(8) a. Ah! John left Manhattan in order that she could date someone new!
   b. *Ah! John was hysterical 'cause she was dating someone new!

Again, though, exclamatives are possible inside complex NPs when they are
on a right branch:

(9) a. Ah! John talked to someone who said she was dating someone new!
   b. Ah! John heard a rumor that she was dating someone new!

According to Erteschik-Shir (2007, 164), Morgan (1975) actually discussed
fragment replies, not direct replies. Erteschik-Shir claims these are also
sensitive to islands:

(10) Q: Did the man who Tricia fired leave town?
     a. *No, Thelma.
     b. No, the man who Thelma fired (left town).

This test seems to work a little better, since fragment replies are impossible
with complex NPs on a right branch (11), but the correlation is still not
perfect. It seems to me that a fragment reply is possible inside an indefinite
subject (12):

(11) Q: Did you see the man who fired Tricia?
     a. *No, Thelma.
     b. No, the man who fired Thelma.

(12) Q: Was a statue of Tricia built in Poughkeepsie?
     a. No, Thelma.

  b. No, a statue of Thelma (was).
     (cf. *Who was a statue of built in Poughkeepsie?)

Fragment replies also work with clause-initial *if*-clauses:

(13) Q: Did you say that if you see Tricia at the party, you'll leave?
      a. No, Thelma.
      b. No, if I see Thelma (I will).
         (cf. *Who did you say that if you see at the party you'll leave?)

Once again, then, phenomena that are claimed to be sensitive to the same
islands as movement are actually not.
    Moreover, it seems to me that any discourse-based account of islands
faces an insurmountable problem from sluicing contexts. Consider the
following dialogs:

(14) A: Yesterday I met a man who claimed that John stole something.
      B1: What?
      B2: *What did you meet a man who claimed that John stole?

(15) A: John was furious because his wife had taken something of his.
      B1: What?
      B2: *What was John furious because his wife had taken?

(16) A: We've been assigned to read a book and write a certain kind of paper.
      B1: What kind of paper?
      B2: *What kind of paper have we been assigned to read a book and write?

In each of these cases, A makes a statement containing an indefinite.
B seeks to determine the referent of that indefinite. B can do that with
sluicing in all of the (B1) cases. B cannot do that by repeating the entire
sentence, with extraction of a wh-phrase corresponding to the indefinite
(the B2 cases). Yet the discourse contexts for B1 and B2 are *identical*. It is
simply impossible to explain the contrast between B1 and B2 as being due
to discourse.
    I conclude from all of the above that discourse approaches to islands
simply do not work, and should be abandoned.

6 Data compiled by Peter Culicover, and presented in Culicover (2008), from which
   I draw freely here.
7 Example due to Townsend and Bever (2001).
8 This is quite true of features in general, as I discuss in Boeckx (2010a, 2011b).
9 Sprouse, Wagers, and Phillips (to appear) also point out that this is far from an
   innocent assumption in processing accounts. In particular, they note that processing accounts of island effects often rely on the assumption that such effects
   arise when two processes each independently imposing a certain processing load
   must be simultaneously deployed. But, as Sprouse *et al.* write, "to our knowledge
   the complexity of the definition of 'simultaneous' in the capacity-based theory
   has not been addressed in the literature."
10 Sprouse, Wagers, and Phillips (to appear) point out that several key assumptions
   are not always made explicit in many processing accounts, and some may not
   even be as robust as is often claimed. For example, Sprouse *et al.* found out that
   the alleged processing cost with certain structures (the 'island' domains) is not
   always robustly attested in experiments for all such structures. Thus, Sprouse

et al. noted that the island-structure cost is only reliably present in the acceptability judgments of *wh(ether)*-islands, and is reliably absent in complex NP islands and subject islands.

11 For relevant discussion surrounding the meaning of standard acceptability judgments, see, in addition to Phillips's own work (e.g., Phillips 2009), Marantz (2005), Sprouse (2007a,b, 2011), and Sprouse and Almeida (2011).

12 For additional experimental arguments against Stepanov's specific claim, see Jurka 2010.

13 See, however, the attempt by Sprouse, Fukuda, Ono, and Kluender (2011), to account for certain island effects with in situ *wh*-phrases in English multiple wh-questions in terms of a backward search that is in certain ways similar to the forward search found in standard filler-gap constructions.

For the idea that wh-in-situ may be standard wh-movement 'in reverse,' see Boeckx (2008a). See also the discussion in Chapter 4, Section 4.2.

14 Goldberg (2006) claims that the island-effects induced by wh-in-situ are not 'stable' across speakers, and therefore cannot be taken as arguments against reductionist accounts that fail to capture them. Goldberg's claim strikes me as untenable, judging from the extensive literature documenting robust island effects in wh-in-situ languages, most of which reporting on research done by native speakers; see Watanabe (2001) and Simpson (2000) for excellent reviews.

15 Norbert Hornstein (p.c.) points out that it is not immediately out of the question that a processing account may capture the relevant contrast, if it could be shown that the 'island' structure used in (22) poses less processing difficulties than the one used in (23).

On the other hand, Sprouse, Wagers, and Phillips (to appear) found out that even robust islands fail to pose the processing problems that reductionist accounts rely on.

16 I won't go into the details of this graph, and just want to focus on the superadditive effect. Thus, I will not delve into the issues of how (un)acceptability is measured and represented graphically. For valuable discussion, see Sprouse (2007a).

17 Sprouse *et al.* point out that given that they only tested two capacity measures, it is logically possible that a different capacity measure could be found that does indeed correlate with the strength of island effects. They acknowledge this potential limitation, but stress that such an objection is undermined by the fact that most working memory measures are known to be highly correlated.

18 The discussion that follows draws on Abrusán's work (see Abrusán 2007, 2011a, 2011b), as well as Szabolcsi (2006). Unless otherwise noted, the examples used here for illustration of the basic intuitions behind semantico-pragmatic accounts are taken from these works.

19 Other notions have been appealed to by syntacticians, but these are equally vague and/or equally 'semanticy': Pesetsky's (1987) notion 'D-linking' or Starke's (2001) notion of 'specificity.' I should also point out that prior to Rizzi's Relativized Minimality treatment, syntacticians like Huang (1982), Lasnik and Saito (1984), and Chomsky (1986) sought to account for the selectivity of weak islands in terms of conditions on (proper) government that ultimately implicated thematic-role assignment. This, however, led to many analyses where what looked like bona fide arguments were denied a theta-role to account for their sensitivity to weak islands.

Notes on Chapter 3

1 Norbert Hornstein points out (p.c.) that there may be another reason to disfavor filter-based explanations in syntax. According to him,

> if one assumes in minimalist context that all filters are bare output conditions, i.e., properties of the interfaces, then any filter must seem like a

plausible feature of that interface. This is not an easy thing to show for most filters as there is no earthly reason why most of them, e.g. Island conditions, minimality etc. make no sense as outputs on the conceptual or intentional objects of cognition, whereas they make sense as limitations on the computational system. This is the biggest and most serious issue concerning filters right now. Of course none of this means they don't exist, but it does mean we should hope that they don't.

Hornstein's comment seems to me to reflect a bias in linguistic theorizing (going back to Chomsky's early subjacency account), according to which islands are constraints to be interpreted as the consequences of efficient computational properties. As I will show in the next chapter, plausible, interface-based explanations can be offered, provided one is willing to abandon long-standing theoretical habits.

2 It is interesting to note that Richards (2011), the most detailed attempt to address Boeckx and Grohmann's (2007) qualms to date, is forced to drastically rethink the notion of phase in order to avoid the consequences pointed out by Boeckx and Grohmann (see Richards's rejection of the very notion of 'phase head' in his section 4, p. 83).

3 For an antecedent of the PIC, see van Riemsdijk's 1978 "Head Constraint":

> No rule may involve Xi (Xj) and Y in the structure
> $\ldots X_i\ldots[_\alpha\ldots Y\ldots]\ldots X_j\ldots$
> if Y is c-commanded by the head of α, where α ranges over V, N, A, P.

4 There are actually two versions of the PIC, the one I present in the text, and put forth in Chomsky 2000, and another, proposed in Chomsky 2001, according to which the complement domain of a given phase only becomes inaccessible once the next higher phase head is introduced into the derivation. The two versions are given in (i) and (ii), respectively.

> (i) PIC (Chomsky 2000:108)
>   In phase α with head H, the domain of H is not accessible to operations outside α; only H and its edge are accessible to such operations.
> (ii) PIC (Chomsky 2001:14)
>   [Given the structure $[_{ZP}\, Z\, [_{HP}\, \alpha\, [H\, YP]]]$, with H and Z the heads of phases]: The domain of H is not accessible to operations at ZP; only H and its edge are accessible to such operations.

The versions of the PIC in (i) and (ii) are designed to yield two different search spaces for non-phase heads (e.g., T or any functional head sandwiched between v^* and C): only the 2001 version of the PIC allows for T to establish Agree with an element inside v^*P.

Though potentially significant, this modification of the PIC suggested by Chomsky does not affect the point I make in the text. Therefore I set this issue aside here.

5 This remark by Chomsky seems to me to indicate that he intends phases to capture island conditions. Norbert Hornstein (p.c.) is less sure, as he interprets Chomsky's ambivalent characterization of 'island' nodes like D and P regarding their phasal status as a sign that Chomsky wants to keep phases separate from the issue of islandhood.

I take it that Chomsky's more recent (2007, 2008) discussion of CED effects in the context of phases, as well as his characterization of D as phasal, as a sign that he does indeed intend phases to be responsible for island effects.

6 Abels (2003) argues that this is too permissive: movement of the entire phase complement to the phase edge is disallowed, as this movement would violate the

ban on too short a movement ('Anti-locality'), which prohibits phrase-internal movement (forcing the moving category to cross at least one full phrase boundary).

7 For another attempt, see den Dikken (2007), and for a critique of the latter, see Boeckx 2007.

8 Not surprisingly, several studies have proposed a Phase Edge condition, according to which complex units *in phase edges* become internally frozen (see Fortuny 2008, Gallego and Uriagereka 2007a,b). This is still stipulative, of course, but at least it seems to make the right empirical cut.

9 The material in this section reproduces the bulk of Boeckx and Gallego (2011). Credit for any argument in this section should be given to both authors.

10 Because of this choice, Müller's system essentially eliminates any difference between the two versions of the PIC found in the literature (cf. note 4).

11 Some remarks are in order. First, it seems that Müller's (2010) system has more than one type of EF (Müller talks of inherent and non-inherent EFs), but he does not elaborate on this. Second, as Müller himself admits, EF insertion violates Chomsky's (1995) *inclusiveness* (the condition that bans addition of syntactically relevant material that is not present in the pre-syntactic lexical entries), but he assumes that inclusiveness can be violated in favor of (8a). Finally, as stated in the text, EF assignment is related to having "an effect on the outcome," but Müller is also silent in this respect, pointing out that "an important question is what it means for edge feature insertion to have 'an effect on the outcome'. However I will not focus on this issue in what follows since it is orthogonal to the main plot of this paper" (p. 37). I will not elaborate on any of these points, but I want to note that such issues ultimately have to be dealt with.

12 It is worth noting that the operation in (14) is impossible in Chomsky's (2000 *et seq.*) system, as it would require for v^* to look into its own specifier, which is out of its complement domain. The relevant search procedure would require a specifier–head dependency (i.e., m-command), which is dispensed with from Chomsky (2000) onwards.

13 An immediate question that arises after considering Müller's (2010) proposal is what would prevent the relevant phase head from carrying an extra EF so that the merger of the external argument does not consume all EFs of the phase head. This of course depends on one's conception of EFs, to which I return.

14 Note that, in these cases, adjuncts involve a non-finite clause. Truswell (2007) takes adjuncts of this type to be low in the v^*P structure, which would be consistent with Müller's (2010) account of freezing effects: if they are not last merged, adjuncts can circumvent islandhood. Be that as it may, it is not entirely clear how this approach would explain that adjuncts that need to be low in the v^*P too to license NPIs (in Larson 2004, they are first merged within the v^*P), block extraction:

(i) John didn't talk [after any of our meetings]
(ii) *What meetings$_i$ didn't John talk [after any of t$_i$]?

15 Interestingly, as Hornstein (2001) further notes, extraction is impossible if the conditional clause occupies a final (truly adjoined) position:

(i) *[Which book$_i$ did you say [that Quinn would abandon linguistics [if he ever read t$_i$]]]?

16 Müller's (2010) proposal is very similar to Epstein and Seely's (2002), who develop a framework where every application of Merge is followed by an immediate application of transfer.

17 It is somewhat unfortunate that Chomsky uses the term "feature." Under the assumption that features have values, match, and delete, an EF — just like the EPP of the GB era – cannot qualify as a feature.

Notes on Chapter 4

1 More recently (Uriagereka 2011), Uriagereka has come to the conclusion that this particular motivation, based as it was on Kayne's (1994) Linear Correspondence Axiom, may not be as central as his original paper made it look.

  For different implementations of Uriagereka's central insight, see Nunes and Uriagereka (2000), Johnson (2002), and Zwart (2007). For an attempt to address some of the empirical difficulties faced by Uriagereka's account, one unfortunately accompanied by a significant weakening of the original proposal (to which I will return in note 8), see Sheehan (to appear).

  Fox and Pesetsky (2005) also hint at the role of cyclic linearization in the context of certain islands, to which I will also come back.

  Finally, for a quite different articulation of Uriagereka's intuition, one that lets the system choose between early spell-out of phase edges or phase complements (either option allowing the derivation to retain its monotonic character), thereby enlarging the set of possible extractions from non-complements, see Narita (2011).

2 Uriagereka (1999a) suggests that early spell-out turns the complex unit into a 'word,' but as Norbert Hornstein has pointed out to me (p.c.), island domains have none of the phonological properties of words, other than the fact that none of their internal members can be reordered. Other approaches that rely on cyclic linearization to account for island effects, such as Fox and Pesetsky (2005) (to be discussed below), seem to me to get around this problem by adopting somewhat different linearization assumptions from the one Uriagereka assumed, while preserving his insight. Since this is not a major issue when it comes to sketching the logic of Uriagereka's account, I will refrain from elaborating on this point here.

3 For numerous examples of the same ilk, drawn from many languages, see Narita (2011) and Stepanov (2007).

4 Uriagereka's approach, unlike the standard subjacency account, does not make use of escape hatches, indeed cannot make use of these, as it is the entire complex left-branch/adjunct, including its 'edge,' that undergoes early spell-out and compactification, nullifying the escape-through-the-edge strategy.

5 As a matter of fact, Narita (2011) and Sheehan (to appear) have exploited exactly this possibility to account for the lack of CED-effects with certain adjuncts and (in the case of Narita) certain specifiers. The problem for such proposals is how to constrain the choice of which complex part of the tree to atomize to continue to rule out unwanted extractions.

6 To be sure, there are alternative non-movement accounts of the relevant phenomena, to which Uriagereka could resort, but, as I will discuss below, none of these alternatives are as natural or as comprehensive as the now standard movement + deletion/resumption approach mentioned in the text. For very accessible discussion of the superiority of movement + deletion accounts of ellipsis (in repair contexts), see Merchant (2010, 2011) and Lasnik (2007).

7 The repair problem just discussed in the text extends to analyses that do not necessarily rely on cyclic spell-out. Thus, several authors have sought to account for the island status of certain domains like adjuncts by taking them to be introduced into the syntactic derivation after all the operations that would lead to movement have already taken place, thus rendering movement out of adjuncts impossible (see Stepanov 2001, 2007 for such as 'late insertion' analysis); alternatively, adjunction has been said to result in a domain that cannot be inspected by any material belonging to the main spine of the tree, making it impossible for material inside the adjunct to be attracted by elements outside of it, much like what happens to elements trapped in a black hole. The invisibility of adjuncts has

been blamed on the fact that adjuncts reside in a different structural plane/ dimension (Chomsky 2004), or on the fact that adjoined structures lack a label, and only labeled elements can be probed from outside (Hornstein and Nunes 2008, Hornstein 2009).

All of these analyses suffer from the fact that extraction can take place out of adjuncts in the presence of a resumptive pronoun. In other words, they suffer from the same 'repair' problem that plagues Uriagereka's early compactification account.

8 See also Sheehan (to appear). Apart from allowing for the main spine of the tree to undergo early atomization (thereby allowing extraction from otherwise opaque domains such as adjuncts), Sheehan departs from Uriagereka's original account in resorting to labeling considerations *in addition to* early atomization to allow for instances of subextraction (i.e., freezing the head of the phrase in the relevant specifier position, but not say the complement of that head). The system Sheehan develops is quite complex (I refer the reader to her paper for details), and essentially dispenses with the idea of early compactification of the non-complements that characterized Uriegereka's proposal. Not surprisingly, Sheehan's analysis covers a wider range of data, but at the cost of seriously weakening the type of theory (island induced by early spell-out) envisaged by Uriagereka.

9 Although studying contexts where expected island effects do not materialize may seem puzzling at first (why study phenomena where islands don't arise if one is trying to understand why they do?), the situation is no different from what biologists do when they study cases of deficits, accidents, mutants, and other situations where something goes 'wrong' to understand what typically happens ('normals'). This is what Alberch (1989) called the logic of monsters. It's, after all, standard experimental science, where one studies minute manipulations to test theory-informed predictions.

10 I am incapable of judging how well the repair effects under discussion fit with processing-based accounts of the sort reviewed in Chapter 2. Much depends on how resumptive and elided dependencies are processed. I know of no leading candidate theory in this domain.

11 Readers are also encouraged to think of *pro*-drop languages, which surely offer compelling cases of null elements inside island domains.

12 Fox and Pesetsky depart from Chomsky's phase-based system reviewed in the previous chapter in that they assume that the phonological component processes the content of the entire phase (in particular, it fixes the linear order of all the elements at the phase edge), not just the phase complement. While non-trivial, this difference will be ignored here.

13 Hornstein, Lasnik and Uriagereka do not address issues such as those discussed in the previous section of this chapter, such as why it is the domains corresponding to strong islands that must be linearized early, while the main spine of the tree need not be, even though it would equally well solve the 'departure-from-monotonic-derivation' problem.

14 Tsai's and Reinhart's suggestions boil down to a mechanism of long-distance binding, but alternatives have been suggested over the years, such as the idea that the island is circumvented because the entire island domain is pied-piped covertly (see Nishigauchi 1986, Richards 2000).

15 See the contributions in Rouveret (2011), as well as Aoun and Li (2003), and Boeckx (2003a) for relevant data and discussion in the context of resumption; for ellipsis, see Fox and Lasnik (2003) and Merchant (2008); for wh-in-situ, see Simpson (2000) and Watanabe (2001). For pied-piping, I recommend Heck (2008) and Cable (2010).

16 I remember giving a talk as a graduate student arguing for a movement analysis of resumption in island contexts and being told by a senior and prominent member of the theoretical linguistic community during the question period that the analysis was doomed from the start, given that "one thing we know for sure is that islands block movement." It should be clear to the readers of this book that one cannot be so confident about this statement any more; indeed, after Ross's careful discussion in his thesis, one should never have been so confident about islands blocking movement.

17 For groundbreaking work in this area, see Aoun and Li (2003), who argue on the basis of Lebanese Arabic data that reconstruction under resumption only obtains outside island contexts, and take this fact to rule out a movement account of resumption in islands (but see Boeckx and Hornstein 2008 for a movement account of the relevant data); for a more nuanced state of affairs, which differentiates among various types of reconstruction effects, and finds some of these to obtain even inside islands for at least some languages, see Guilliot (2006, 2007), Rouveret (2008), and Guilliot and Malkawi (2006), and several contributions in Rouveret (2011).

18 I should point out that Merchant's and Lasnik's treatments differ in an important way when it comes to the effect of ellipsis on island violations. Though often lumped together, Merchant's and Lasnik's differ in that Merchant does not offer a uniform treatment of island repair under ellipsis, whereas Lasnik does. According to Merchant, whereas some islands can be repaired by ellipsis, other apparent cases of island repair arise from the fact that there was never any island domain in the ellipsis site. For empirical, as well as theoretical, arguments against Merchant's weaker position, and in favor of a unified treatment according to which all types of islands can be repaired under ellipsis, see Lasnik (2005).

19 It stands to reason that alternative analyses, leading to very different architectural conclusions, are, of course, possible. Perhaps some of these constraints, such as superiority, are representational conditions but on the semantic side, rather than on the phonological side of the grammar, and so remain unaffected by ellipsis, understood as PF-deletion/lack of pronunciation (see Chierchia 1991 and Hornstein 1995 for semantic treatments of superiority). Alternatively, what looks like an adherence to the superiority condition may be nothing more than a parallelism requirement holding between the ellipsis site and the antecedent clause, hence orthogonal to the locality issue under discussion.

Finally, I should point out that in recent years, the unrepairability of the ban on preposition stranding mentioned in the text has been questioned on empirical grounds (see Boeckx 2008a for references concerning a number of languages). If it is repairable, this constraint may be amenable to a treatment along the lines suggested here for more standard islands. This latter point illustrates the need to understand repair environments much better.

20 Alongside the resumption alternative that I am about to sketch, it may also be worth reconsidering the pseudocleft-based analysis of sluicing ((ii), as opposed to (i)).

(i)   a. John saw someone but I don't know who (deleted: John saw __)
      b. John ate ham and something else but I can't remember what (deleted: John ate ham and __)
(ii) a. John saw someone but I don't know who (deleted: it was)
      b. John ate ham and something else but I can't remember what (deleted: it was)

Van Craenenbroeck (2008) raised this possibility again recently by pointing out that some of the strongest arguments that Merchant provided in favor of the island structure being present in the ellipsis site under sluicing (e.g., the case markers of the *wh*-remnant illustrated in (14) in the text) turn out not to be so strong if certain slightly different assumptions are made. In fact, van Craenenbroeck claims that the only argument that truly remains is the case-marking on wh-remnants in languages with morphological case like German. All the other arguments are easily circumvented.

Accordingly, van Craenenbroeck claims that if the pseudocleft analysis turns out to be tenable, one cannot exclude the possibility that in many situations, what looks like the deletion of an entire portion of the sentence containing the ellipsis site may just be a copula clause, with no island to begin with. This, of course, would nullify the island-repair potential of sluicing. But I would like to point out that a 'middle' way may be worth looking into according to which movement also takes place from within the island structure in pseudocleft contexts, as in (iii):

> (iii) a. John saw someone but I don't know who (deleted: it was that John saw __)
>   b. John ate ham and something else but I can't remember what (deleted: it was that John ate ham and __)

21 Interestingly, absence of an overt 'correlate' in the 'antecedent' clause (so-called 'sprouting' contexts) robs sluicing of some of its most interesting properties, as discussed by Chung (2006). For example, Chung observes that the absence of an overt correlate bans preposition stranding:

> (i) They are jealous, but it's unclear *who/of who
> [as opposed to "They are jealous of someone, but it's unclear who"]

22 I write 'initial plausibility' instead of something stronger like 'explanatory force' because, as I noted above, exactly what the phonological problem with (non-elided) gaps is has never been made clear in the relevant literature. It is in fact quite interesting that both Lasnik (2001) and Merchant (2001), the major works on repair by ellipsis, remain completely silent on the issue. Both simply adopt Chomsky's (1972) idea that deletion alleviates islands because it removes the offending violation caused by movement from the representation used to judge the well-formedness of the sentence. Chomsky metaphorically spoke of ellipsis removing the * (the symbol used to mark a sentence as ill-formed) from the sentence, but the source of the * was left open. Lasnik and Merchant continue to speak of repair-via-*-deletion (taking the * to be "some PF uninterpretable feature"), but, of course, this only begs the question.

23 As originally observed by Doron (1982) in the context of Hebrew restrictive relatives, optional resumptive pronouns in object position restrict the range of possible interpretations with respect to those allowed by gap relatives. This is shown by the contrast in (i): the gap relative (ia) is ambiguous between a non-specific and a specific interpretation of the relative 'head,' whereas the resumptive relative (ib) is unambiguous, and only allows for the specific interpretation:

> (i) a. Dani yimca et   ha-iša   še   hu mexapes.
>   Dani will   find the woman that he seeks.
>   b. Dani yimca et   ha-iša   še   hu mexapes *ota.*
>   Dani will   find the woman that he seeks   her.

A second type of 'specificity effect' found with resumptive pronouns concerns single vs. multiple individual readings in examples like (ii):

(ii) a. ha-iša   še   kol   gever   hizmin _   hodeta   lo.
         the woman that every   man   invited   thanked   him.
      b. ha-iša   še   kol   gever   hizmin   *ota*   hodeta   lo.
         the woman that every   man   invited   her   thanked   him.

The gap relative (iia) allows for both a single individual reading of the relative 'head,' involving the same woman for all the men, and a multiple individual reading, such that for every man there is a possibly different woman that he invited. The resumptive relative (iib), however, only allows for the single individual reading.

24 Needless to say, it may well be that some resumptive patterns do not fit the description under discussion (recall my warning above about the complexity of repair phenomena). For instance, it may be that some resumptive elements really are just overt versions of gaps. But if this is so, I predict that these will be island-sensitive.

25 See Demirdache (1991) for what is perhaps the first hint at such a relationship between resumption and wh-in-situ, since Demirdache takes resumptive pronouns to be in-situ operators moving covertly much like in-situ wh-phrases were assumed to do in the 1980s.

26 Cable suggests that the difference between 'wh-in-situ' vs. 'wh-movement' languages lies in the fact in the former, the Q-element adjoins to the unit containing the 'wh'-sounding element, leaving the latter behind when it moves, whereas in 'wh-movement' languages, the Q-element projects a QP when it merges with the unit containing the 'wh'-sounding element, and takes it along with it when it moves.

27 Needless to say, not all problems about pied-piping disappear with Cable's suggestion. Constraints on what can, must, or cannot be pied-piped ought to follow from conditions governing the possible attachment sites of the Q-element. The precise formulation of these conditions remains a task for the future (see Cable's own work for relevant suggestions).

28 Cable's main empirical motivation for this type of analysis comes from the obligatory presence of a particle accompanying the wh-word in wh-fronting contexts, such as the particle *sá* in the following example from Tlingit:

(i) Wáa   sá   sh tudinookw i   éesh?
    how   Q   he.feels   your   father
    How is your father feeling?

29 Cable himself does not consider this movement/reprojection alternative. By base-generating Q where he does, Cable wants to avoid instances of movement across islands in pied-piping contexts. In fact, Cable considers that in languages where pied-piping does not void island effects, Q enters into an agreement-at-a-distance relation with the wh-sounding element.

30 Johnson's suggestion builds on the lack of reconstruction effects under resumption documented for Lebanese Arabic in Aoun and Li (2003) in the context of island-free resumptive structures. However, as I mentioned in the previous section, more recent literature on the topic (see especially Rouveret 2011) suggests that the facts are more complex than what Aoun and Li suggested. At the moment it is not clear that all reconstruction effects are blocked in resumptive structures within islands.

31 Boeckx and Hornstein (2008) suggest that reconstruction is only possible when some agreement operation underlies movement, which is precisely what Boeckx

(2003a) suggested cannot be the case when movement crosses an island boundary (an idea to be reviewed in the main text momentarily). If correct, Boeckx and Hornstein's analysis would derive Johnson's suggestion without blaming islands on reconstruction per se.

32 Subsequent to Boeckx's (2003a) study, Chomsky (2004) offered a very strong conceptual argument for viewing move as just another instance of merge ('internal merge'), thus reducing 'copy + merge' to a single operation (remerge). Chomsky essentially pointed out that if merge is an operation that is virtually conceptually necessary, it would take an extra constraint to prevent merge from remerging an element that has already been merged; since movement is nothing but another name for internal merge, this means that it would take an extra condition to ban movement. A grammar without such an extra condition is obviously to be preferred over one that arbitrarily rules out movement. Thus, the possibility of movement follows immediately from the existence of merge (which everyone must recognize). Although it's rarely been pointed out, I think that Chomsky's suggestion shows that there is no meaningful distinction to be made between movement and base-generation, if movement is merge.

33 On the freezing effect of agreement, see also Donati (2006). Gallego (2007, 2010) refines Boeckx's (2003a) characterization of the type of agreement that causes freezing, and suggests that it's full agreement (including case) that has this effect. I won't go into such details here.

34 Data taken from McCloskey (2002), for Irish, and Adger and Ramchand (2005), for Scottish Gaelic.

35 Rackowski and Richards (2005) offer a different account of island effects based on agreement. Alongside Boeckx (2003a), they re-characterize the CED in terms of agreement: opaque domains are those that do not allow agreement to reach into them. Rackowski and Richards seek to derive the generalization that opaque domains are non-complements from Chomsky's (2000) suggestion that agreement can only take place from a head into that head's complement domain, not into its specifier or into adjoined material. The proposal suffers from the same proposal we noted in the context of Uriagereka (1999a) earlier in this chapter: the fact that not all specifiers are opaque. It also suffers from the fact that specifiers can enter into an agreement relation with a higher, c-commanding head. It therefore becomes crucial for Rackowski and Richards to characterize the relevant agreeing heads precisely, but at the moment I do not know of any non-stipulative way of achieving this. (The issue is reminiscent of how to characterize barriers/bounding cnodes/phase-heads accurately.)

36 The notion of 'strong' feature-checking relations goes back to Chomsky (1993).

37 Although the assumption is not completely unproblematic, if the existence of movement into theta-positions, and arguments bearing multiple theta-roles, is recognized (a possibility that is hard to rule out in a non-stipulative fashion in a minimalist context; see Hornstein 2001, among others).

38 Like Boeckx (2003a), Rizzi and Shlonsky resort to resumption to license chains that would otherwise be too strong.

39 Boeckx (2008a) discusses the GB antecedents of this idea, most prominently, Kayne (1984) (who imposed licensing conditions on chains in terms of (unambiguous) 'government projections') and Koster (1987) (and his notion of 'dynasties'). Chomsky's (1986) idea of well-formedness conditions on chain compositions arguably also belongs to this family of approaches. On chains as superprojections, see also Uriagereka (1998).

40 Boeckx (2008a) shows how resumptive elements allow otherwise illegitimate chains to be licensed, relying on Boeckx's (2003a) intuition that resumptive

elements essentially free up the chains formed by their antecedents from being defined in terms of unconnected sisters. The idea developed in Boeckx (2008a) assimilates resumptive chains to parasitic gaps.

41 This approach would also straightforwardly incorporate Truswell's (2007) generalization concerning licit cases of extraction out of adjuncts (cf. the data discussed in (40), Chapter 1), dubbed the Single Event condition, according to which "an 'A'-dependency is legitimate only if the minimal constituent containing the head and foot of the chain describes a single event."

42 Another particularly salient shortcoming arises from Boeckx's (2008a) reliance on a rigid X-bar schema like that of Chomsky (1970) or Kayne (1994). Representational conditions on the format of projections, and by transitivity those on the format of chains, should, however, be derived.

43 In a certain sense, Chomsky's (1986) idea that certain blocking categories become barriers (by inheritance) went in the same direction, but it did not implicate the role of the moving element to define this inheritance.

44 Prima facie, the statement just made appears to be factually wrong: there are, after all, well-known instances of long-distance A-bar dependencies that have extended a previously established A-chain, as in (i).

(i) Who did John say [__ was arrested __]

However, I think this is only an apparent problem for the view I am trying to defend. As I have pointed out in Boeckx (2003a, 2008a), cases like (i) are known to be quite distinct from, say, long-distance A-bar movement of arguments that did not undergo A-movement prior to the A-bar dependency, like (ii), even if on the surface they seem to be on a par.

(ii) Who did John say [Bill arrested __]

The most obvious difference is that one case (i) is subject to the *that*-trace effect (it is sensitive to the overt presence of the complementizer), whereas the dependency in (ii) is not.

Why should this be? The answer that strikes me as the most promising is that the overt complementizer that induces the *that*-trace effect, and whose absence licenses the extraction in (i), is the element that truly defines the clause internal movement as an A-relation (A-chain). Since I will defend the idea that only A-chains (as opposed to, say, chains formed by successive cyclic movement) are those that cannot be extended, the absence of C in (i) would allow for chain extension, if I am correct that it is *that* that types the chain as A-chain.

Incidentally, the idea that it is C that truly defines the A-relation is an idea that is gaining support. For example, Chomsky (2007, 2008) provides several arguments in favor of taking the complementizer C that induces A-movement to SpecIP for case/agreement purposes (i.e., A-chain). Put another way, not any movement to, say, SpecIP, qualifies as the formation of an A-chain, and therefore (i) does not immediately invalidate the claim I am putting forward: that once an unambiguously A-type chain has been formed, further A-bar movement of the element heading the A-chain (or of any element contained by it) is blocked.

One last point: readers wondering if finite verb agreement in (i) does not indicate that an A-relation was established should bear in mind that in the framework assumed here, roughly that of Chomsky (2000 *et seq.*), agreement relations can be established in the absence of movement, hence cannot reliably be used as evidence that an A-chain was established. Presence of the complementizer is what appears to force movement for the agreement relation to take place (for reasons discussed in the text below); in the absence of the complementizer, agreement can be established at a distance.

45 I will qualify this somewhat below, and suggest, along with recent proposals in the literature, that some adjuncts need not form Pair-Merge structures, depending on their adjunction sites.

46 For the same reason, adjuncts can be thought of as residing on a different plane/ dimension (Chomsky 2004, relying on a sizeable literature that takes adjunction to require syntactic representations in three dimensions).

47 For a much earlier claim that (some instances of) agreement induces early spell-out, see Uriagereka (1999b).

48 For Chomsky, Inheritance is required because it is only the complement of the phase head C, and not C itself that can undergo spell-out (cf. the discussion in Section 3.1 regarding the difference between the phase edge and the phase complement).

49 By hypothesis, the type of agreeing objects that induce islands, of the sort illustrated in (31) above, from Basque, must undergo movement.

50 In Boeckx (2010a) I argue that movement is required so as to void what would otherwise be a minimality situation caused by Inheritance. As this is not a crucial point in the argument presented in the text, I will set this issue aside here.

51 For Chomsky (2007) and Richards (2007), cyclic spell-out is tied to inheritance, and would therefore be induced in the case of object agreement, but since no A-chain would be included in the transferred portion, by hypothesis, no island effect would arise.

52 There are various reasons for why subjects need not move in certain constructions: presence of an expletive, a null subject *(pro)*, lack of features on C to be inherited, etc. (see Boeckx 2010a for discussion of several additional options).

53 Boeckx (2010a) claims that whether an adjoined structure is formed by Pair-Merge or set-Merge depends on the adjunction site: if adjunction takes place to the phase edge, a Pair-Merge structure results; if adjunction is to the phase complement, a set-Merge structure results. This roughly captures the difference between high (opaque) adjuncts and low (transparent) adjuncts.

54 The adjoined status of the resumptive pronoun could perhaps account for the lack of full-blown reconstruction effects of the sort first discussed by Aoun and Li (2003).

55 I am here pursuing a long-standing idea of mine (see Boeckx 2003a, 2007), where I divorce intermediate movement steps from cyclic/phasal nodes, and regard intermediate movement steps as non-feature-driven, which is crucial for the solution offered in the text, for feature-driven displacement would lead to early spell-out of the chain.

56 For readers familiar with the phase literature: only chains contained in the phase-head complement, not those reaching the phase edge, are the problematic (island-inducing) ones.

57 For example, one might seek to relate the analysis of strong islands offered here to the structure of memory and the limited number of elements that can be included in the 'focus of attention' during processing (see Wagers 2008), and relate Wagers's up-to-date discussion to Chomsky's (1965) idea, quoted above, that "the perceptual device ... is unable (or finds it difficult) to utilize a procedure ϕ while it is in the course of executing ϕ."

Notes on Appendix

1 This appendix reproduces the core of an argument first presented in Boeckx (2008a), and relies on empirical arguments presented in Broekhuis (2006), Gallego (2007, 2010), and Gallego and Uriagereka (2007a).

2 On some prepositions that look DP-internal, but aren't, see Kayne (2005) (who explicitly discussed cases involving *of*).

3 Sheehan's (to appear) analysis of examples like those discussed in Chomsky (2007) could lead to the conclusion that the relevant *wh*-element originated in a base-generated, 'satellite' position (though Sheehan herself does not endorse this position, maintaining that the extraction took place from the in-situ copy of the subject DP).

4 Gallego (2007) also shows that a similar asymmetry between displaced (opaque) and non-displaced (transparent) arguments obtains in the realm of objects, as the approach developed in Chapter 4 predicts.

5 The Torrego-effects are one of the only two cases of acceptable extraction out of A-bar chains that I know of. The other instance, which, unlike the Torrego effects, gives rise to fairly robust acceptability across speakers, comes from the literature on Japanese scrambling.

   Takahashi (1994) observes that it is possible to scramble out of scrambled phrases, as shown in (i).

> (i) [Sono hon-o]$_i$ John-ga [Mary-ga t_i katta   to]$_j$ Bill-ga   itta to
>   this book-Acc John-Nom Mary-Nom bought that Bill-Nom said that
>   omotteiru   [Japanese]
>   think
>   'That book, John thinks that [that Mary bought] Bill said'.

Bošković and Takahashi (1998) explain away this exception of the ban on extraction out of displaced constituents by analyzing scrambled phrases as being base-generated in their surface positions. Alternatively, it has been claimed that (phonetically null) resumption may underlie at least some instances of Japanese-type scrambling (see Boeckx 2003b; Lee 2006). Either of these two analyses would explain away the problem posed by Japanese for the approach defended in Chapter 4.

6 The examples discussed by Chomsky and Lasnik and Saito involve stranding of the preposition *of*, as in (i).

> (i) ??Which author do you wonder [how many books of <which author>] Bill read <how many books of which authors>?

Though marginal, (i) is reported to be better than (ii).

> (ii) *which author do you believe that many books of <which author> will be read by Bill?

Most speakers I consulted judge (i) and (ii) as equally unacceptable. I do not have an explanation for why some speakers find (i) somewhat better.

References

Abels, K. 2003. Successive-cyclicity, anti-locality, and adposition stranding. Doctoral dissertation, University of Connecticut.

Abels, K. and K. Bentzen. 2009. A note on the punctuated nature of movement paths. *Catalan Journal of Linguistics* 8: 19–40.

Abrusán, M. 2007. Contradiction and grammar: the case of weak islands. Doctoral dissertation, MIT.

  (2011a) Wh-islands in Degree Questions. *Semantics and Pragmatics* 4: 1–44.

  (2011b) Presuppositional and negative islands: a semantic account. *Natural Language Semantics* 19: 257–321.

Adger, D. 2003. *Core Syntax.* Oxford University Press.

Adger, D. and G. Ramchand. 2005. Merge and Move: Wh-dependencies revisited. *Linguistic Inquiry* 36: 161–193.

Alberch, P. 1989. The logic of monsters: Evidence for internal constraint in development and evolution. *Geobios, mémoire spécial* no. 12: 21–57.

Aoun, J. and Y.-H. A. Li. 2003. *Essays on the Representational and Derivational Nature of Grammar: The Diversity of Wh-constructions.* Cambridge, Mass.: MIT Press.

Arsenijević, B. and W. Hinzen. To appear. On the absence of X-within-X recursion in human grammar. *Linguistic Inquiry.*

Beck, S. 1996. Quantified structures as barriers for LF-movement. *Natural Language Semantics* 4: 1–46.

  2006. Intervention effects follow from focus interpretation. *Natural Language Semantics* 14: 1–56.

Berwick, R. and A. Weinberg. 1984. *The Grammatical Basis of Linguistic Performance.* Cambridge, Mass.: MIT Press.

Bever, T. G. 1970. The cognitive basis for linguistic structures. In *Cognition and the Development of Language*, ed. J. R. Hayes, 279–362. New York: Wiley.

Boeckx, C. 2003a. *Islands and Chains.* Amsterdam: John Benjamins.

  2003b. Free word order in minimalist syntax. *Folia Linguistica* 37: 77–102.

  2006. *Linguistic Minimalism: Origins, Concepts, Methods, and Aims.* Oxford University Press.

  2007. *Understanding Minimalist Syntax: Lessons from Locality in Long-distance Dependencies.* Oxford: Blackwell.

2008a. *Bare Syntax*. Oxford University Press.

2008b. Islands. *Language and Linguistics Compass* 2: 151–167.

2008c. *Aspects of the Syntax of Agreement*. London: Routledge.

2008d. No Merge is an island. Presented at Mayfest 2008: *Perspectives on Islands,* May 2008.

2009. Merge alpha: Merging and filtering. Presented at the conference on Minimalist approaches to syntactic locality. August 2009. [A version of this talk to appear in *Minimalist Approaches to Syntactic Locality*, ed. B. Suranyi. Cambridge University Press.]

2010a. Defeating lexiconcentrism. Ms., ICREA/UAB.

2010b. Linguistic minimalism. In *Oxford Handbook of Grammatical Analysis*, ed. B. Heine and H. Narrog, 485–505. Oxford University Press.

(ed.) 2011a. *The Oxford Handbook of Linguistic Minimalism*. Oxford University Press.

2011b. Review of A. Kibort and G. Corbett (2010) *Features. Perspectives on a key notion in linguistics. Journal of Linguistics*.

2011c. Narrow syntax unchained. Presented at the "Chains in Minimalism" workshop, February 2011.

Boeckx, C. and A. Gallego. 2011. Deriving CED effects from phases: some reasons for skepticism. Ms., ICREA/UAB.

Boeckx, C. and K. K. Grohmann. 2007. Putting phases in perspective. *Syntax* 10: 204–222.

Boeckx, C. and N. Hornstein. 2008. Superiority, reconstruction, and islands. In *Foundational Issues in Linguistic Theory*, ed. R. Freidin, C. Otero, and M. L. Zubizarreta. Cambridge, Mass.: MIT Press.

Boeckx, C. and Y. Jeong. 2004. The fine structure of intervention in syntax. In *Issues in Current Linguistic Theory: A Festschrift for Hong Bae Lee*, ed. C. Kwon and W. Lee, 83–116. Seoul: Kyunchin.

Boeckx, C. and H. Lasnik. 2006. Intervention and repair. *Linguistic Inquiry* 37: 150–155.

Bošković, Ž. and D. Takahashi. 1998. Scrambling and last resort. *Linguistic Inquiry* 29: 347–366.

Brandi, L. and P. Cordin. 1989. Two Italian dialects and the null subject parameter. In *The Null Subject Parameter*, ed. O. Jaeggli and K. Safir, 111–142. Dordrecht: Kluwer.

Brody, M. 1995. *Lexico-logical Form*. Cambridge, Mass.: MIT Press.

2003. *Towards an Elegant Syntax*. London: Routledge.

Broekhuis, H. 2006. Extraction from subjects: some remarks on Chomsky's "On Phases." In *Organizing Grammar*, ed. H. Broekhuis, N. Corver, and R. Huybregts, 59–68. Berlin: Mouton de Gruyter.

Browning, M. 1987. Null operator constructions. Doctoral dissertation, MIT.

Cable, S. 2010. *The Grammar of Q*. Oxford University Press.

Carnie, A. 2006. *Syntax: A Generative Introduction* (2nd edition). Malden: Wiley-Blackwell.

Cattell, R. 1976. Constraints on movement rules. *Language* 52: 18–50.

Ceplova, M. 2001. Minimalist islands: restricting P-features. Ms., MIT.

Chametzky, R. A. 2000. *Phrase Structure*. Oxford: Blackwell.

2003. Phrase structure. In *Minimalist Syntax*, ed. R. Hendrick, 192–225. Oxford: Blackwell.

Chierchia, G. 1991. Functional WH and weak crossover. In *Proceedings of WCCFL* 10. Stanford, Calif.: CLSI, pp. 44–55.

Chomsky, N. 1955. The logical structure of linguistic theory. Ms., Harvard/ MIT. [Published in part, 1975, New York: Plenum.]

1957. *Syntactic Structures*. The Hague: Mouton.

1964. *Current Issues in Linguistic Theory*. The Hague: Mouton.

1965. *Aspects of the Theory of Syntax*. Cambridge, Mass.: MIT Press.

1966. *Cartesian Linguistics*. New York: Harper and Row.

1970. Remarks on nominalization. In *Readings in English Transformational Grammar*, ed. R. Jacobs and P. Rosenbaum, 184–221. Waltham, Mass.: Ginn.

1972. Some empirical issues in the theory of transformational grammar. In *Goals of Linguistic Theory*, ed. S. Peters. Englewood Cliffs, NJ: Prentice Hall.

1973. Conditions on transformations. In *A Festschrift for Morris Halle*, ed. S. Anderson and P. Kiparsky, 232–286. New York: Holt, Rinehart, and Winston.

1977. On wh-movement. In *Formal Syntax*, ed. P. Culicover, T. Wasow, and A. Akmajian, 71–132. New York: Academic Press.

1980. *Rules and Representations*. New York: Columbia University Press.

1981. *Lectures on Government and Binding*. Dordrecht: Foris.

1986. *Barriers*. Cambridge, Mass.: MIT Press.

1993. A minimalist program for linguistic theory. In *The View from Building 20*, ed. K. Hale and S. J. Keyser, 1–52. Cambridge, Mass.: MIT Press. [Reprinted in Chomsky, N. 1995. *The Minimalist Program*, 167–217.]

1994. Bare phrase structure. Ms., MIT. [Published in Webelhuth, G. (ed.) 1995. *Government and Binding and the Minimalist Program*, 385–439. Oxford: Blackwell.]

1995. Categories and transformations. In Chomsky, N. *The Minimalist Program*, 219–394. Cambridge, Mass.: MIT Press.

2000. Minimalist inquiries: the framework. In *Step by Step*, ed. R. Martin, D. Michaels, and J. Uriagereka, 89–155. Cambridge, Mass.: MIT Press.

2001. Derivation by phase. In *Ken Hale: A Life in Language*, ed. M. Kenstowicz, 1–50. Cambridge, Mass.: MIT Press.

2004. Beyond explanatory adequacy. In *Structures and Beyond*, ed. A. Belletti, 104–131. Oxford University Press.

2007. Approaching UG from below. In *Interfaces + Recursion = Language? Chomsky's Minimalism and the View from Syntax-Semantics*, ed. U. Sauerland and M. Gärtner, 1–30. Berlin: Mouton de Gruyter.

2008. On phases. In *Foundational Issues in Linguistic Theory*, ed. R. Freidin, C. Otero, and M.-L. Zubizarreta, 133–166. Cambridge, Mass.: MIT Press.

Chomsky, N. and M. Halle. 1968. *The Sound Pattern of English*. Cambridge, Mass.: MIT Press.

Chomsky, N., M. Halle, and F. Lukoff. 1956. On accent and juncture in English. In *For Roman Jakobson: Essays on the Occasion of his Sixtieth Birthday*, ed. M. Halle, H. G. Lunt, H. McLean, and C. H. van Schooneveld, 65–80. The Hague: Mouton.

Chomsky, N. and H. Lasnik. 1977. Filters and control. *Linguistic Inquiry* 8: 425–504.

  1993. The theory of principles and parameters. In *Syntax: An International Handbook of Contemporary Research*, Vol. I. ed. J. Jacobs *et al.*, 506–569. Walter de Gruyter.

Chung, S. 1994. Wh-agreement and "referentiality" in Chamorro. *Linguistic Inquiry* 25: 1–44.

  2006. Sluicing and the lexicon: the point of no return. In *BLS 31: General Session and Parasession on Prosodic Variation and Change*, ed. R. T. Cover and Y. Kim, 73–91. Berkeley, Calif.: Berkeley Linguistics Society.

Chung, S., W. A. Ladusaw, and J. McCloskey. 1995. Sluicing and logical form. *Natural Language Semantics* 3: 239–282.

Cinque, G. 1978. Towards a unified treatment of island constraints. In *Proceedings of the 12th International Congress of Linguistics*, Insbrucker Beitrage zur Sprachwissenschaft, W. Dressler and W. Meid (eds.), 344–348.

  1990. *Types of A-bar dependencies*. Cambridge, Mass.: MIT Press.

  1993. A null theory of phrase and compound stress. *Linguistic Inquiry* 24: 239–298.

  1999. *Adverbs and Functional Heads*. Oxford University Press.

Comorowski, I. 1988. Discourse linking and the wh-island constraint. *Proceedings of the 19th meeting of NELS*.

Craenenbroeck, J. van. 2008. What does silence look like? Talk given at the University of Chicago, December 2008.

Culicover, P. W. 2008. Beyond simpler syntax: processing complexity and explaining island phenomena. Talk given at Mayfest, May 2008.

Culicover, P. W. and P. M. Postal (eds.). 2001. *Parasitic Gaps*. Cambridge, Mass.: MIT Press.

Dayal, V. 1996. *Locality in WH Quantification*. Dordrecht: Kluwer.

Deane, P. 1991. Limits to attention: a cognitive theory of island phenomena. *Cognitive Linguistics* 2: 1–63.

Demirdache, H. 1991. Resumptive chains in restrictive relatives, appositives, and dislocation structures. Doctoral dissertation, MIT.

Demonte, V. 1987. C-command, prepositions, and predications. *Linguistic Inquiry* 18: 147–157.

Den Dikken, M. 2007. Phase extension, contours of a theory of the role of head. Movement in phrasal extraction. *Theoretical Linguistics* 33: 1–41.

Donati, C. 2006. On wh-head-movement. In *WH-movement: Moving On*, ed. L. Cheng and N. Corver, 21–46. Cambridge, Mass.: MIT Press.

Doron, E. 1982. On the syntax and semantics of resumptive pronouns. *Texas Linguistic Forum* 19: 1–48.

Embick, D. and R. Noyer. 2001. Movement operations after syntax. *Linguistic Inquiry* 32: 555–595.

2007. Distributed morphology and the syntax-morphology interfaces. In *Oxford Handbook of Linguistic Interfaces*, ed. G. Ramchand and C. Reiss, 289–324. Oxford University Press.

Epstein, S. D. 1999. Un-principled syntax: the derivation of syntactic relations. In *Working Minimalism*, ed. S. D. Epstein and N. Hornstein, 317–345. Cambridge, Mass.: MIT Press.

Epstein, S. D., H. Kitahara, and T. D. Seely. 2010. Structure building that can't be. Ms., University of Michigan, Keio University, and Michigan State University.

Epstein, S. D. and T. D. Seely. 2002. Rule applications as cycles. In *Derivation and Explanation in the Minimalist Program*, ed. S. D. Epstein and T. D. Seely, 65–89. Oxford: Blackwell.

Erteschik-Shir, N. 1973. On the nature of island constraints. Doctoral dissertation, MIT.

2007. *Information Structure: The Syntax-Discourse Interface.* Oxford University Press.

Etxepare, R. 1999. On null complementizers in Spanish. *International Journal of Basque Linguistics and Philology* 32(2): 469–496.

Feynman, R. 1965. *The Character of Physical Law.* Cambridge, Mass.: MIT Press.

Fortuny, J. 2008. *The Emergence of Order in Syntax.* Amsterdam: John Benjamins.

Fox, D. 2000. *Economy and Semantic Interpretation.* Cambridge, Mass.: MIT Press & MITWPL.

Fox, D. and M. Hackl. 2003. Successive cyclic movement and island repair: the difference between sluicing and VP-ellipsis. *Linguistic Inquiry* 34: 143–154.

2007. The universal density of measurement. *Linguistics and Philosophy* 29: 537–586.

Fox, D. and D. Pesetsky. 2005. Cyclic linearization of syntactic structure. *Theoretical Linguistics* 31: 1–46.

Freidin, R. 1992. *Foundations of Generative Syntax.* Cambridge, Mass.: MIT Press.

Frisch, S. 1999. Review of Thomas Berg, ed., *Linguistic Structure and Change: An Explanation from Language Processing.* Oxford: Clarendon Press, 1998. *Journal of Linguistics* 35: 579–655.

Fukui, N. 1997. Attract and the A-over-A principle. In *UCI Working Papers in Linguistics* #3, 51–67.

Gallego, A. 2007. Phase theory and parametric variation. Doctoral dissertation, Universitat Autonoma de Barcelona.

2010. *Phase Theory.* Amsterdam: John Benjamins.

Gallego, A. and J. Uriagereka. 2007a. Conditions on sub-extraction. In *Selected Papers from XVI Colloquium on Generative Grammar*, ed. L. Eguren and O. Fernandez-Soriano. Amsterdam: John Benjamins.

2007b. Freezing effects. Ms., Universitat Autonoma de Barcelona and University of Maryland.

Gazdar, G. 1981. Unbounded dependencies and coordinate structures. *Linguistic Inquiry* 12: 155–184.

Givon, T. 1979. *On Understanding Grammar*. New York: Academic Press.

Goldberg, A. 2006. *Constructions at Work*. Oxford University Press.

Goodall, G. 1987. *Parallel Structures in Syntax*. Cambridge University Press.

Grimshaw, J. 1990. *Argument Structure*. Cambridge, Mass.: MIT Press.

Grohmann, K. K. 2003. *Prolific Domains*. Amsterdam: John Benjamins.

Guilliot, N. 2006. La reconstruction à l'interface de la syntaxe et sémantique. Doctoral dissertation, University of Nantes.

2007. Reconstruction: the islands' puzzle. In *Proceedings of the XXXII Incontro di Grammatica Generativa*, ed. M. C. Picchi and A. Pona, 107–118. Alessandria: Edizioni dell'Orso.

Guilliot, Nicolas and N. Malkawi. 2006. When resumption determines reconstruction. *Proceedings of the 25th West Coast Conference on Formal Linguistics*, 168–176. Somerville, Mass.: Cascadilla Press.

Haegeman, L. 1991. *An Introduction to Government-and-Binding Theory (2nd edition)*. Malden: Wiley-Blackwell.

Hagstrom, P. 1998. Decomposing questions. Doctoral dissertation, MIT.

Halle, A. and M. Marantz. 1993. Distributed morphology and the pieces of inflection. In *The View from Building* 20, ed. K. Hale and S. J. Keyser, 111–176. Cambridge, Mass.: MIT Press.

Harley, H. and R. Noyer. 1999. State-of-the-article: distributed morphology, *GLOT International* 4(4): 3–9.

Hauser, M. D., N. Chomsky, and W. T. Fitch. 2002. The faculty of language: what it is, who has it, and how did it evolve? *Science* 298: 1569–1579.

Hawkins, J. A. 1999. Processing complexity and filler-gap dependencies across grammars. *Language* 75: 244–285.

Heck, F. 2008. *On Pied-piping*. Berlin: Mouton/de Gruyter.

Hinzen, W. 2006. *Minimal Mind Design*. Oxford University Press.

2007. *An Essay on Names and Truth*. Oxford University Press.

Hofmeister, P. and I. Sag. 2010. Cognitive constraints and island effects. *Language* 86: 366–415.

Honcoop, M. 1998. *Dynamic Excursions on Weak Islands*. The Hague: Holland Academic Graphics.

Hornstein, N. 1995. *Logical Form*. Oxford: Blackwell.

2001. *Move! A Minimalist Theory of Construal*. Oxford: Blackwell.

2009. *A Theory of Syntax*. Cambridge University Press.

Hornstein, N., H. Lasnik, and J. Uriagereka. 2007. The dynamics of islands: speculations on the locality of movement. *Linguistic Analysis* 33: 149–175.

Hornstein, N. and J. Nunes. 2008. Some thoughts on adjunction. *Biolinguistics* 2: 57–86.

Hornstein, N., J. Nunes, and K. K. Grohmann. 2006. *Understanding Minimalism*. Cambridge University Press.

Hornstein, N. and A. Weinberg. 1981. Case theory and preposition stranding. *Linguistic Inquiry* 12: 55–91.

Huang, C.-T. J. 1982. Logical relations in Chinese and the theory of grammar. Doctoral dissertation, MIT.

Irurtzun, A. 2007. The grammar of focus at the interfaces. Doctoral dissertation, University of the Basque Country.

Jackendoff, R. 1972. *Semantic Interpretation in Generative Grammar*, Cambridge, Mass.: MIT Press.

James, D. 1972. Some aspects of the syntax and semantics of interjections. Paper presented at the 8th Regional Meeting of the Chicago Linguistic Society.

Johnson, K. 2002. Towards an etiology of adjunct islands. Ms., University of Massachusetts, Amherst.

   2008. Fitting islands into the semantics of movement. Talk given at Mayfest, May 2008.

   2009. Why movement? Talk given at Chicago Linguistics Society meeting, April 2009.

Jurka, J. 2010. The importance of being a complement: CED effects revisited. Doctoral dissertation, University of Maryland.

Kato, T. 2006. Symmetries in coordination. Doctoral dissertation, Harvard University.

Kayne, R. S. 1984. *Connectedness and Binary Branching*. Dordrecht: Foris.

   1994. *The Antisymmetry of Syntax*. Cambridge, Mass.: MIT Press.

   2002. Pronouns and their antecedents. In *Derivation and Explanation in the Minimalist Program*, ed. S. D. Epstein and T. D. Seely, 133–166. Oxford: Blackwell.

   2005. *Movement and Silence*. Oxford University Press.

Kehler, A. 1996. Coherence and the coordinate structure constraint. In *Proceedings of the 22nd Annual Meeting of the Berkeley Linguistics Society*, 220–231. Berkeley Linguistics Society, University of California, Berkeley.

Kluender, R. 1991. Cognitive constraints on variables in syntax. Doctoral dissertation, University of California, San Diego.

   1992. Deriving island constraints from principles of predication. In *Island Constraints: Theory, Acquisition, and Processing*, ed. H. Goodluck and M. Rochemont, 223–258. Dordrecht: Kluwer.

   1998. On the distinction between strong and weak islands: a processing perspective. In *Syntax and Semantics 29, the Limits of Syntax*, ed. P. W. Culicover and L. McNally, 241–279. New York: Academic Press.

   2004. Are subject islands subject to a processing account? In *Proceedings of WCCFL 23*, 475–499. Somerville, Mass.: Cascadilla Press.

Kluender, R. and M. Kutas. 1993. Subjacency as a processing phenomenon. *Language and Cognitive Processes* 8: 573–633.

Koster, J. 1978a. *Locality principles in syntax*. Dordrecht: Foris.

   1978b. Why subject sentences don't exist. In *Recent Transformational Studies in European Languages*, ed. S. J. Keyser, 53–64. Cambridge, Mass.: MIT Press.

1987. *Domains and Dynasties*. Dordrecht: Foris.

2010. Theories of language. Ms., University of Groningen.

Kroch, A. 1989. Amount quantification, referentiality, and long wh-movement. Ms. University of Pennsylvania.

Kuno, S. 1973. Constraints on internal clauses and sentential subjects. *Linguistic Inquiry* 4: 363–385.

Kuno, S. and K. Takami. 1997. Remarks on negative islands. *Linguistic Inquiry* 28: 553–576.

Kush, D. 2010. On the escapability of islands in Scandinavian. Ms. University of Maryland.

Kush, D. and F. Lindahl. 2011. On the escapability of islands in Scandinavian. Presented at the LSA annual meeting, Jan. 7, 2011.

Larson, R. 1988. The double object construction. *Linguistic Inquiry* 19: 335–391.

Lasnik, H. 1999. On the locality of movement: formalist syntax position paper. In *Functionalism and Formalism in Linguistics*, ed. M. Darnell, E. Moravcsik, F. Newmeyer, M. Noonan, and K. Wheatley, 33–54. Amsterdam: John Benjamins.

2000. *Syntactic Structures Revisited*. Cambridge, Mass.: MIT Press.

2001. When can you save a structure by destroying it? In *Proceedings of NELS 31*, 301–320. University of Massachusetts, Amherst: GLSA.

2003. *Minimalist Investigations in Syntactic Theory*. London: Routledge.

2005. Review of Jason Merchant, *The Syntax of Silence*. *Language* 81: 259–265.

2006. Conceptions of the cycle. In *Wh-Movement Moving On*, ed. L. Cheng and N. Corver, 197–216. Cambridge, Mass.: MIT Press.

2007. On ellipsis: The PF approach to missing constituents. *University of Maryland Working Papers in Linguistics* 15: 143–153.

Lasnik, H. and M. Saito. 1984. On the nature of proper government. *Linguistic Inquiry* 15: 235–289.

1992. *Move α*. Cambridge, Mass.: MIT Press.

Lee, M. K. 2006. Scrambling in Korean and topicalization in Spanish as instances of resumptive chain. In *Proceedings of Harvard Studies in Korean Linguistics XI*, 617–630. Department of Linguistics, Harvard University.

Levine, R. and T. Hukari. 2006. *The Unity of Unbounded Dependency Constructions*. Stanford, Calif.: CSLI.

Lin, V. 2001. A way to undo A-movement. In *Proceedings of the 20th West Coast Conference on Formal Linguistics*, 358–371. Somerville, Mass.: Cascadilla Press.

Manzini, M. R. 1992. *Locality*. Cambridge, Mass.: MIT Press.

Marantz, A. 1984. *On the Nature of Grammatical Relations*. Cambridge, Mass.: MIT Press.

2005. Generative linguistics within the cognitive neuroscience of language. *The Linguistic Review* 22: 429–445.

McCloskey, J. 1988. Syntactic theory. In *Linguistics: The Cambridge Survey, vol. I*, ed. F. Newmeyer. Cambridge University Press.

2002. Resumption, successive cyclicity, and the locality of operations. In *Derivation and Explanation in the Minimalist Program*, ed. S. D. Epstein and T. D. Seely, 184–226. Oxford: Blackwell.

Merchant, J. 2001. *The Syntax of Silence*. Oxford: Oxford University Press.

2008. Variable island repair under ellipsis. In *Topics in Ellipsis*, ed. K. Johnson, 132–153. Cambridge University Press.

2010. Ellipsis. Ms., University of Chicago. (A version of which to appear in *Handbook of Contemporary Syntax*, 2nd edition, ed. A. Alexiadou, T. Kiss, and M. Butt. Berlin: Walter de Gruyter.)

2011. Diagnosing ellipsis. Ms., University of Chicago. (A version of which to appear in *Diagnosing Syntax*, ed. L. Cheng and N. Corver. Oxford University Press.)

Miller, G. and N. Chomsky. 1963. Finitary models of language users. In *Handbook of Mathematical Psychology*, ed. R. D. Luce, R. Bush, and E. Galanter, 419–491. New York: Wiley.

Moltmann, F. 1992. Coordination and comparatives. Doctoral dissertation, MIT.

Morgan, J. L. 1975. Some interactions of syntax and pragmatics. In *Syntax and Semantics Volume III: Speech Acts*, ed. P. Cole and J. L. Morgan, 289–304. New York: Academic Press.

Muadz, H. 1991. Coordinate structures: a planar representation. Doctoral dissertation, University of Arizona.

Müller, G. 2010. On deriving CED effects from the PIC. *Linguistic Inquiry* 41: 35–82.

Munn, A. 1993. Topics in the syntax and semantics of coordinate structures. Doctoral dissertation, *University of Maryland, College Park*.

Narita, H. 2011. Phasing in full interpretation. Doctoral dissertation, Harvard University.

Nishigauchi, T. 1986. Quantification in syntax, Ph.D. dissertation, University of Massachusetts, Amherst.

Nunes, J. and J. Uriagereka. 2000. Cyclicity and extraction domains. *Syntax* 3: 20–43.

Obenauer, H.-G. 1984. On the identification of empty categories. *The Linguistic Review* 4: 153–202.

Ott, D. 2010. Grammaticality, interfaces, and UG. In *Exploring Crash-proof Grammars*, ed. M. T. Putnam, 89–104. Amsterdam/New York: John Benjamins.

Perlmutter, D. 1971. *Deep and Surface Structure Constraints in Syntax*. New York: Holt, Rinehart, and Winston.

1972. Evidence for shadow pronouns in French relativization. In *The Chicago Which Hunt: Papers from the Relative Clause Festival*, 73–105. Chicago Linguistic Society.

Pesetsky, D. 1987. Wh-in-situ: movement and unselective binding. In *The Representation of (In)definiteness*, ed. E. Reuland and A. ter Meulen 98–129. Cambridge, Mass.: MIT Press.

Phillips, C. 2006. The real-time status of island constraints. *Language* 82: 795–823.

2009. Should we impeach armchair linguists? In S. Iwasaki, ed., *Japanese-Korean Linguistics* 17. Stanford: CSLI.

2011. Some arguments and non-arguments for reductionist accounts of syntactic phenomena. *Language and Cognitive Processes* 26: 1–32.

Pietroski, P. In press. *Semantics without Truth-values*. Oxford University Press.

Postal, P. M. 1986. Foreword. In *Infinite Syntax!*, by J. R. Ross, xvii–xix. Norwood, NJ: Ablex.

1997. Islands. Ms., NYU.

1998. *Three Investigations of Extraction*. Cambridge, Mass.: MIT Press.

Pritchett, B. 1991. Subjacency in a principle-based parser. In *Principle-based Parsing: Computation and Psycholinguistics*, ed. R. Berwick, S. Abney, C. Tenny, 301–345. Dordrecht: Kluwer.

Rackowski, R. and N. Richards. 2005. Phase edge and extraction: a Tagalog case study. *Linguistic Inquiry* 36: 565–599.

Raposo, E. 2002. Nominal gaps with prepositional modifiers in Portuguese and Spanish: a case for Quick Spell-Out. *Cuadernos de Lingüística del I. U. Ortega y Gasset* 9: 127–144.

Reinhart, T. 1998. Wh-in-situ in the framework of the minimalist program. *Natural Language Semantics* 6: 29–56.

2006. *Interface Strategies*. Cambridge, Mass.: MIT Press.

Reuland, E. 2011. *Anaphora and Language Design*. Cambridge, Mass.: MIT Press.

Richards, M. 2007. On feature-inheritance: An argument from the Phase Impenetrability Condition. *Linguistic Inquiry* 38: 563–572.

2011. No phase is an island(?). Ms., University of Leipzig.

Richards, N. 2000. An island effect in Japanese. *Journal of East Asian Linguistics* 9: 187–205.

2001. *Movement in Language*. Oxford University Press.

2010. *Uttering Trees*. Cambridge, Mass.: MIT Press.

van Riemsdijk, H. 1978. *A Case Study in Syntactic Markedness*. Dordrecht: Foris.

2008. Identity avoidance. In *Foundational Issues in Linguistic Theory*, ed. R. Freidin, C. Otero, and M. L. Zubizarreta. Cambridge, Mass.: MIT Press.

Rizzi, L. 1978. Violations of the wh-island constraint in Italian and the subjacency condition. *Montreal Working Papers in Linguistics* 11: 155–190.

1982. *Issues in Italian Syntax*. Dordrecht: Foris.

1990. *Relativized Minimality*. Cambridge, Mass.: MIT Press.

1997. The fine structure of the left periphery. In *Elements of Grammar*, ed. L. Haegeman, 281–337. Dordrecht: Kluwer.

2004. Locality and left periphery. In *Structures and Beyond*, ed. A. Belletti, 223–251. Oxford University Press.

2006. On the form of chains: criterial positions and ECP effects. In *WH-movement: Moving On*, ed. L. Cheng and N. Corver, 97–133. Cambridge, Mass.: MIT Press.

2009. Movement and concepts of locality. In *Of Minds and Language*, ed. M. Piattelli-Palmarini, J. Uriagereka, and P. Salaburu, 155–168. Oxford University Press.

2011. Minimality. In *The Oxford Handbook of Linguistic Minimalism*, ed. C. Boeckx, 220–238. Oxford University Press.

Rizzi, L. and U. Shlonsky. 2007. Strategies of subject extraction. In *Interfaces + Recursion = Language? Chomsky's Minimalism and the View from Syntax-semantics*, ed. U. Sauerland and M. Gaertner, 115–160. Mouton: de Gruyter.

Roberts, I. 1997. *Comparative Syntax*. London: Arnold.

Rosenbaum, P. 1970. A principle governing deletion in English sentential complementation. In *Readings in English Transformational Grammar*, ed. R. Jacobs and P. Rosenbaum, 222–272. Waltham, Mass.: Blaisdell Publishing.

Ross, J. R. 1967. Constraints on variables in syntax. Doctoral dissertation, MIT. (Published 1986 as *Infinite Syntax!* Norwood, NJ: Ablex.)

1969. Guess who? In *Proceedings of CLS* 5, 252–286. Chicago Linguistic Society.

1984. Inner islands. In Claudia Brugman and Monica Macauley et al. (Eds.) *Proceedings of the Tenth Annual Meeting of the Berkeley Linguistics Society*, ed. C. Brugman, M. Macauley *et al.*, 258–265. Berkeley Linguistics Society, University of California, Berkeley.

Rouveret, A. 2008. Phasal agreement and reconstruction. In *Foundational Hypotheses*, ed. R. Freidin, C. Otero, and M. L. Zubizarreta, 167–196. Cambridge, Mass.: MIT Press.

(ed). 2011. *Resumptive Pronouns at the Interfaces*. Amsterdam: John Benjamins.

Rullmann, H. 1995. Maximality in the semantics of wh-constructions, University of Massachusetts at Amherst: Ph.D. Dissertation.

Ruys, E. 1993. The scope of indefinites. Doctoral dissertation, Universiteit Utrecht.

Sag, I. 2010. Feature geometry and predictions of locality. In *Proceedings of the Workshop on Features*, ed. G. Corbett and A. Kibort, 236–271. Oxford University Press.

Scheer, T. 2011. Aspects of the development of generative phonology. In *The Continuum Companion to Phonology*, ed. B. Botma, N. C. Kula and K. Nasukawa, 397–446. New York: Continuum.

Sheehan, M. To appear. The resuscitation of CED. In *Proceedings of NELS 40*.

Simpson, A. 2000. *Wh-movement and the Theory of Feature-Checking*. Amsterdam: John Benjamins.

Snyder, W. 2000. An experimental study of syntactic satiation effects. *Linguistic Inquiry* 31: 575–582.

Sportiche, D. 1998. *Atoms and Partitions of Clause Structure*. London: Routledge.

Sprouse, J. 2007a. A program for experimental syntax. Doctoral dissertation, University of Maryland.

2007b. Continuous acceptability, categorical grammaticality, and experimental syntax. *Biolinguistics* 1: 118–129.

2009. Revisiting satiation. *Linguistic Inquiry* 40(2): 329–341.

2011. A test of the cognitive assumptions of magnitude estimation: commutativity does not hold for acceptability judgments. *Language* 87(2): 274–288.

Sprouse, J. and D. Almeida. 2011. A formal experimental investigation of the empirical foundation of generative syntactic theory. Ms. UC Irvine.

Sprouse, J., S. Fukuda, H. Ono, and R. Kluender. 2011. Reverse island effects and the backward search for a licensor in multiple wh-questions. *Syntax*.

Sprouse, J., M. Wagers, and C. Phillips. To appear. A test of the relation between working memory capacity and syntactic island effects. *Language*.

Starke, M. 2001. Move dissolves into merge: a theory of locality. Doctoral dissertation, University of Geneva.

Stepanov, A. 2001. Cyclic domains in syntactic theory. Doctoral dissertation, University of Connecticut.

2007. The end of CED? Minimalism and extraction domain. *Syntax* 10: 80–126.

Stowell, T. 1981. Origins of phrase structure. Doctoral dissertation, MIT.

Szabolcsi, A. 2006. Weak and strong islands. In *The Syntax Companion*, ed. M. Everaert and H. van Riemsdijk, 479–531. Oxford: Blackwell.

2008. What nature classes of (weak) islands? Talk given at Mayfest, May 2008.

Szabolcsi, A. and M. den Dikken. 2002. Islands. In *The Second State-of-the-Article Book*, ed. L. Cheng and R. Sybesma, 213–240. Berlin: Mouton de Gruyter.

Szabolcsi, A. and F. Zwarts. 1990. Semantic properties of composed functions and The distribution of wh-phrases. In *Proceedings of the Seventh Amsterdam Colloquium*, ed. M. Stokhof and L. Torenvliet, 529–555. Amsterdam: ILLI.

1993. Weak islands and an algebraic semantics for scope taking. *Natural Language Semantics* 1: 235–284.

1997. Weak islands and an algebraic semantics for scope taking. In *Ways of Scope Taking*, ed. A. Szabolcsi, 109–155. Dordrecht: Kluwer.

Takahashi, D. 1994. Minimality of movement. Doctoral dissertation, University of Connecticut.

Torrego, E. 1985. On empty categories in nominals. Ms., University of Massachusetts, Boston.

1998. *The Dependencies of Objects*. Cambridge, Mass.: MIT Press.

Townsend, D. J. and T. G. Bever. 2001. *Sentence Comprehension: The Integration of Habits and Rules*. Cambridge, Mass.: MIT Press.

Truswell, R. 2007. Locality of wh-movement and the individuation of events. Doctoral Dissertation, University College London.

Tsai, D. W.-T. 1994. On economizing the theory of A-bar dependencies. Doctoral dissertation, MIT.

Uriagereka, J. 1988. On government. Doctoral dissertation, University of Connecticut, Storrs.

1998. *Rhyme and Reason*. Cambridge, Mass.: MIT Press.

1999a. Multiple spell-out. In *Working Minimalism*, ed. S. D. Epstein and N. Hornstein, 251–282. Cambridge, Mass.: MIT Press.

1999b. Minimal Restrictions on Basque Movements. *Natural Language and Linguistic Theory* 17: 403–444.

2011. *Spell-Out and the Minimalist Program*. Oxford University Press.

Wagers, M. 2008. The structure of memory meets memory for structure in linguistic cognition. Doctoral dissertation, University of Maryland.

Wang, A. 2007. Sluicing and Resumption. In *Proceedings of NELS 37*. University of Massachusetts, Amherst: GLSA.

Watanabe, A. 1992. Subjacency and S-Structure movement of wh-in-situ. *Journal of East-Asian Linguistics* 1: 255–291.

2001. Wh-in-situ languages. In *Handbook of Contemporary Syntactic Theory*, ed. M. Baltin and C. Collins, 203–225. Oxford: Blackwell.

Wexler, K. and P. W. Culicover. 1980. *Formal Principles of Language Acquisition*. Cambridge, Mass.: MIT Press.

Wilkins, W. 1977. The variable interpretation convention: a condition on variables in syntactic transformations. Doctoral dissertation, UCLA.

1980. Adjacency and variables in transformations. *Linguistic Inquiry* 11: 709–750.

Williams, E. 1974. Rule ordering in grammar. Doctoral dissertation, MIT.

Yang, C. 2011. Three factors in language acquisition. In *The Biolinguistic Enterprise*, ed. A. M. Di Sciullo and C. Boeckx, 155–168. Oxford University Press.

Zubizarreta, M. L. 1998. *Prosody, Focus and Word Order*, Cambridge, Mass.: MIT Press.

Zwart, C. J.-W. 2007. Layered derivations. Ms., University of Groningen.

Index